IMAGES
of America

SLATINGTON, WALNUTPORT, AND WASHINGTON TOWNSHIP

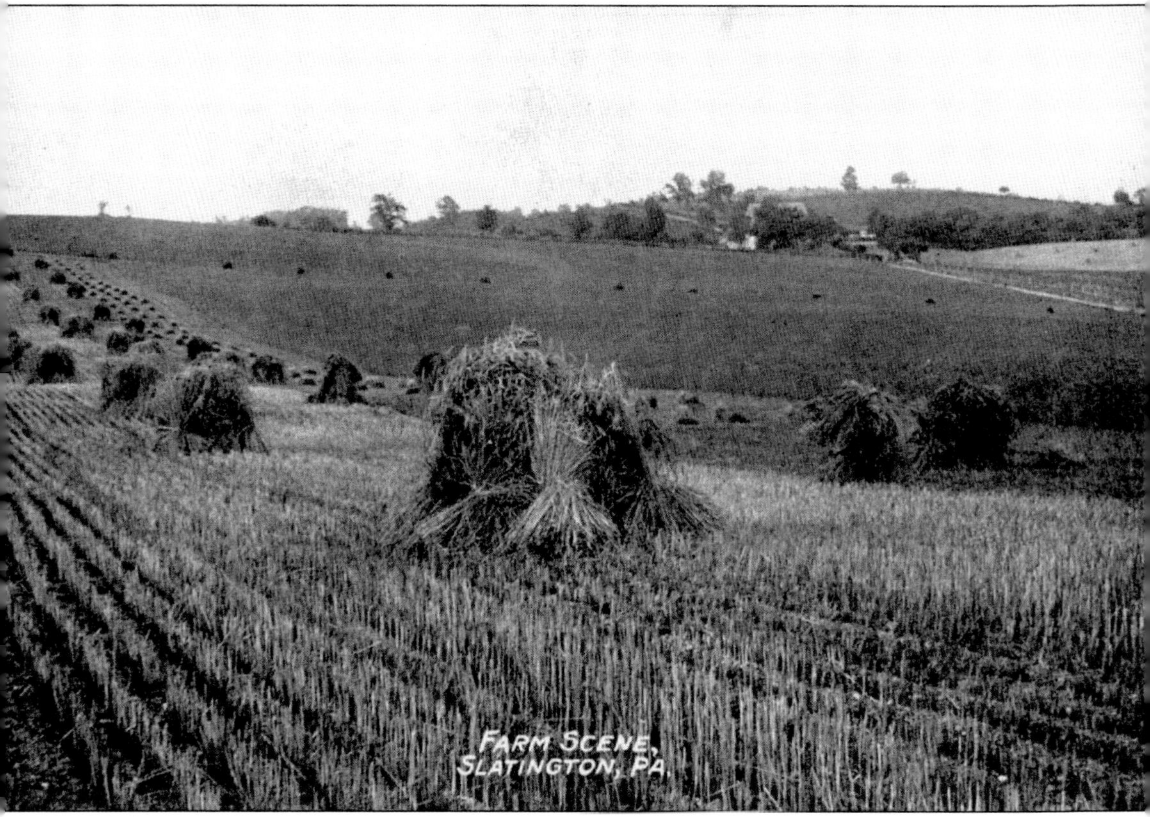

When much of the area looked like this, many of the original settlers coming to the Slatington area were German farmers. (Courtesy of Larry Hillborn.)

On the cover: Please see page 104. (Courtesy of Slatington Public Library.)

IMAGES
of America

SLATINGTON, WALNUTPORT, AND WASHINGTON TOWNSHIP

Sean and Johanna Billings for the Northern Lehigh Future Focus

ARCADIA
PUBLISHING

ISBN 978-0-7385-4489-2

Published by Arcadia Publishing
Charleston, South Carolina

Printed in the United States of America

Library of Congress Catalog Card Number: 2005938518

For all general information contact Arcadia Publishing at:
Telephone 843-853-2070
Fax 843-853-0044
E-mail sales@arcadiapublishing.com
For customer service and orders:
Toll-Free 1-888-313-2665

Visit us on the Internet at www.arcadiapublishing.com

Contents

ACKNOWLEDGMENTS

Northern Lehigh Future Focus collected and copied many of the photographs used in this book. We would like to thank everyone who generously allowed their photographs to be copied. We tried to give credit to each person who donated a photograph to Future Focus and apologize if we missed anyone. It was very difficult to decide which photographs to use because we had far more than we could include.

We would also like to thank Larry Hillborn, who always allows us the use of his collection for our books. Thanks also go to Jim Layland for his photographs of the Lehigh Valley Transit Company trolleys and to the Slatington Public Library for the use of its slate photograph collection. We would also like to acknowledge the Walnutport Canal Association for the use of its canal photographs and Darrin Heckman and Al Ringer for the use of the 1876 *Centennial Atlas* maps. Appreciation also goes out to Everett and Marilyn Kaul, both of whom volunteer their time to improve the Walnutport and Slatington areas.

Introduction

Slate was king in the appropriately named Slatington Borough and surrounding area. The discovery of slate—used for blackboards, shingles, countertops, and many other items—gave way to a thriving industry and towns such as Slatedale, located in Washington Township. More than 100 quarries were located in Slatington, Walnutport, and Washington Township. Families such as the Kerns, Remaleys, and Balliets formed a business and social foundation for the region as early as the 1700s.

In addition to the quarries, many slate-processing factories sprung up to convert the raw material into consumer and business goods. The early establishment of several post offices aided the factories' growth.

The Lehigh River and the construction of the Lehigh Canal assisted the slate industry by providing a means of transporting products to market. These waterways were also important for the transportation of coal from Mauch Chunk (present-day Jim Thorpe) to Philadelphia, bringing people through the area and facilitating trade.

Railroads also played an important role in this hotbed of small industry. Not only did freight trains travel through the area carrying goods, but a trolley service also transported people across the region.

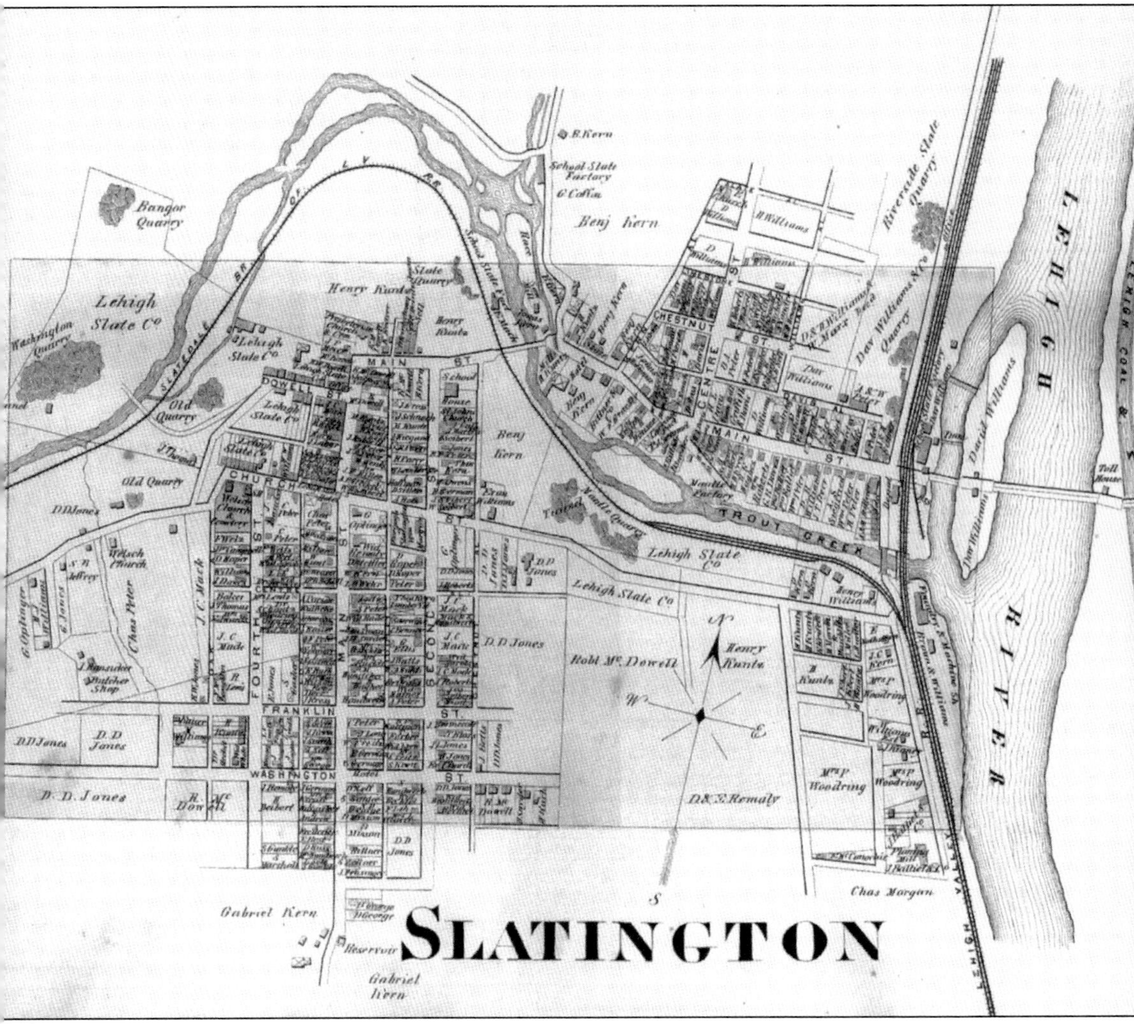

Seen here is a map of Slatington from the 1876 *Centennial Atlas.*

One

Slatington

The origins of the Slatington area can be traced back to Nicholas Kern. He obtained two tracts of land—300 acres in 1737 and 200 acres in 1738—in what was then the Heidelberg District. In 1739, Kern built a gristmill and a sawmill along Trout Creek. In 1752, this area became Heidelberg Township of Northampton County, and in 1812, it became Heidelberg Township of Lehigh County. In 1847, Dallas Township, also in Lehigh County, was formed and the name was changed to Washington Township, Lehigh County, in 1848.

Nicholas Kern and his family built their first home in Slatington. Lower Slatington was settled mostly by their descendants. Ambrose Remaley and his wife, Anna Catharine, obtained land warrants for several hundred acres, including what would become Upper Slatington as well as land in Washington Township, directly south of Slatington. The Remaley descendants settled much of Upper Slatington.

Slate was discovered in 1844. At that time, the nearest post office was in Craig's Store in the village of Lehigh Gap, Carbon County, near the Aquashicola Creek. Slate-related businesses needed mail service to continue growing. In 1851, the Slatington post office opened. The Lehigh Valley Railroad was constructed along the Lehigh River, and the town was incorporated as the borough of Slatington in 1864. Slatington's first mayor was Robert McDowell.

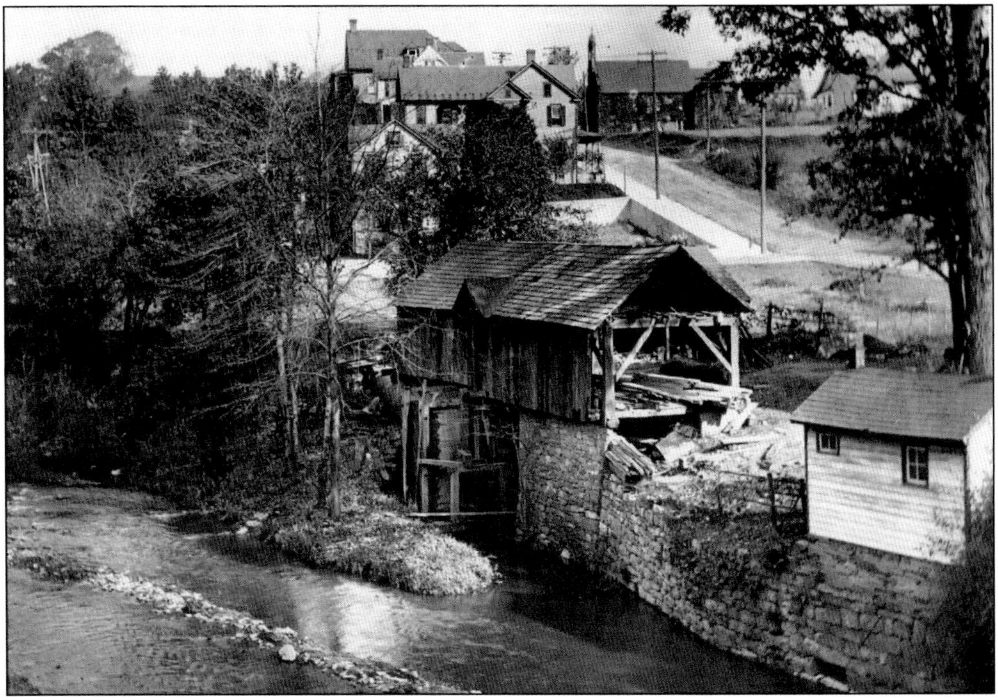

Kern's Mill, located on Trout Creek, was operated by the Kern family for generations. Benjamin Franklin purchased lumber from the mill during the French and Indian War to build Fort Allen in Weissport. Kern's Mill was also known as Trucker's Mill because the local residents of German descent called William Kern *trockener*, meaning "joker" or "person of wit." The name eventually became corrupted as "trucker." (Courtesy of Palmerton Camera Club, Northern Lehigh Future Focus Collection.)

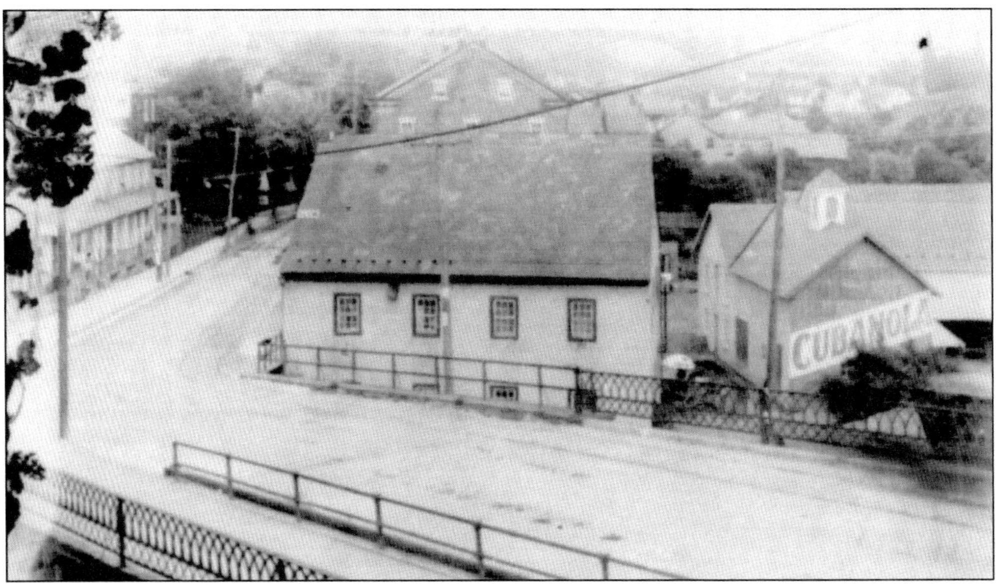

This is how Kern's Mill looked around 1910. The Lehigh Valley Transit trolley tracks are seen crossing the bridge. (Courtesy of Raymond Holland Regional History Collection, Northern Lehigh Future Focus Collection.)

The back of this advertisement for Howard E. Kern states, "Successor to A. J. Kern will continue to give you the good old fashioned service at prices that are right. Phone 151-R-5. Est. 1850." (Courtesy of Larry Hillborn.)

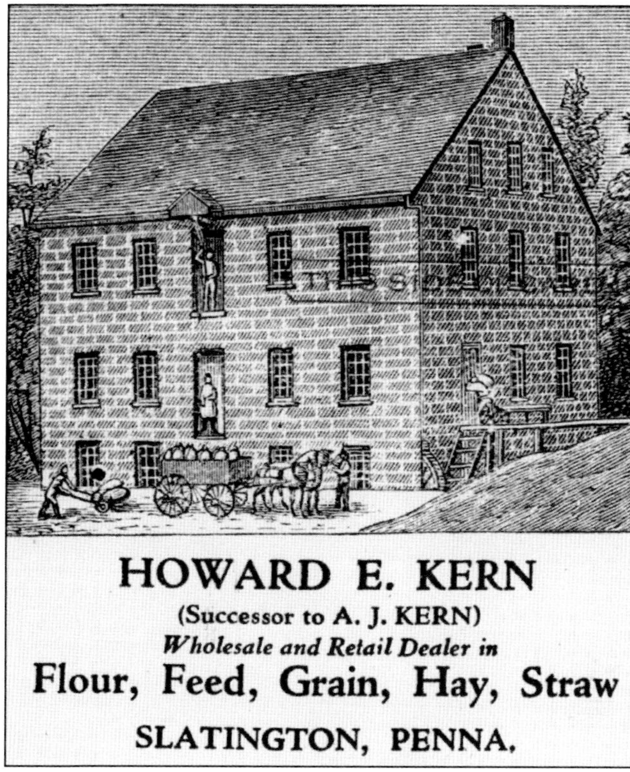

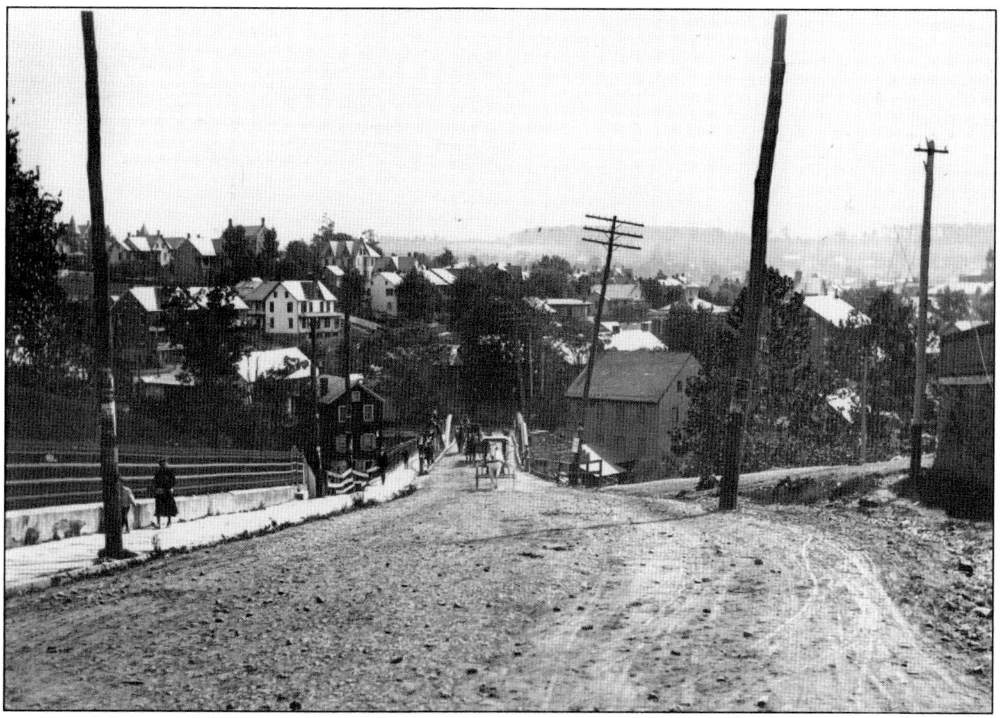

Looking down the Main Street hill in Slatington, Kern's gristmill can be seen on the right. (Courtesy of Palmerton Camera Club, Northern Lehigh Future Focus Collection.)

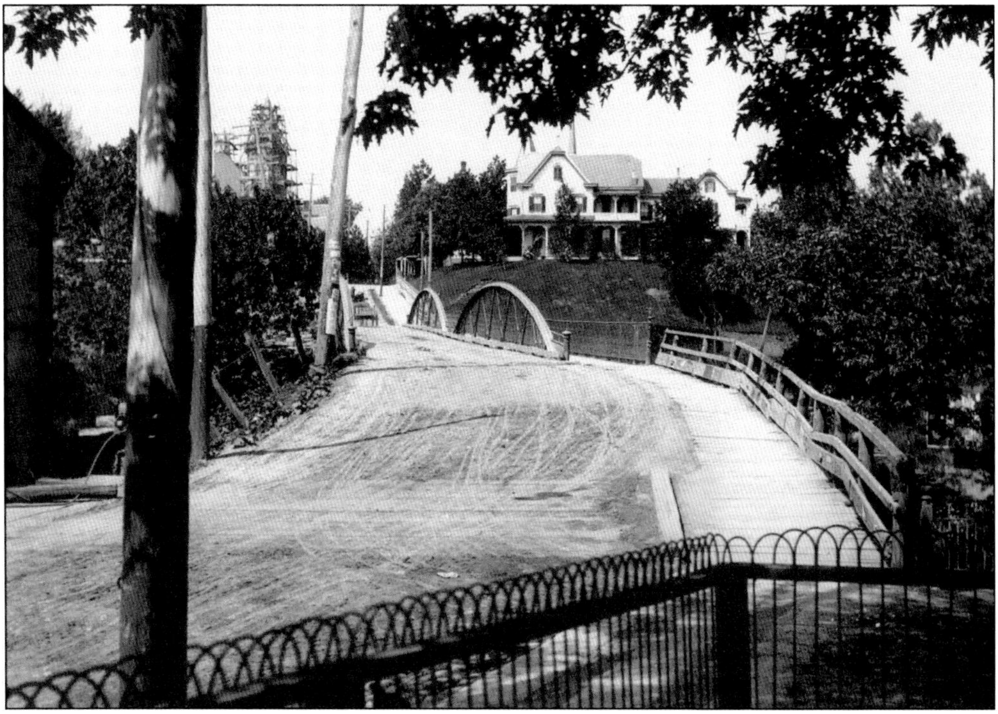

The bridge across Trout Creek was built in 1826. Note the scaffolding around the Baptist church steeple on the left. The steeple was built in 1900, which dates this photograph to that time. (Courtesy of Palmerton Camera Club, Northern Lehigh Future Focus Collection.)

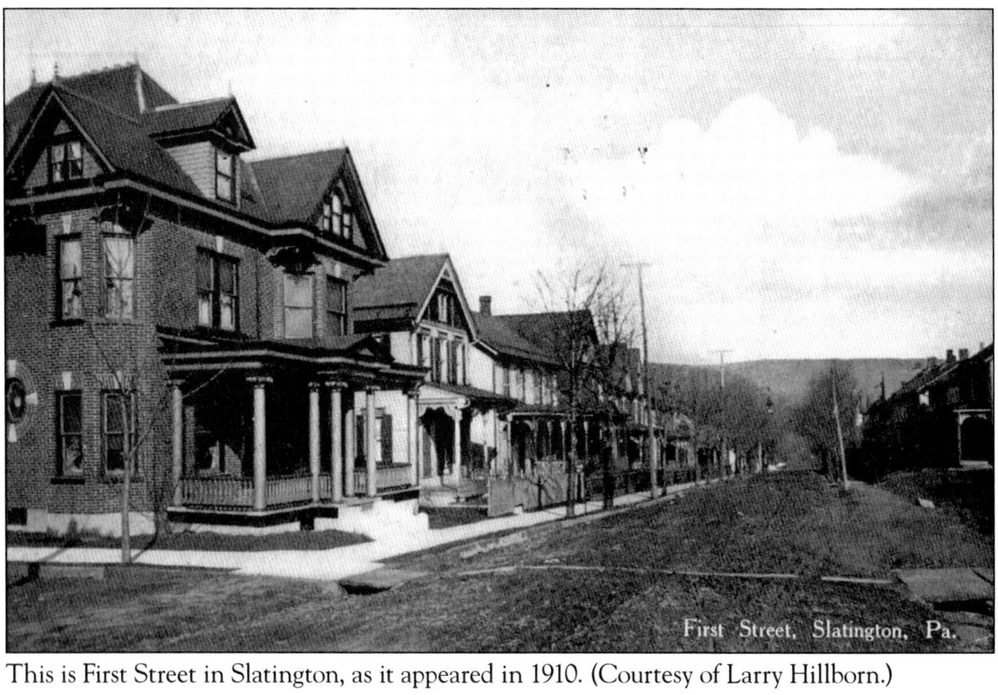

This is First Street in Slatington, as it appeared in 1910. (Courtesy of Larry Hillborn.)

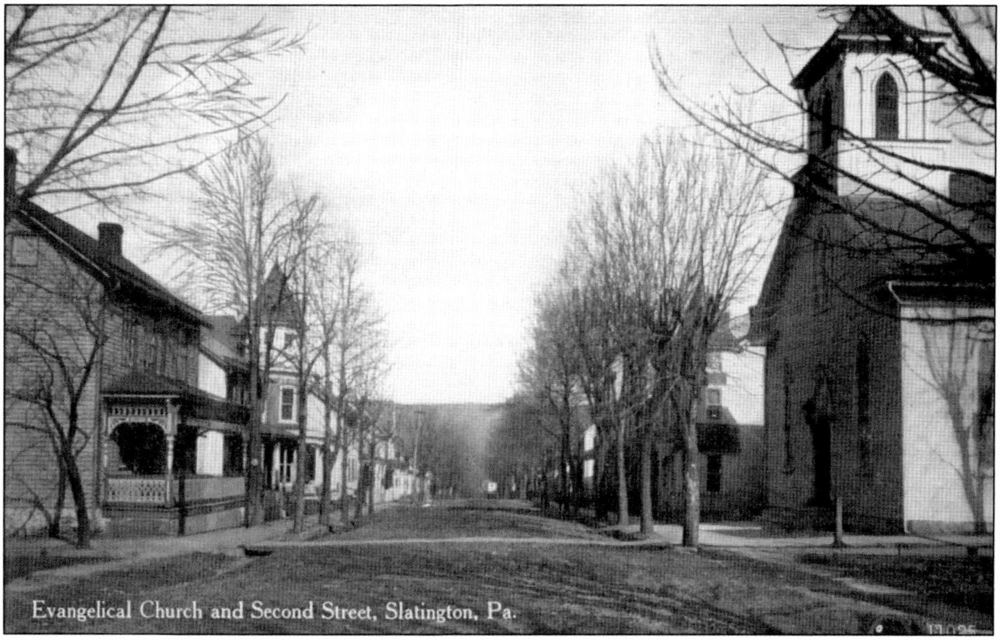

The Evangelical church, along Second Street in Slatington, became the Slatington Women's Club. The building now contains apartments. (Courtesy of Larry Hillborn.)

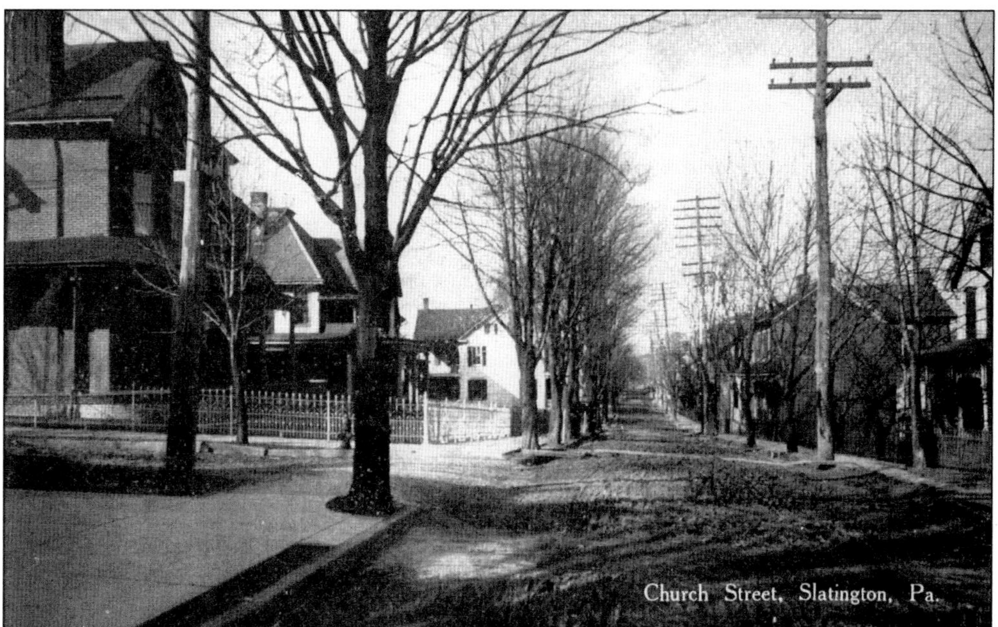

Shown here is a c. 1910 view of Church Street in Slatington. (Courtesy of Larry Hillborn.)

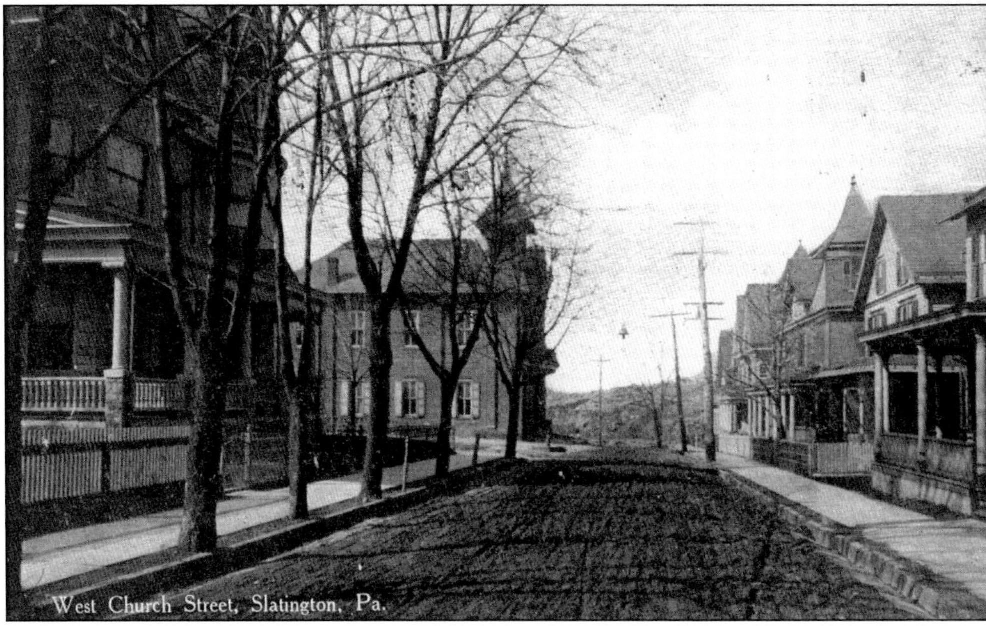

Constructed in 1889, the building on the left at the end of West Church Street is Hose Company No. 1, The building also served as Slatington's first municipal building. (Courtesy of Larry Hillborn.)

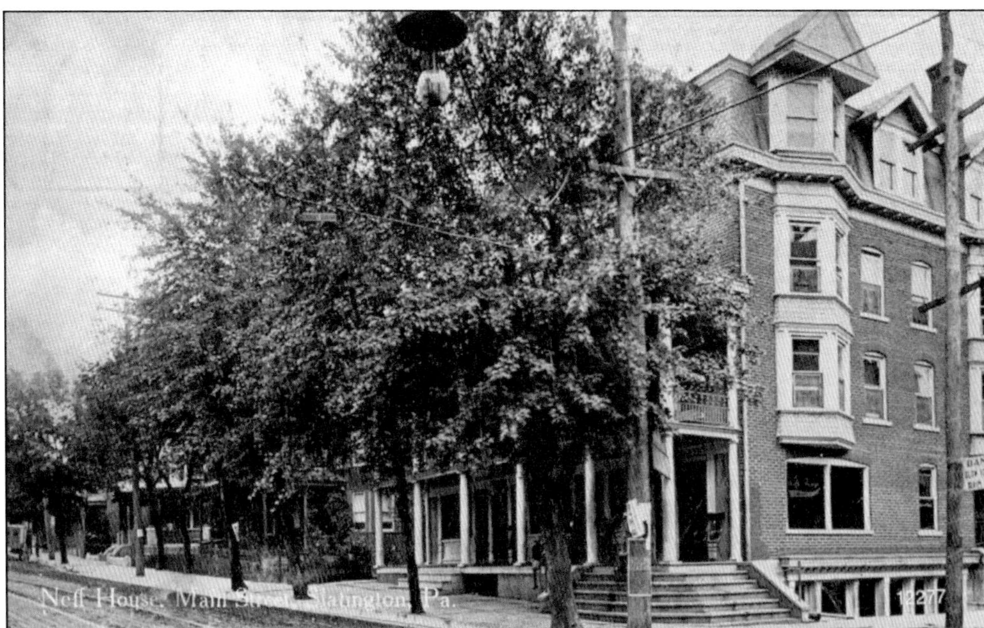

The Neff House, located on Main Street in Slatington, was built in 1850 by John Remaley, great-grandson of Ambrose Remaley. Edward B. Neff renamed it in 1869 after purchasing it. The first election in 1864—when Robert McDowell was elected first burgess of Slatington—took place in this building. (Courtesy of Larry Hillborn.)

The Slatington Post Office, shown here around 1907, was known over the years as Lyceum Hall and the Berlin Building. The structure's upper floors contained offices for J. K. Hower's slate company, the Meadow Brook Slate Company, and, in 1908, the Blue Ridge Slate Company. (Courtesy of Larry Hillborn.)

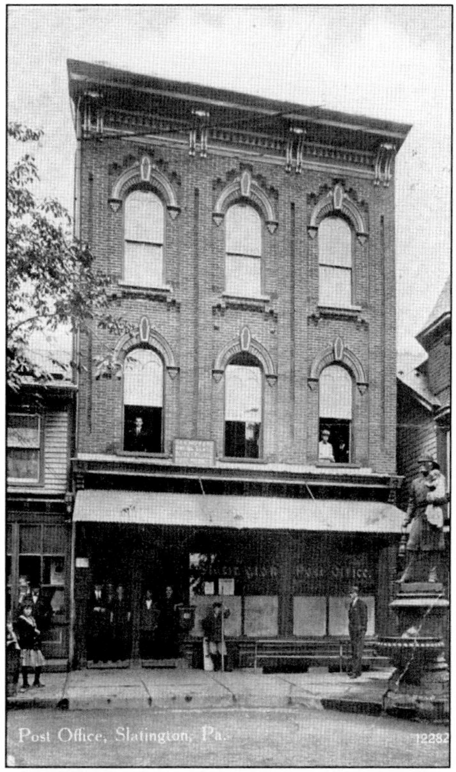

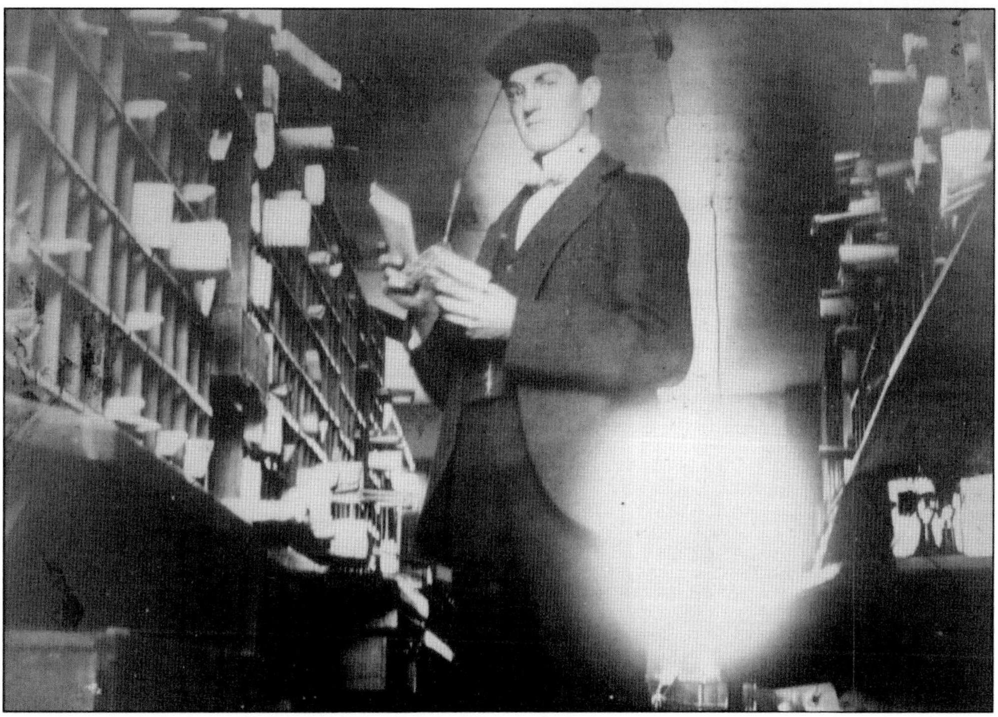

David Lutz served as Slatington postmaster from 1897 to 1903. This photograph is dated 1897. (Courtesy of Slatington Public Library, Northern Lehigh Future Focus Collection.)

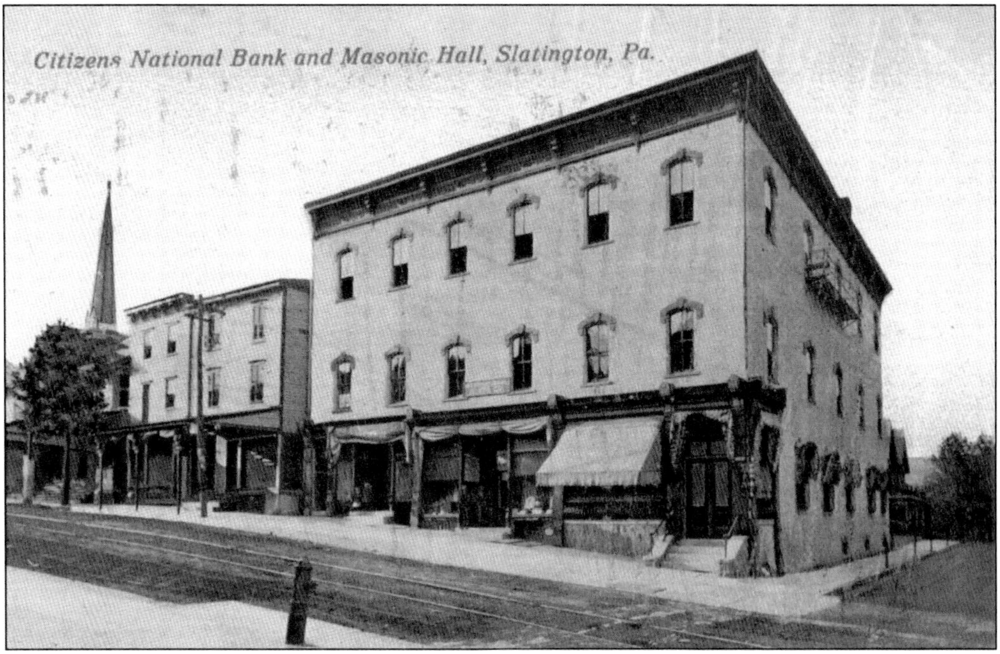

The Citizens National Bank and Masonic Hall in Slatington was built in 1902 and remodeled in 1930. It is shown here around 1923. (Courtesy of Kayleigh Billings.)

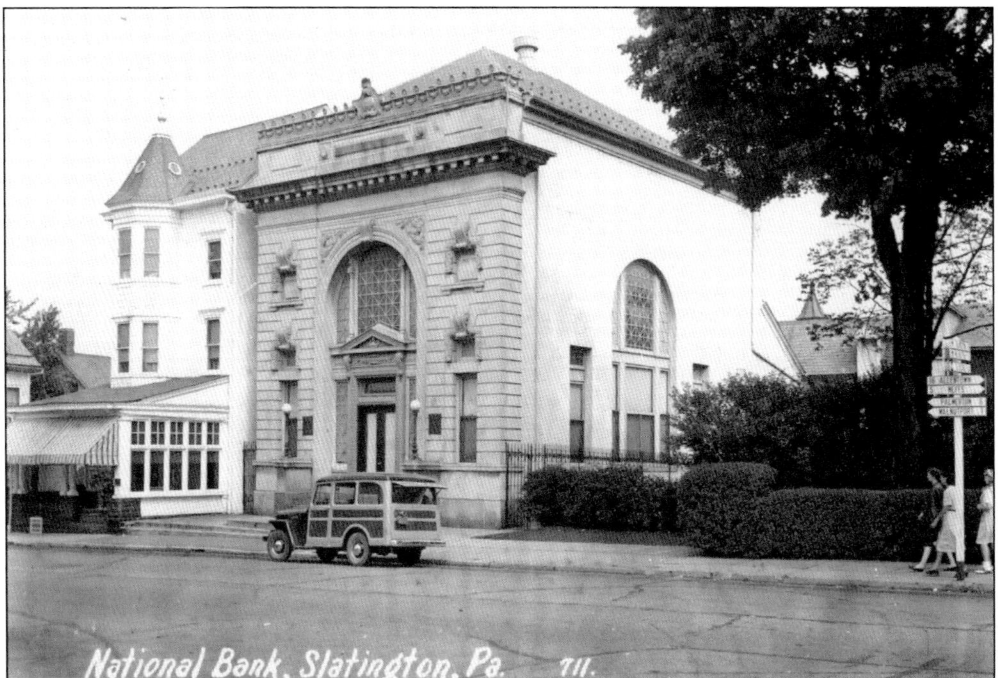

The National Bank in Slatington opened in 1875 and was renovated in 1957. This building was later razed to make way for the current bank. (Courtesy of Larry Hillborn.)

The Premiere Musical Association was located at 650 Main Street in Slatington. Built in 1897, it later became a five-and-dime store. (Courtesy of Larry Hillborn.)

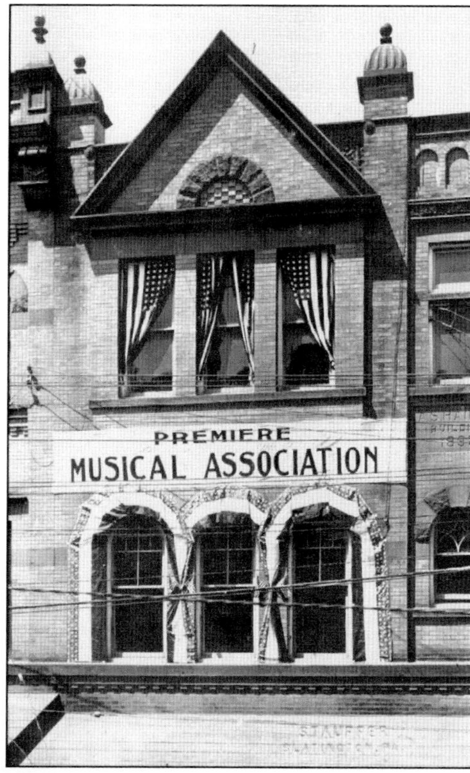

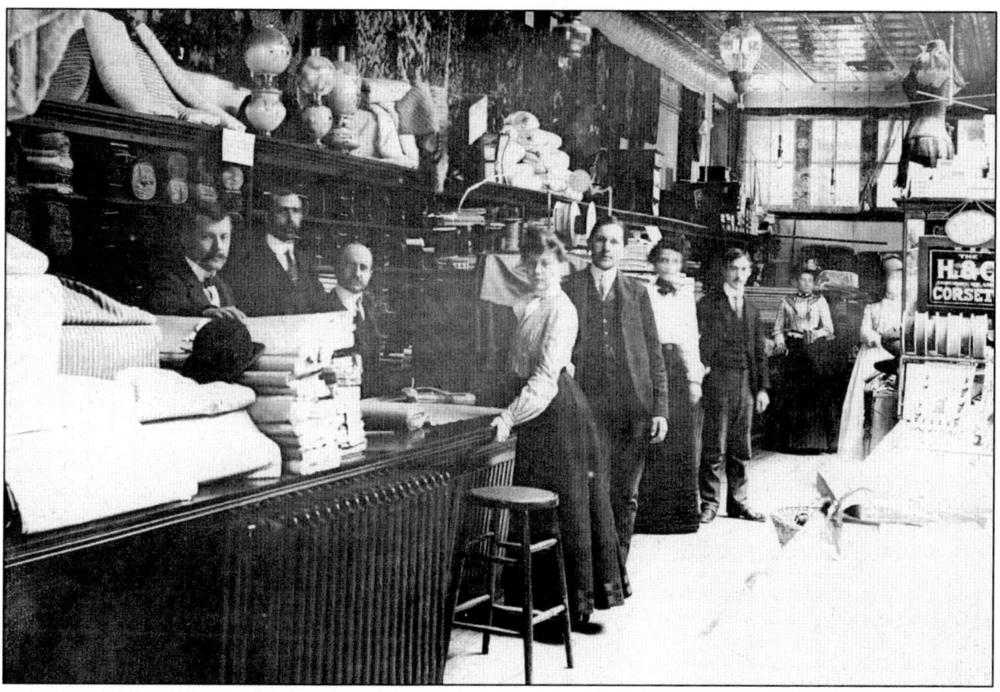

Warren Godshalk, third from the left, is among the people shown inside Haines' Store. The building currently serves as the Slatington Public Library. (Courtesy of Slatington Public Library, Northern Lehigh Future Focus Collection.)

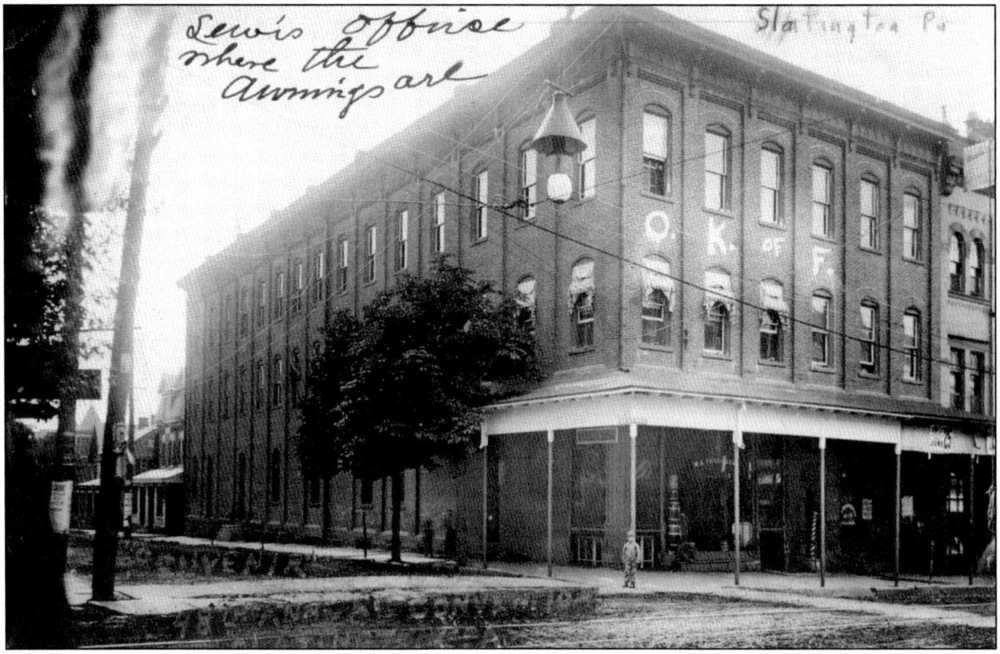

Fritzinger's Hardware was located at the corner of West Church and Main Streets. (Courtesy of Larry Hillborn.)

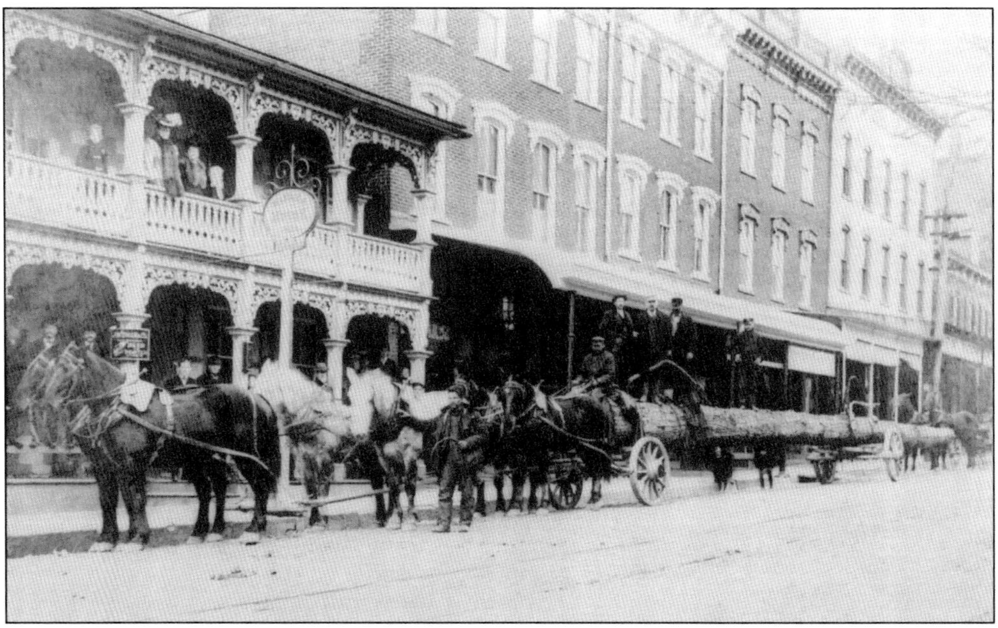

A photograph from 1876 shows a mule team pulling a long lumber wagon in front of the Mansion House Hotel on Main Street in Slatington. The proprietor at this time was R. J. Ringer. The large log may have been going to a slate quarry to be used as a hoist. The Mansion House was located where the borough parking lot is today. (Courtesy of Raymond Holland Regional History Collection, Northern Lehigh Future Focus Collection.)

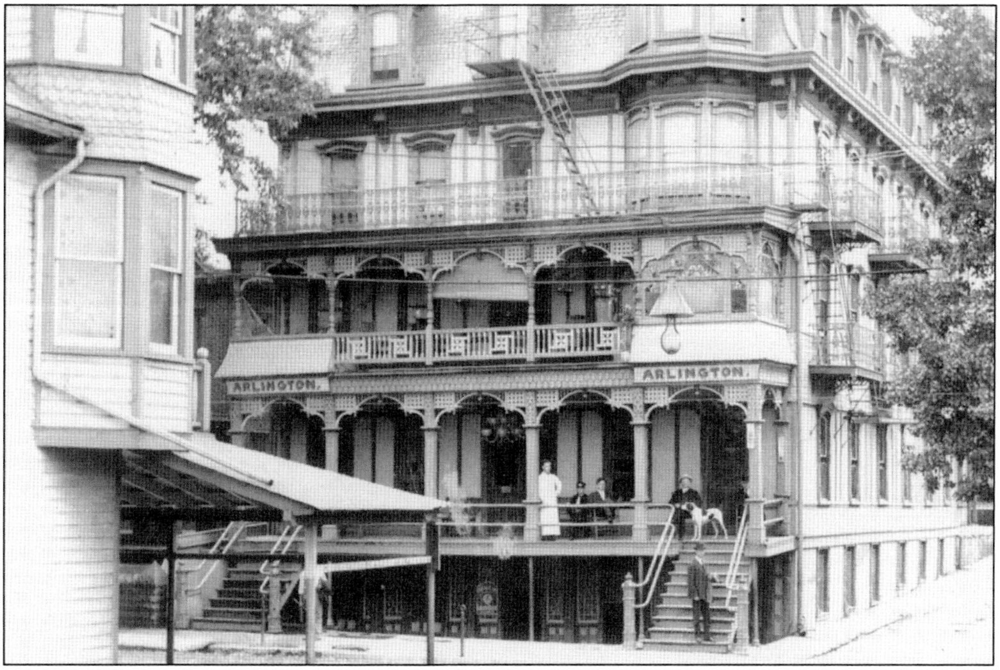

The Arlington Hotel, located at Main and Walnut Streets, was built in 1865. The front of the hotel was removed around 1932 and the remainder burned in the 1970s. L. F. Kuhns and B. F. Craig were two of the proprietors. (Courtesy of Northern Lehigh Future Focus Collection.)

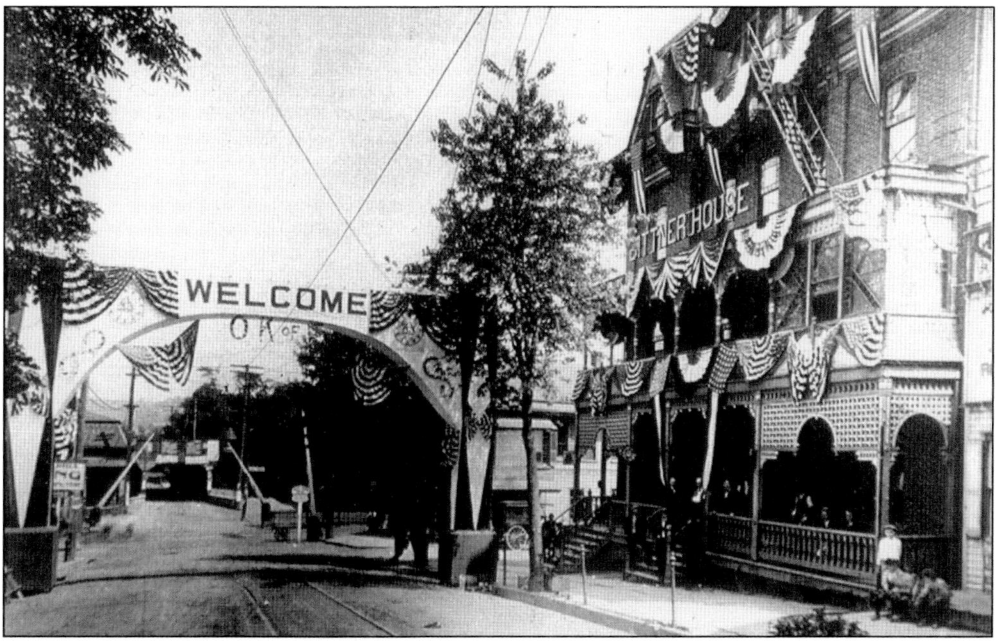

This view is looking down lower Main Street, during the grand session of the Order Knights of Friendship. Taken sometime between August 20 and 24, 1907, the photograph shows the covered bridge in the background crossing the river to Walnutport. The Bittner House Hotel is seen on the right. (Courtesy of St. John's United Church of Christ, Northern Lehigh Future Focus Collection.)

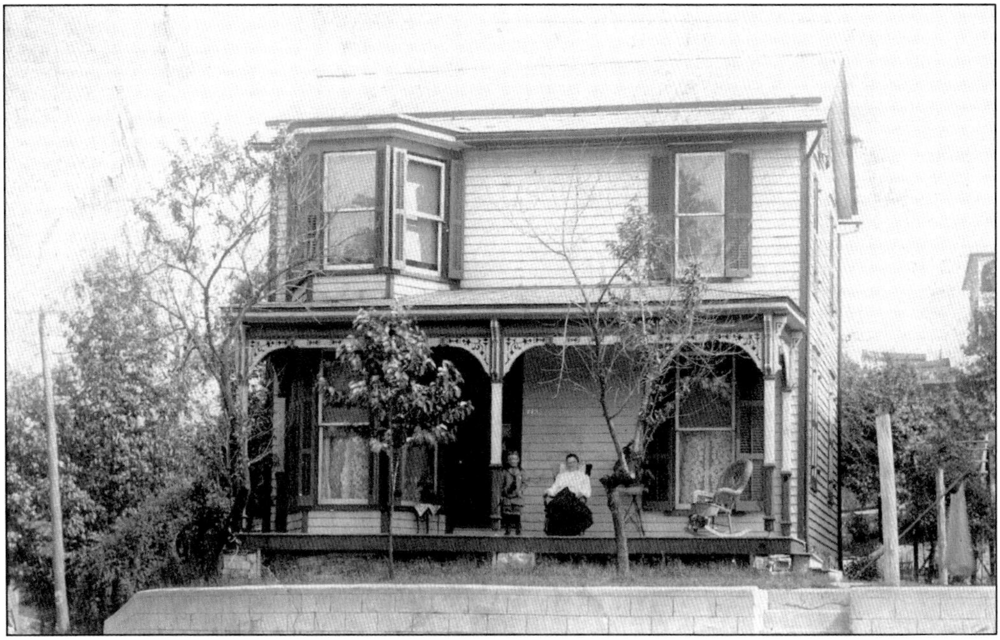

Grandma Hiel and her grandson Clark Hiel look out from their porch at 412 Chestnut Street in Slatington. (Courtesy of Larry Hillborn.)

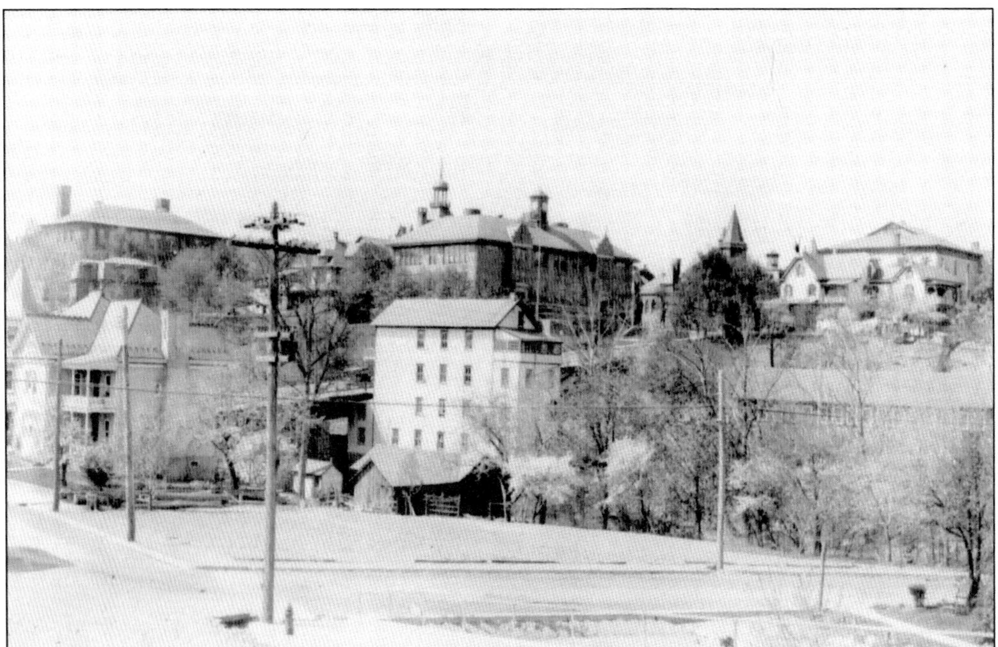

This is a *c.* 1950 view of Main Street in Slatington. The high school is in the center of the photograph. (Courtesy of Raymond Holland Regional History Collection, Northern Lehigh Future Focus Collection.)

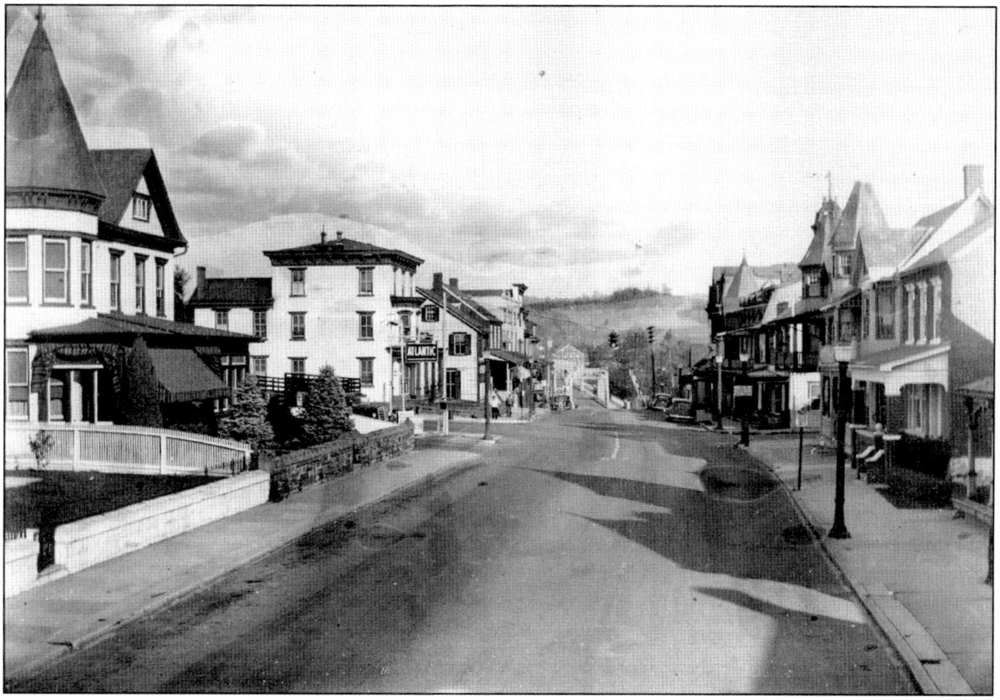

Lower Main Street in Slatington is seen in this photograph looking toward Walnutport. (Courtesy of Larry Hillborn.)

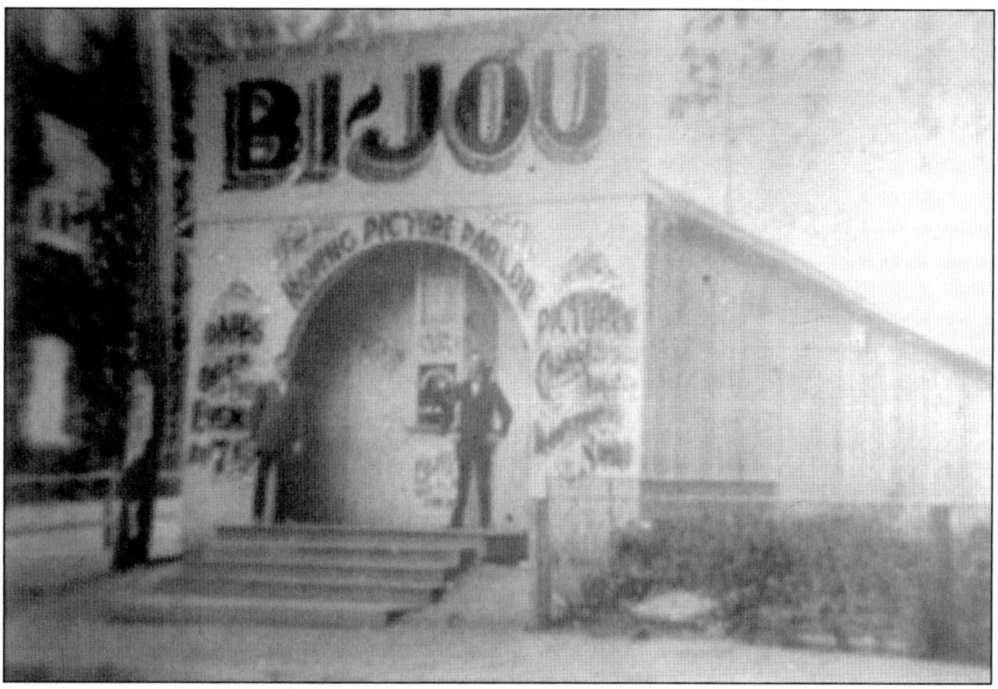

The Bi-Jou Moving Picture Parlor was located on the north side of Main Street at Kern Alley. It showed only silent movies. (Courtesy of Northern Lehigh Future Focus Collection.)

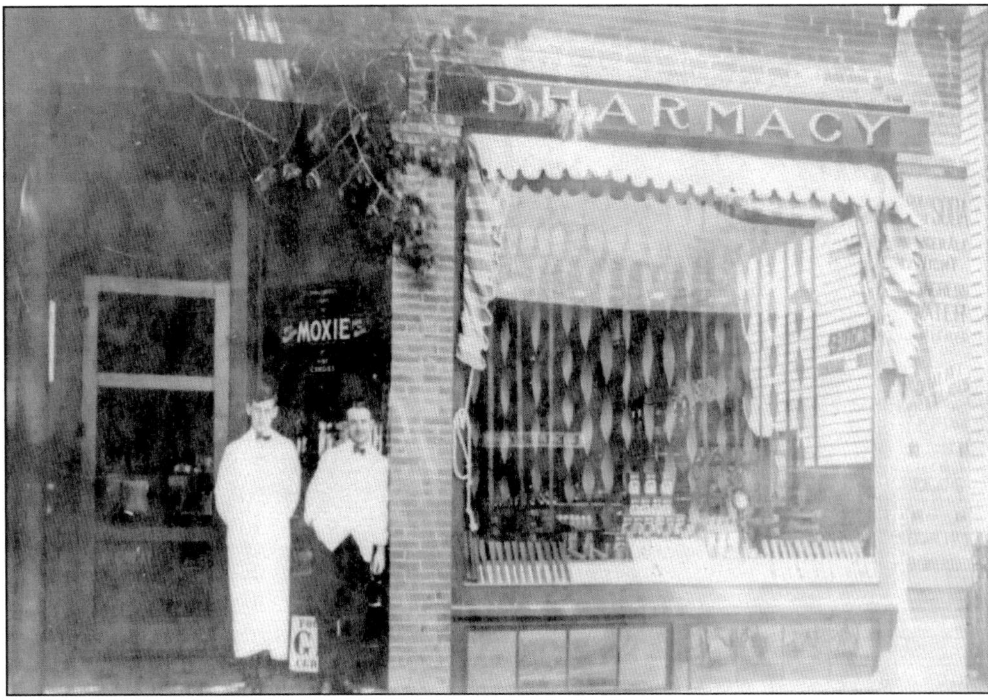

Druggists stand outside Rex's Drug Store, located at 614 Main Street in Slatington, around 1900. (Courtesy of Raymond Holland Regional History Collection, Northern Lehigh Future Focus Collection.)

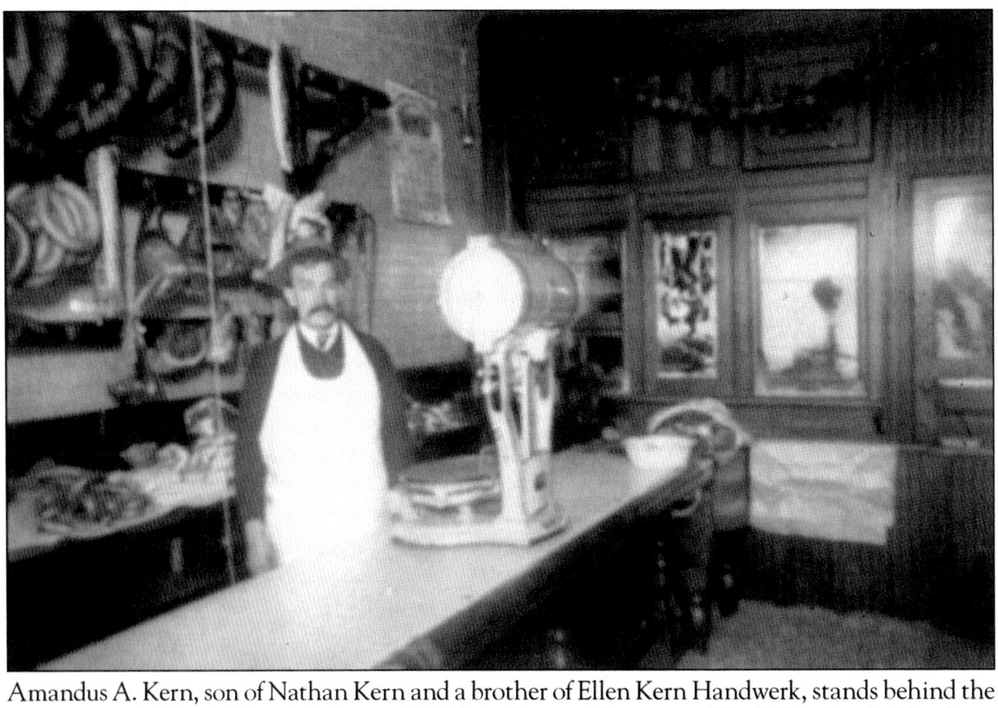

Amandus A. Kern, son of Nathan Kern and a brother of Ellen Kern Handwerk, stands behind the counter inside Kern's Meat Market at 560 Main Street. (Courtesy of Paul Handwerk, Northern Lehigh Future Focus Collection.)

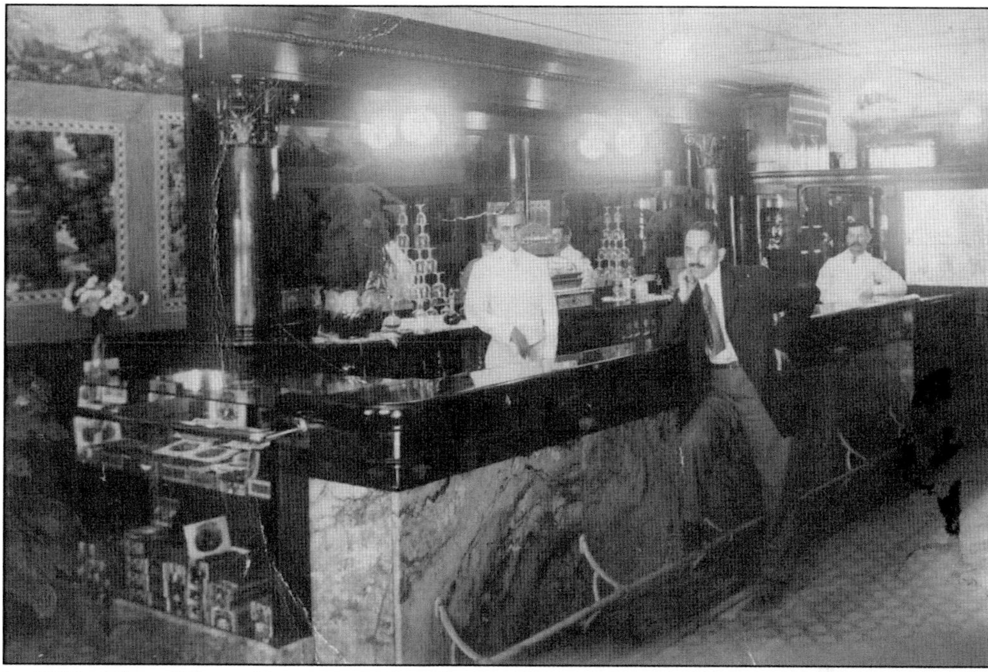

In 1892, Albert Ulysses Kuntz started a saloon and restaurant at 623 Main Street, in which he also sold tobacco and candy. He discontinued the saloon and restaurant in 1919 but continued the tobacco and candy business. (Courtesy of Larry Hillborn.)

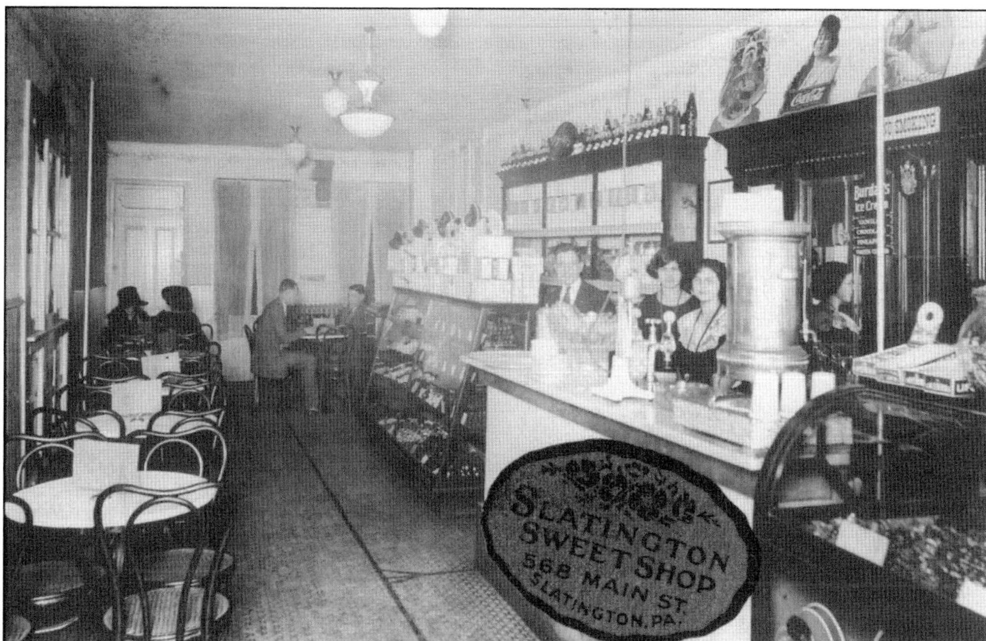

The interior of the Slatington Sweet Shop, 568 Main Street in Slatington, is seen in this photograph. (Courtesy of Larry Hillborn.)

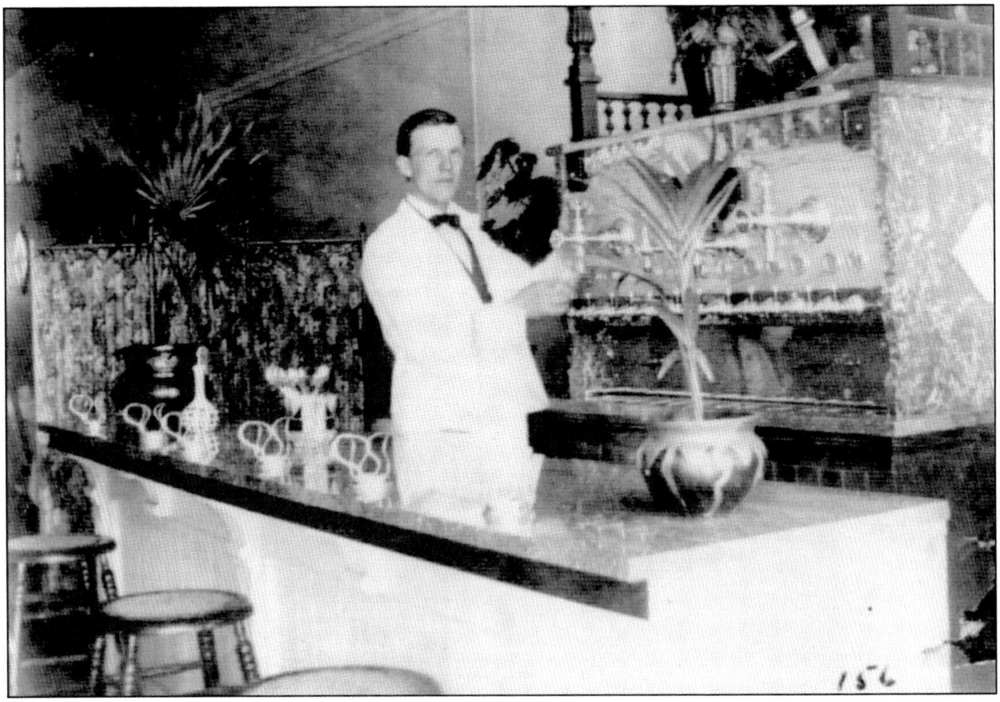

This photograph, taken on March 19, 1898, shows George Grim's soda fountain in Slatington. (Courtesy of Slatington Public Library, Northern Lehigh Future Focus Collection.)

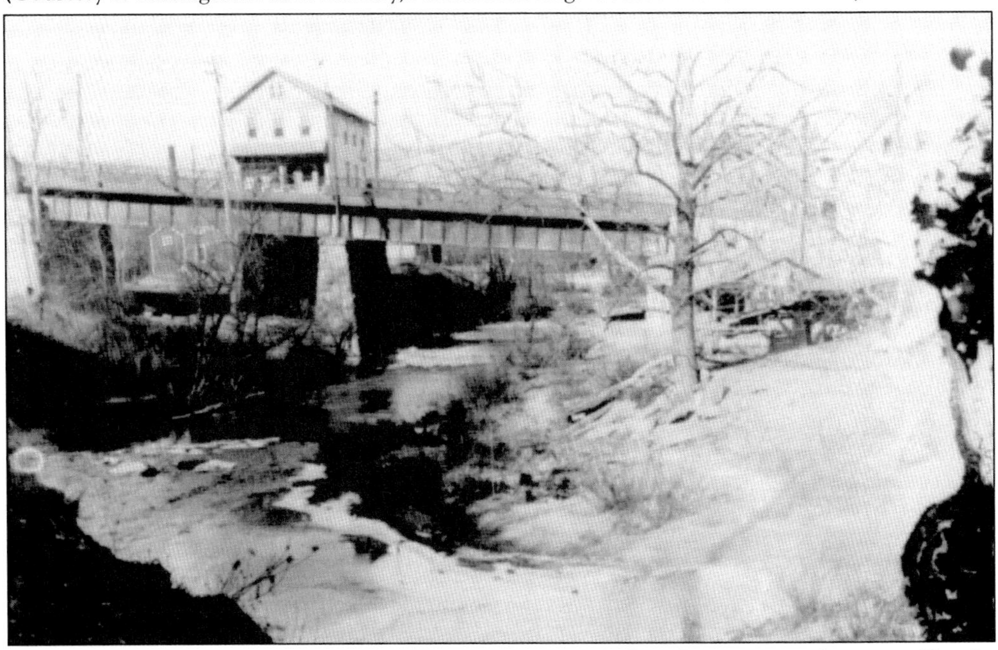

When the Main Street Bridge was built in 1903, James G. Rauch constructed a new office for his newspaper business, moving it from the basement of the Citizens National Bank building. The unique building had access to the street at bridge level. This photograph was taken around 1910. (Courtesy of Raymond Holland Regional History Collection, Northern Lehigh Future Focus Collection.)

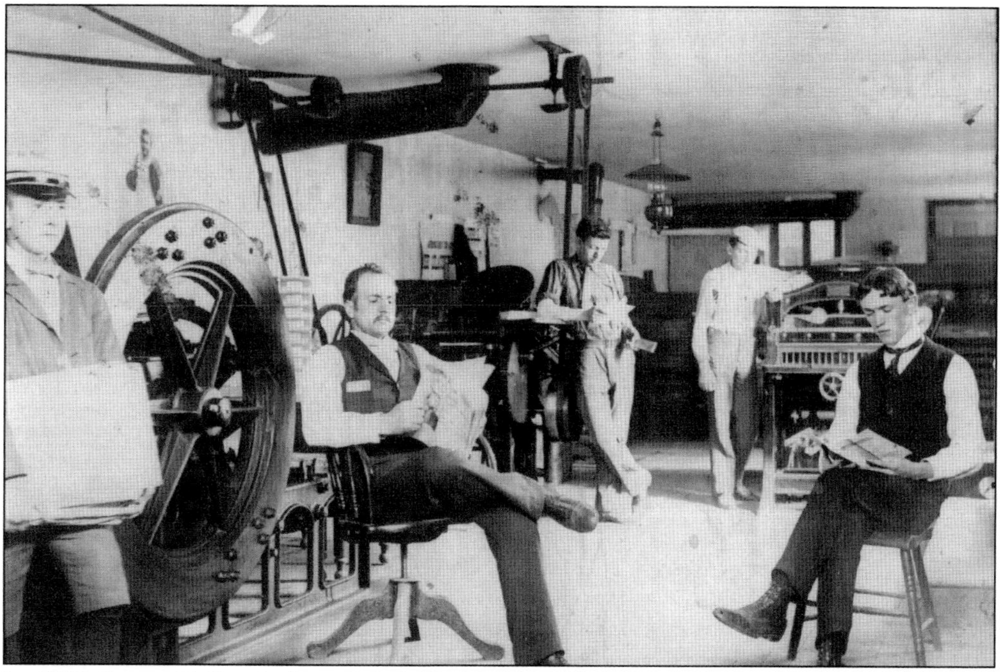

In 1898, James G. Rauch (seated at left) moved to Slatington, purchased a print shop, and published the *Slatington News* until 1985.

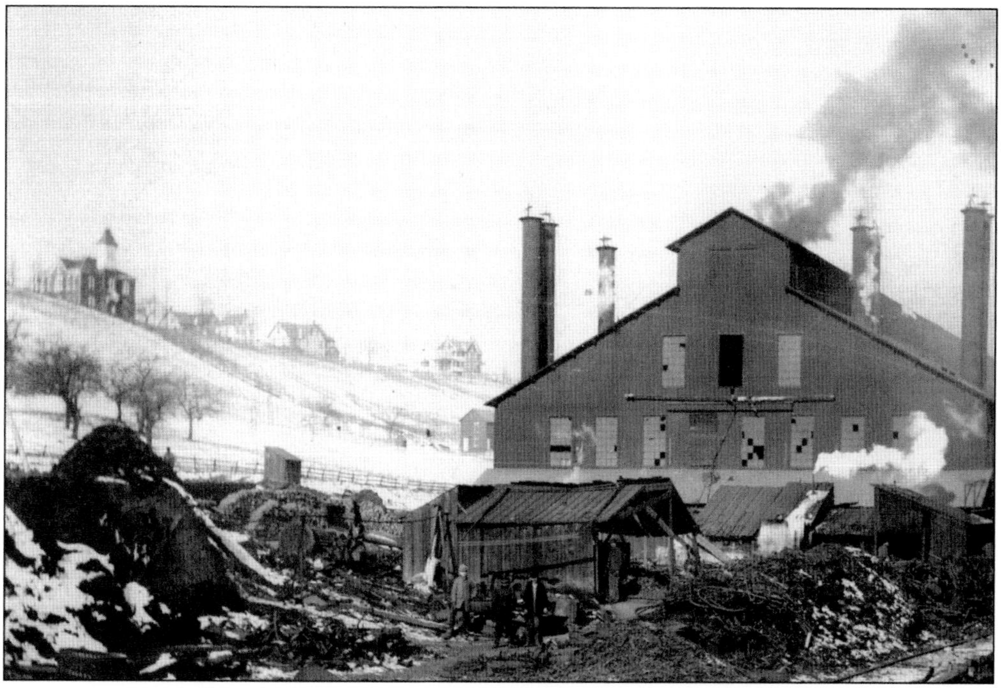

The Slatington Rolling Mill Company was organized in 1890 by William P. Hopkins. Located on South Walnut Street, the company employed 160 people and made steel. The mill went out of business in 1911 and tried to reopen under several names before closing for good in 1922. In 1927, Harry E. Orkin purchased the site to operate his scrap business.

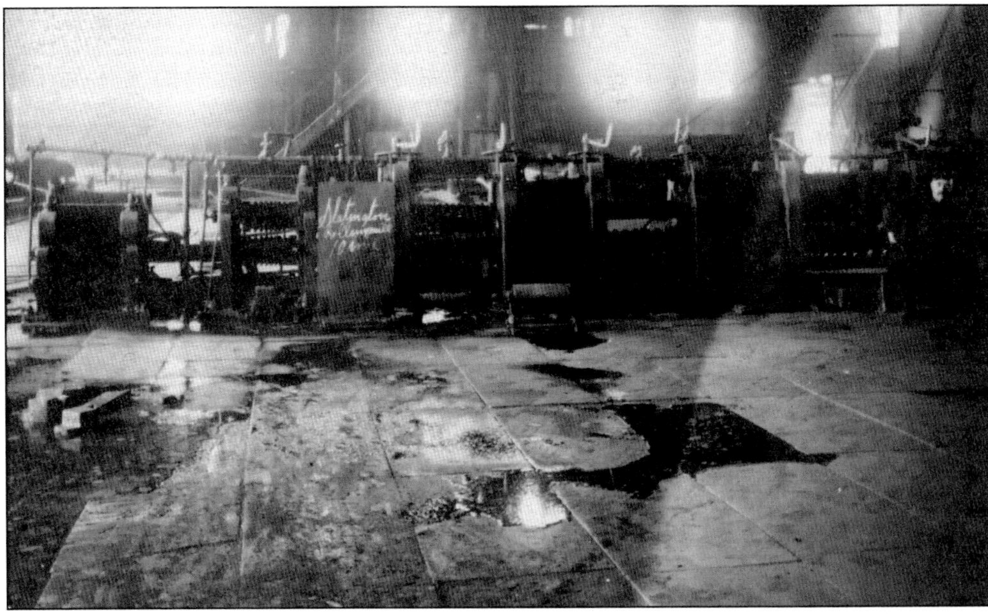

This is the 10-inch train in the Slatington Rolling Mill. (Courtesy of Larry Hillborn.)

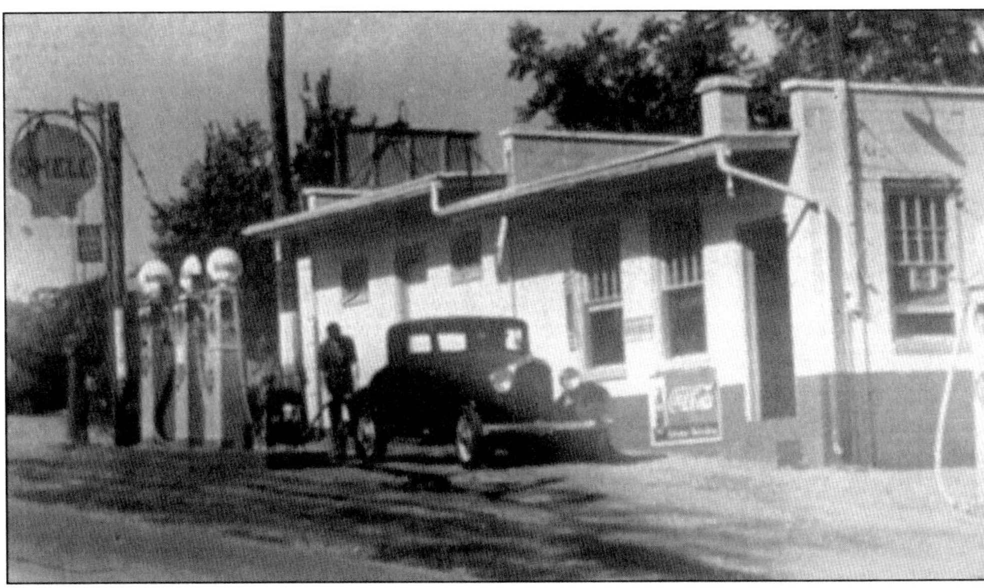

This photograph shows the Shell station, located at the corner of Walnut and Chestnut Streets in Slatington, as it appeared in 1930. (Courtesy of Diana Hoffman, Northern Lehigh Future Focus Collection.)

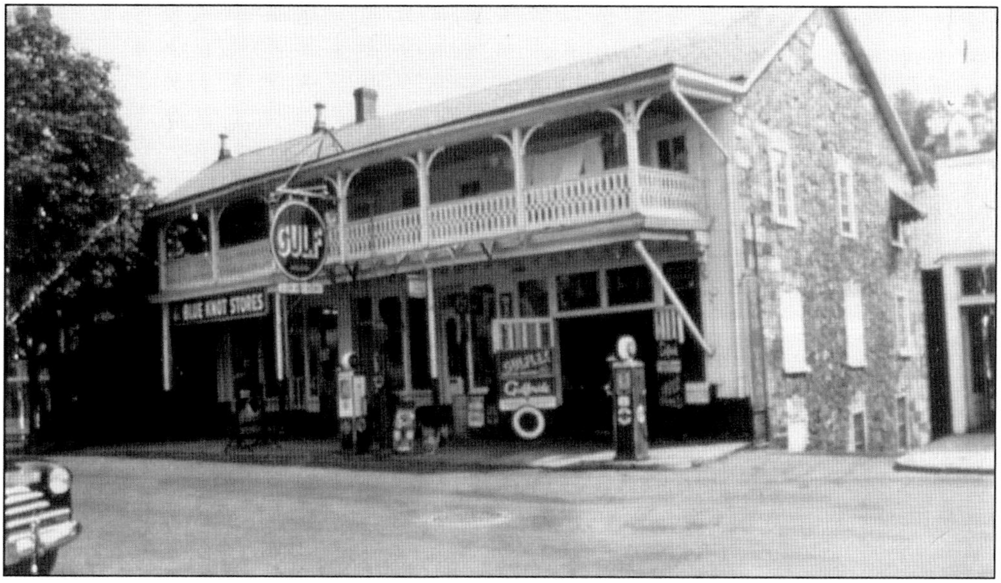

The Slatington Garage, located on lower Main Street, is shown here around 1950. (Courtesy of Jodi Hampton, Northern Lehigh Future Focus Collection.)

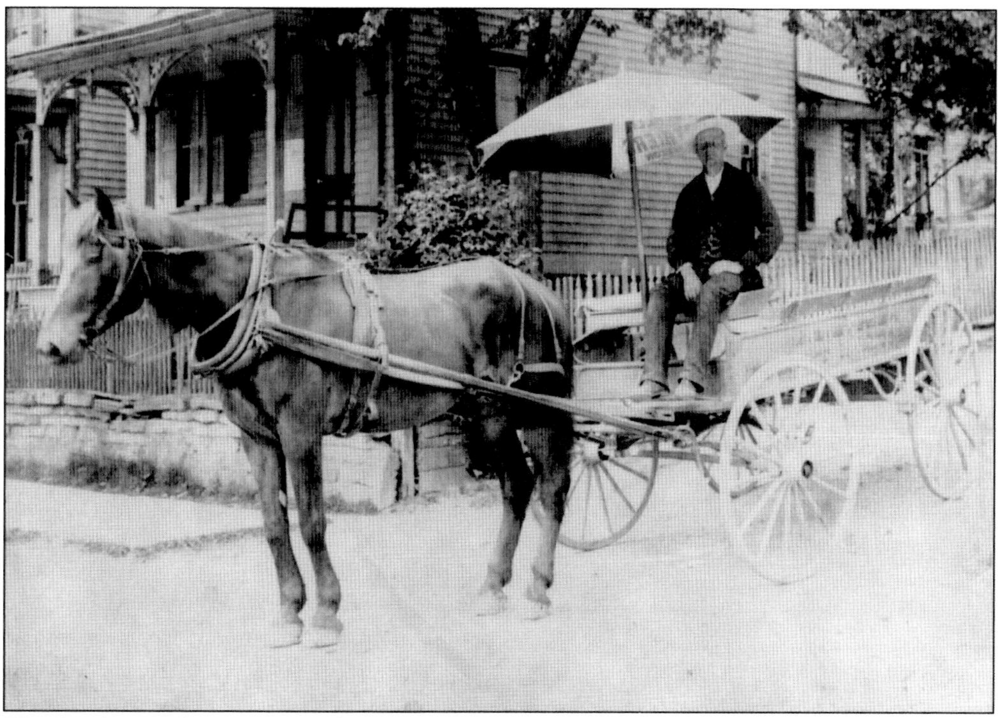

The Snyder Lumber Company delivery wagon looked like this in 1890. (Courtesy of Raymond Holland Regional Historical Collection, Northern Lehigh Future Focus Collection.)

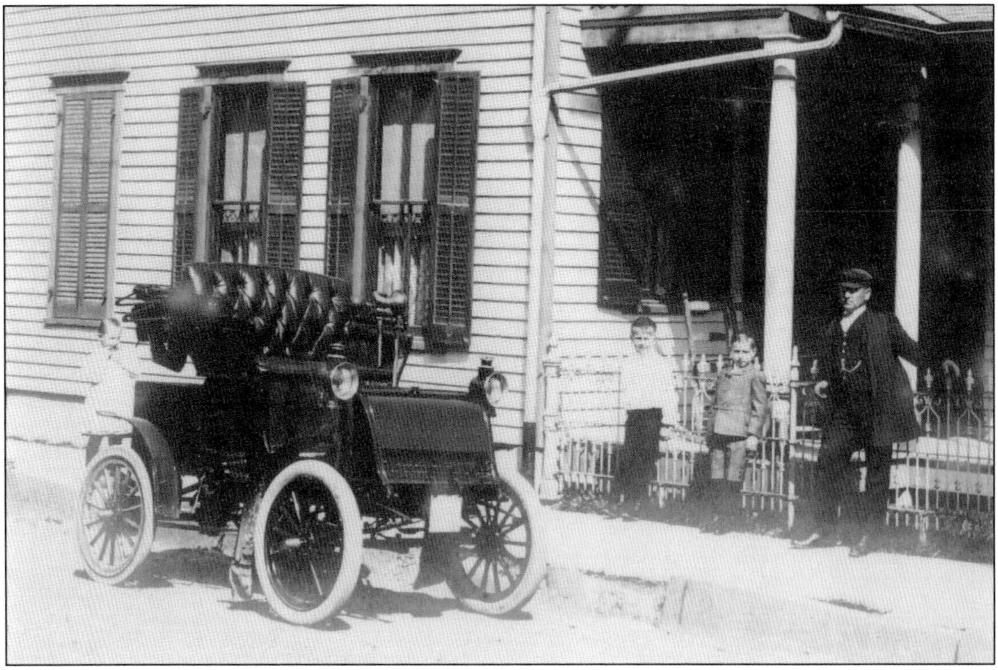

John Paules, right, owned this Elmore automobile, manufactured in Slatington by the Dettmer and Handwerk Motor Company in 1912. The Elmore came in three sizes with up to a 70-horsepower engine. The base model price was $1,250. Lawrence Haines is standing to the left of Paules. (Courtesy of Slatington Public Library, Northern Lehigh Future Focus Collection.)

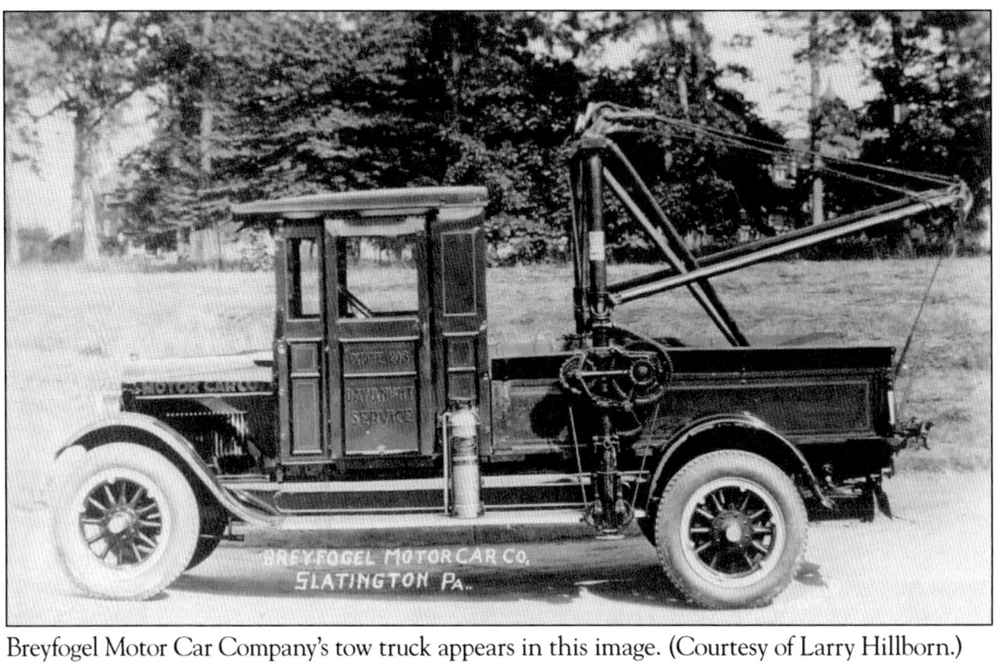

Breyfogel Motor Car Company's tow truck appears in this image. (Courtesy of Larry Hillborn.)

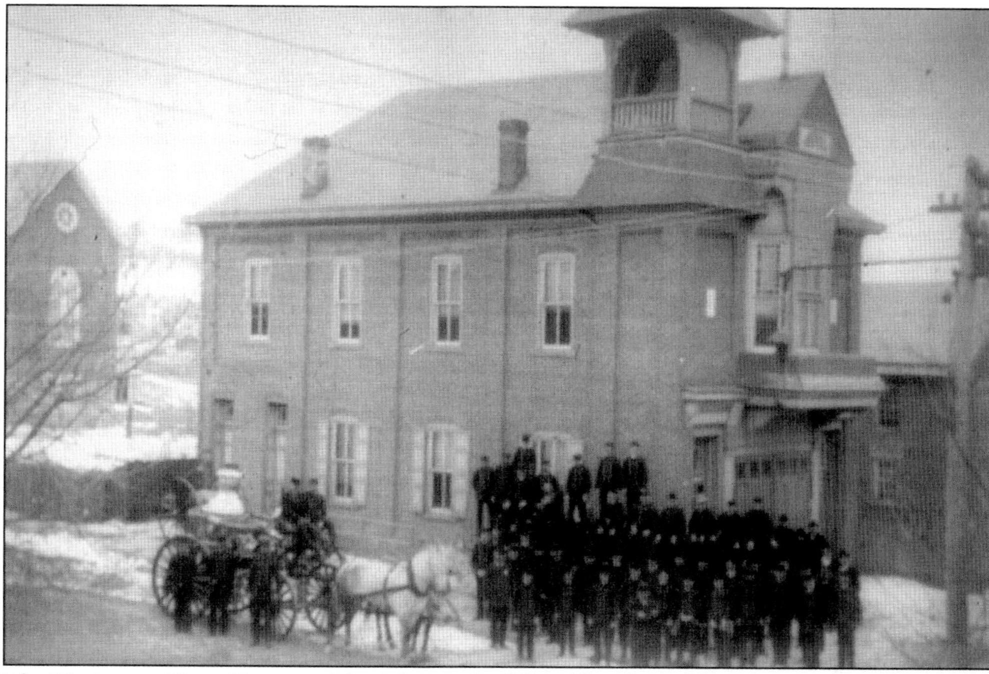

The Slatington Hose Company No. 1, located at West Church and Fourth Streets, is shown here around 1900. The building was constructed in 1889 and also served as the town hall. (Courtesy of Paul Handwerk, Northern Lehigh Future Focus Collection.)

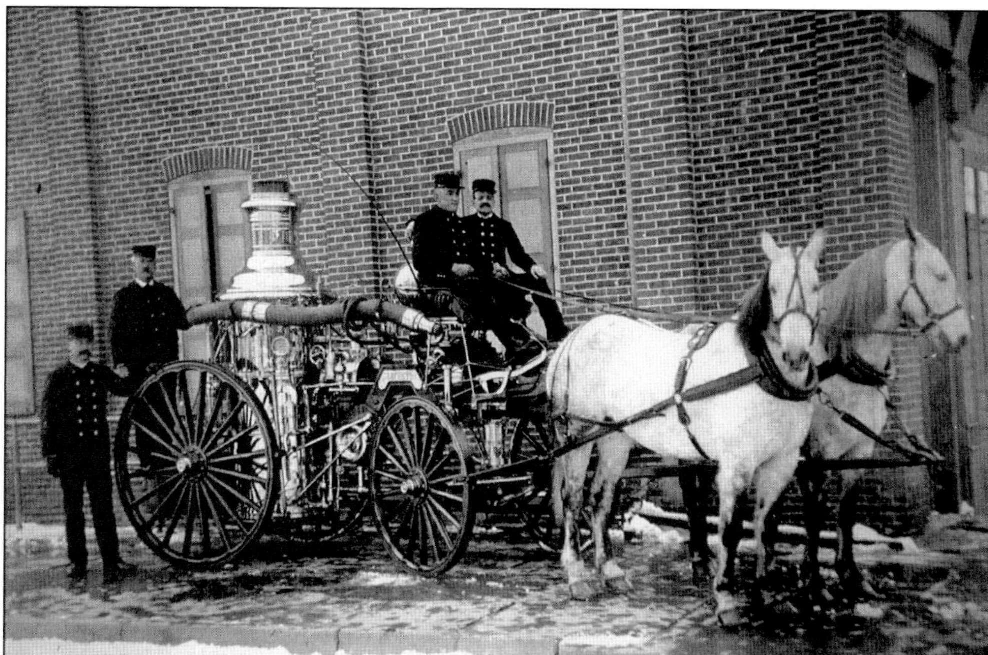

The Hose Company No. 1 horse-drawn fire pump stands ready in front of the firehouse in this c. 1890 photograph. The borough purchased the Silsby steamer in 1889 for $2,691.50. Two specially trained horses, Sam and Dan, pulled it. (Courtesy of Everett and Marilyn Kaul, Northern Lehigh Future Focus Collection.)

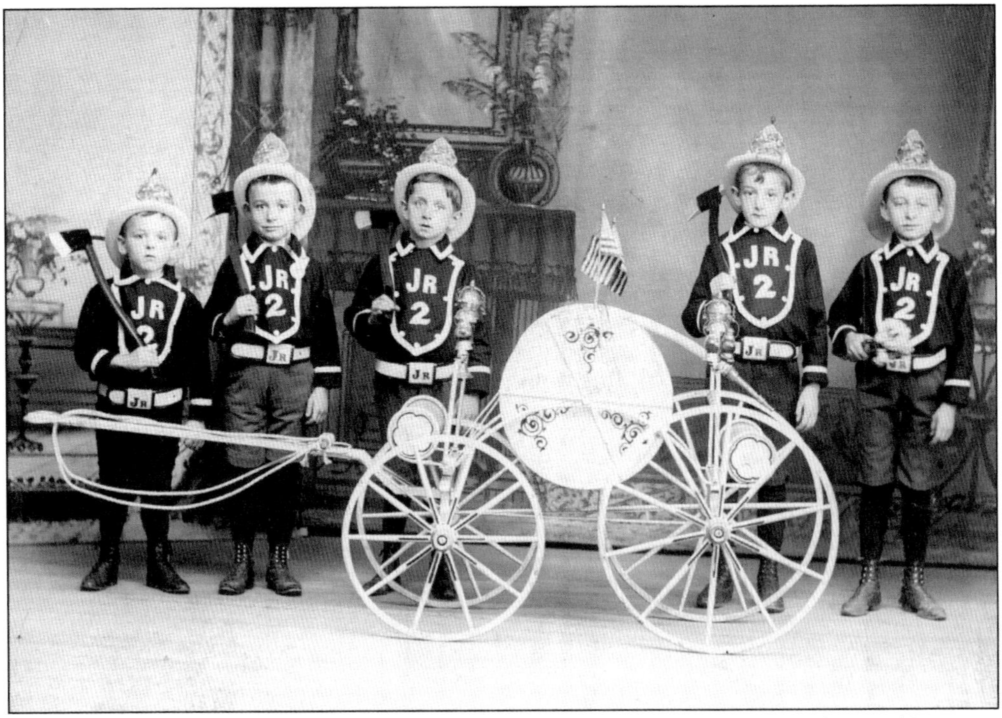

Youngsters pose with the Vigilant Fire Company No. 2 Junior Hose Cart around 1904. (Courtesy of Larry Hillborn.)

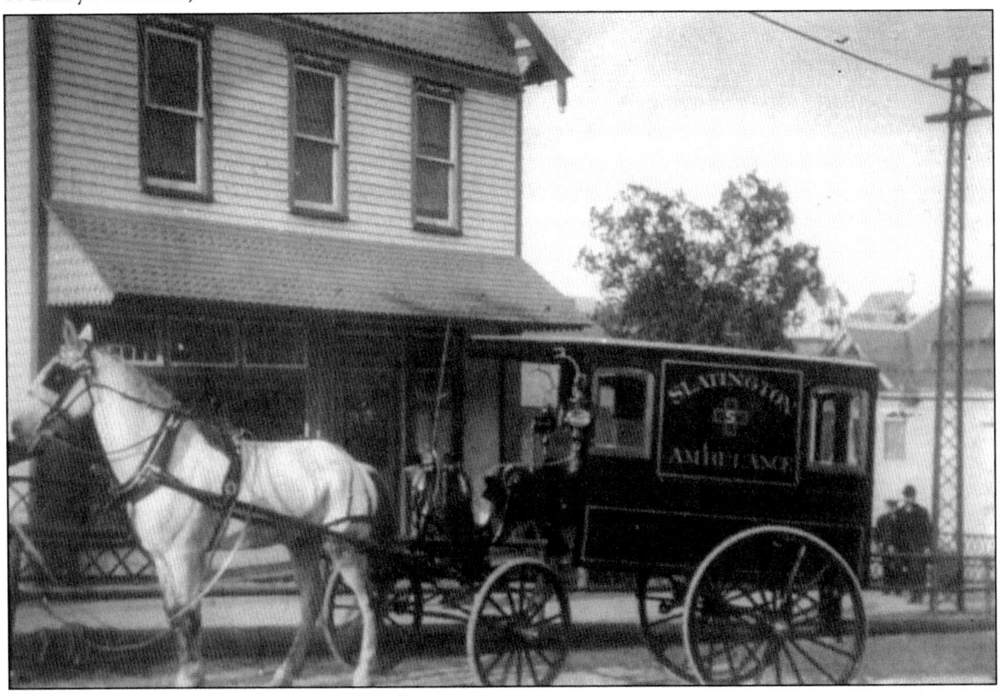

The Slatington ambulance stands in front of the News Publishing Company building on the Main Street Bridge, around 1900. (Courtesy of Paul Handwerk, Northern Lehigh Future Focus Collection.)

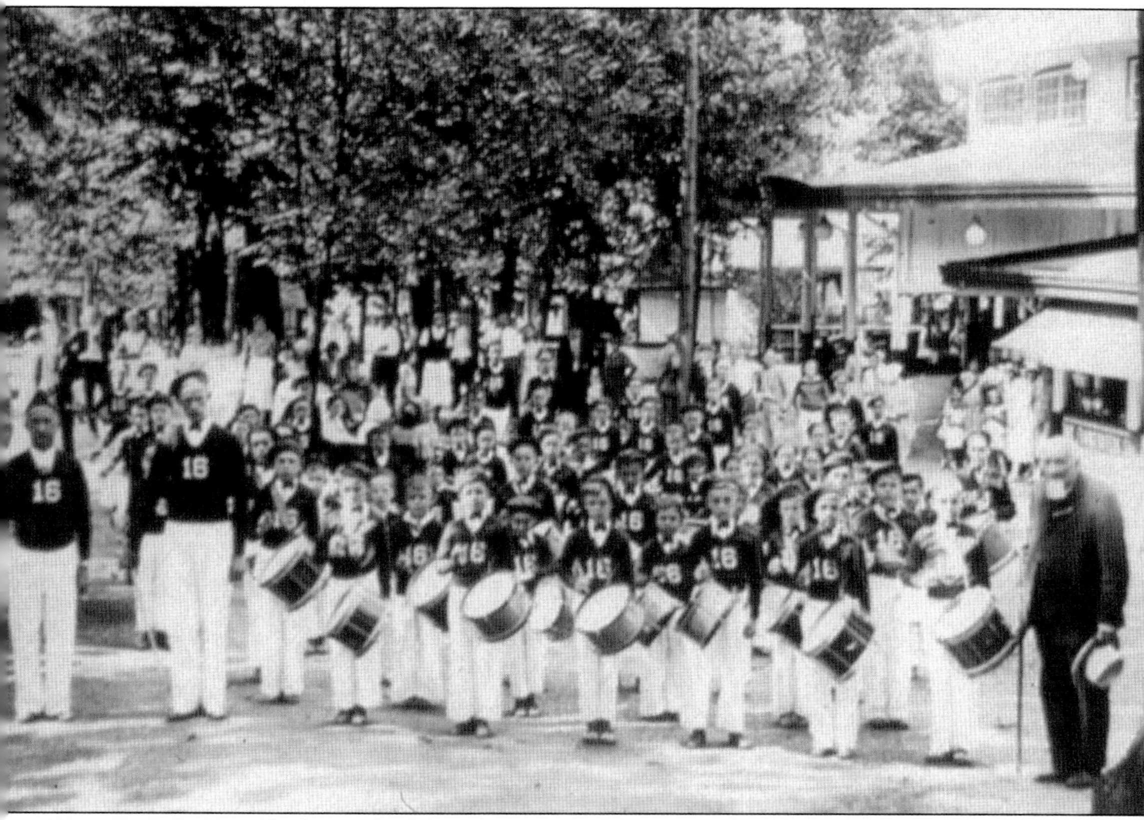

This 1930 photograph shows the last surviving Civil War veteran from the northern Lehigh area, Jerri Oswald, at right. Paul Handwerk is in the third row, second from the right, in this photograph of the Junior Drum and Bugle Corps, taken in Central Park in Allentown. (Courtesy of Paul Handwerk, Northern Lehigh Future Focus Collection.)

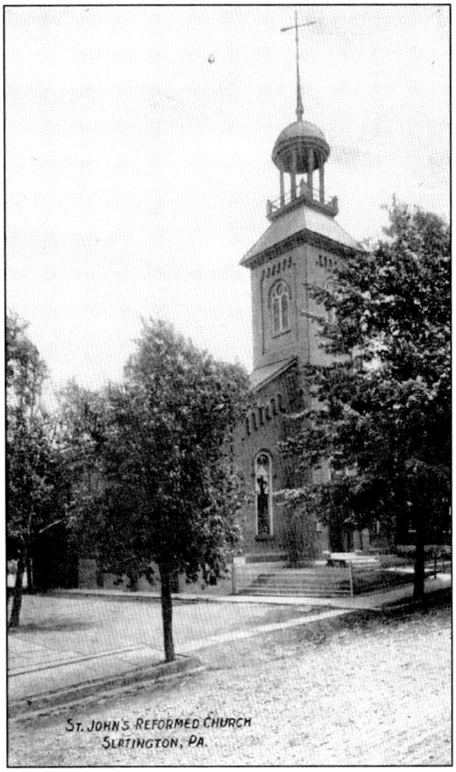

St. John's Reformed Church, shown here around 1908, was built in 1869. The steeple was added in 1900. Now it is a United Church of Christ. (Courtesy of Larry Hillborn.)

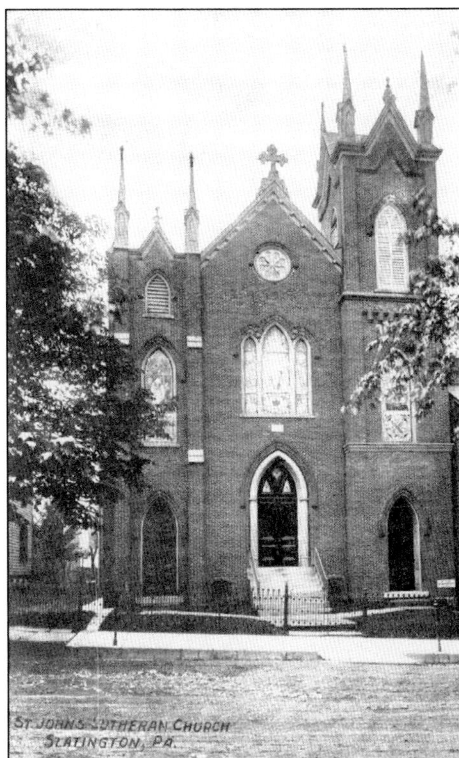

St. John's Lutheran Church in Slatington, built in 1881, is shown here around 1908. (Courtesy of Larry Hillborn.)

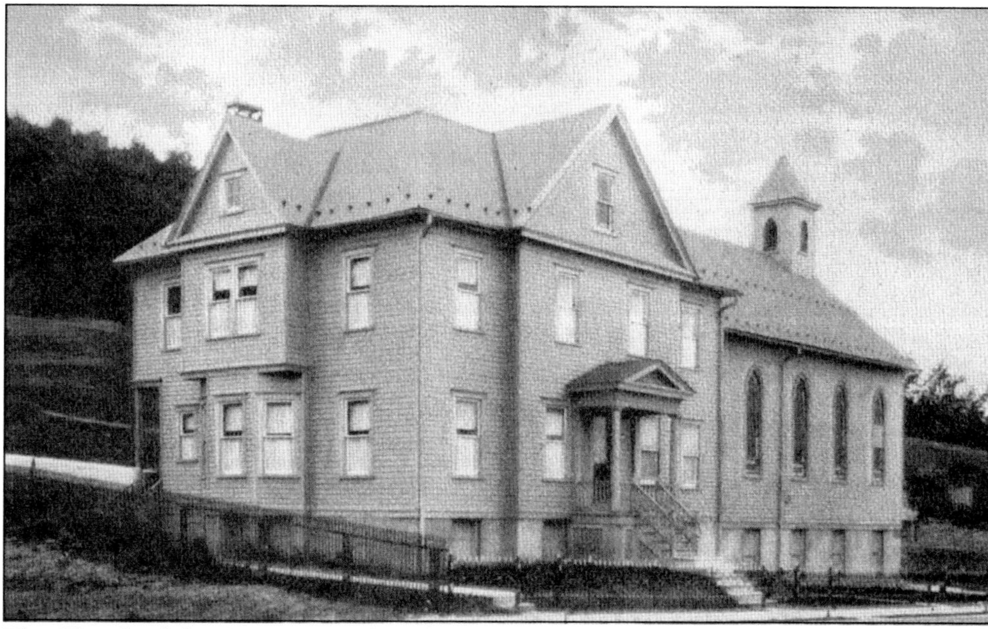

The Church of the Assumption Blessed Virgin Mary was built in 1883, and the rectory was added in 1908. The building was razed in 1986. (Courtesy of Larry Hillborn.)

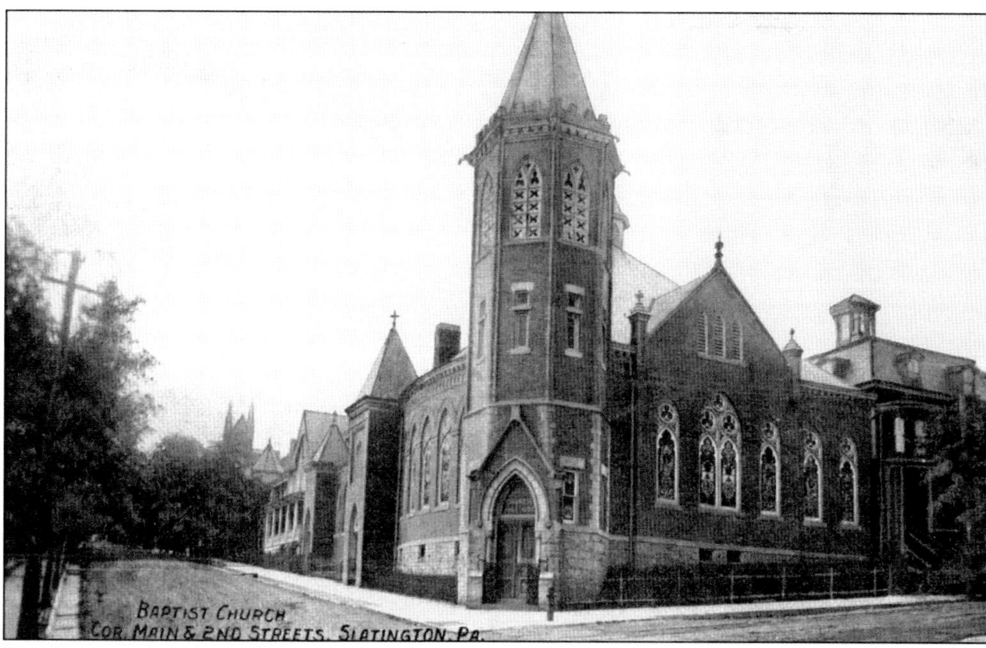

The Baptist church at the corner of Main and Second Streets, Slatington, was built in 1900. (Courtesy of Larry Hillborn.)

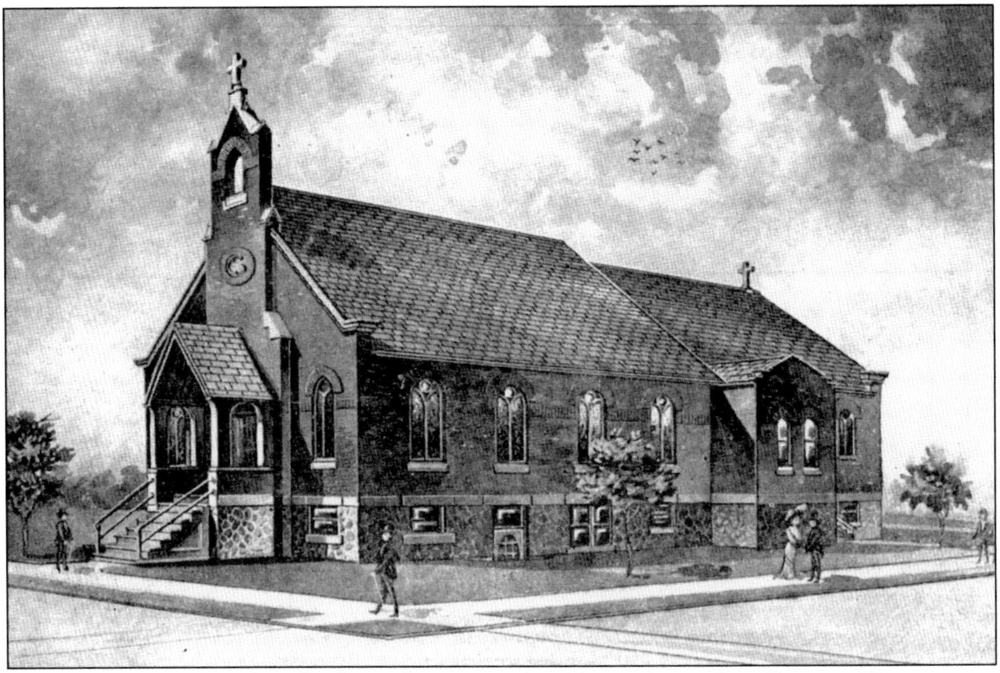

The Christ Episcopal Church, shown here around 1908, was located on Fairview Terrace, now Diamond and Williams Streets, in Slatington. (Courtesy of Larry Hillborn.)

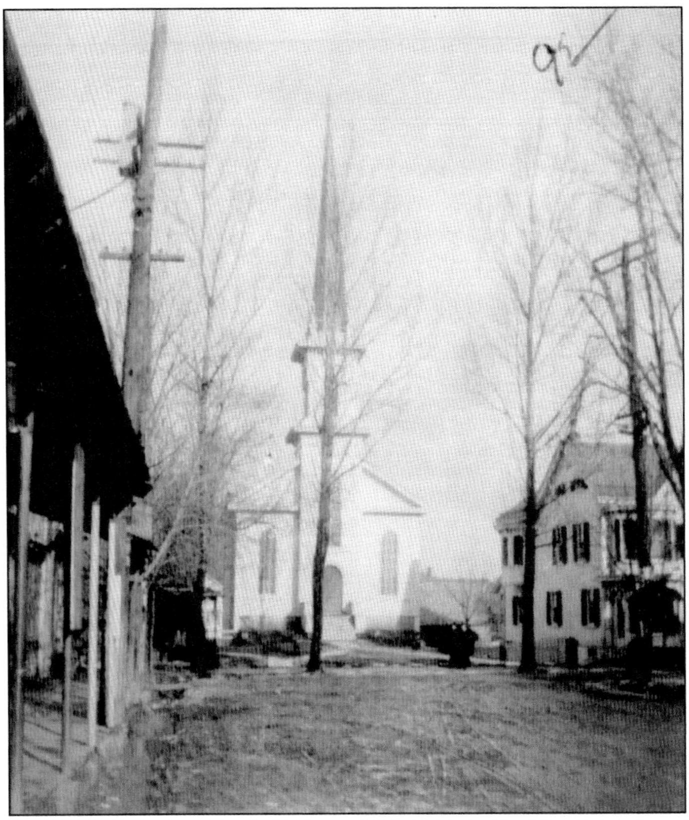

This photograph of the Presbyterian church on Main Street in Slatington was taken on December 5, 1897. (Courtesy of Slatington Public Library, Northern Lehigh Future Focus Collection.)

Two

WALNUTPORT

Walnutport was a village in Lehigh Township until it was officially incorporated as a borough in 1909. It was named for the many walnut trees found along the Lehigh Canal, built in 1829. The canal, built by the Lehigh Navigation Company, and the Central Railroad Company of New Jersey both ran through Walnutport and helped the village grow. The railroad had a combined passenger and freight station in Walnutport.

Walnutport was home to four hotels in the early 1900s—the Anchor Hotel, the Pennsylvania House, the Slate Exchange Hotel, and Marshall's Hotel. The Anchor Hotel and the Pennsylvania House still stand. The Slate Exchange Hotel was razed in the 1940s, and the Diamond Fire Company now stands in its place.

Walnutport had its own electrical plant, which generated hydroelectric power from the canal water. Called the Citizen's Electric Light, Heat and Power Company, its building was torn down in 1910.

The Diamond Fire Company was first organized in 1893 and was located on South Canal Street. It purchased land at Main and Washington Streets in 1902 and, in 1910, built the fire hall on this site using lumber salvaged from the razed Citizen's electric company.

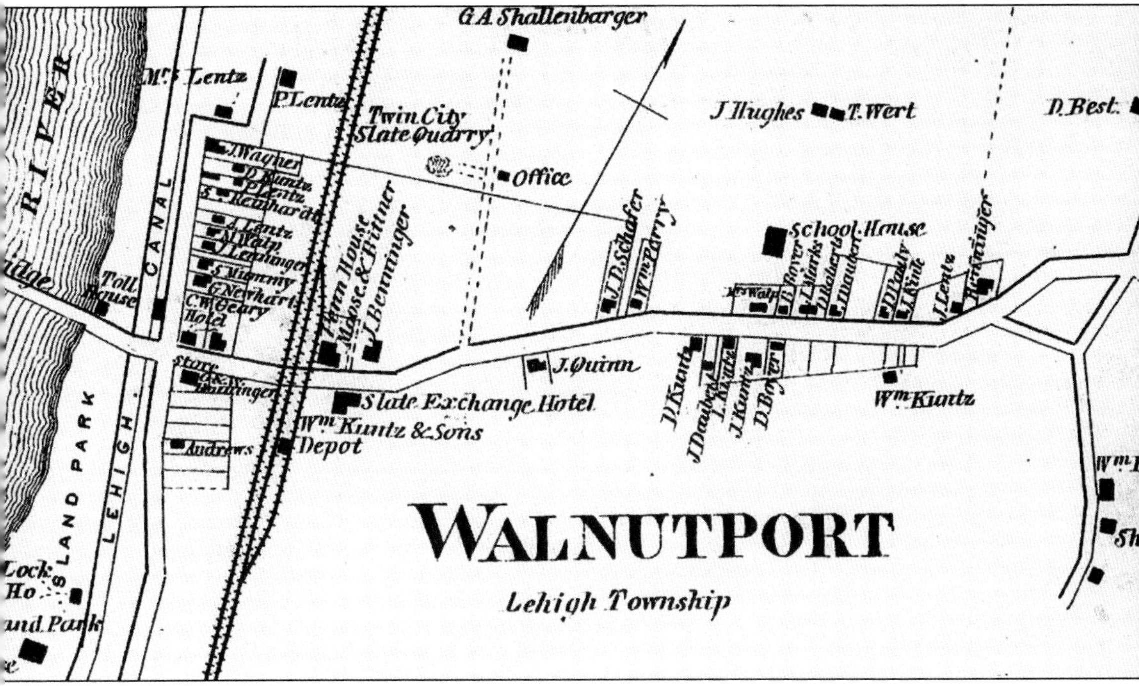

This map of Walnutport is from the 1876 *Centennial Atlas*.

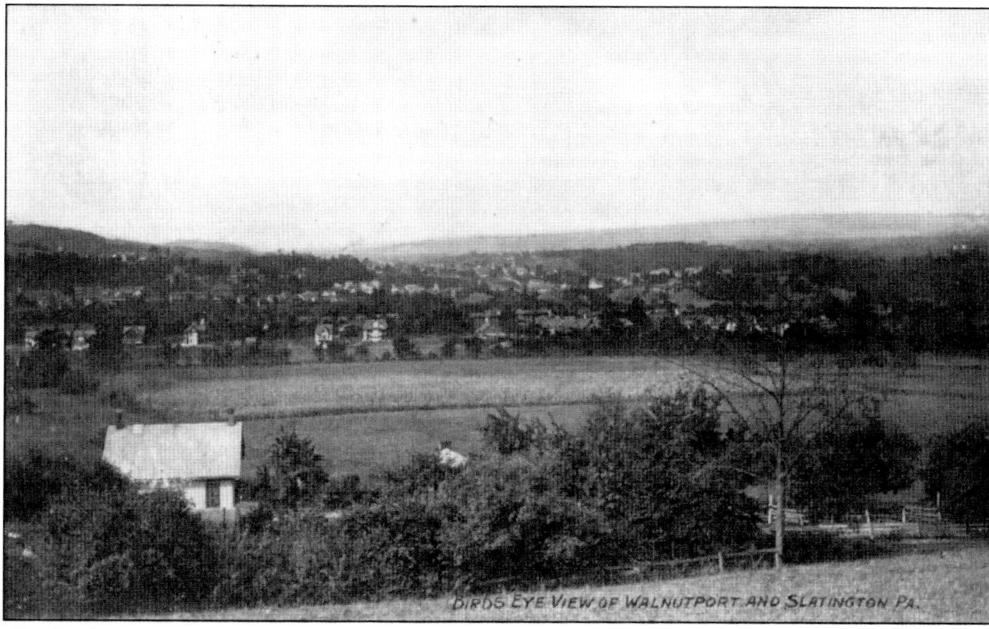

This bird's-eye view shows Walnutport and Slatington around 1909. (Courtesy of Larry Hillborn.)

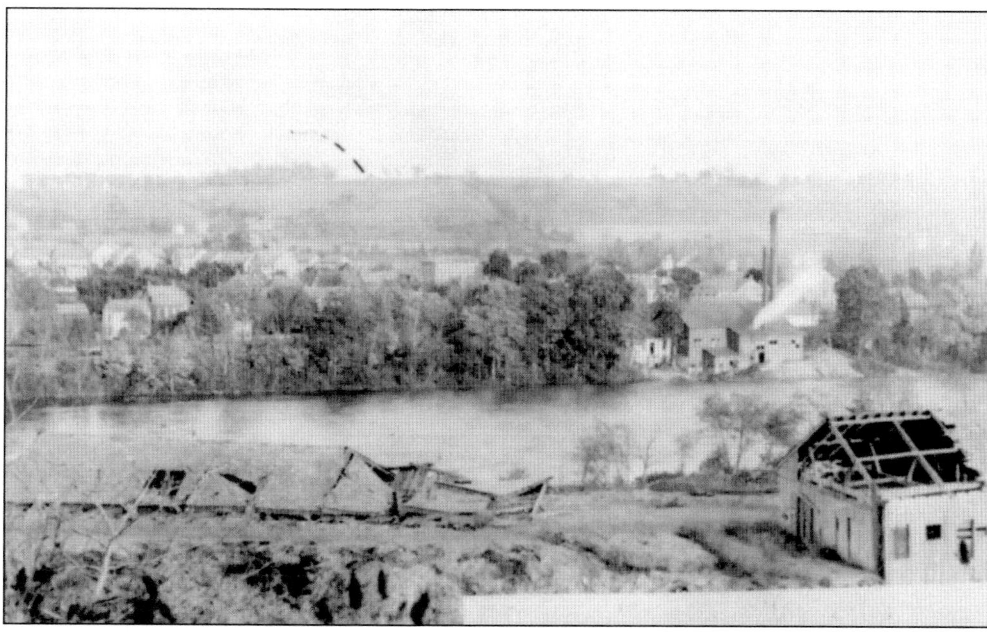

In 1910, industry along the river in Slatington and Walnutport included the Citizen's Electric Light, Heat and Power Company, seen here across the river in Walnutport. (Courtesy of Raymond Holland Regional History Collection, Northern Lehigh Future Focus Collection.)

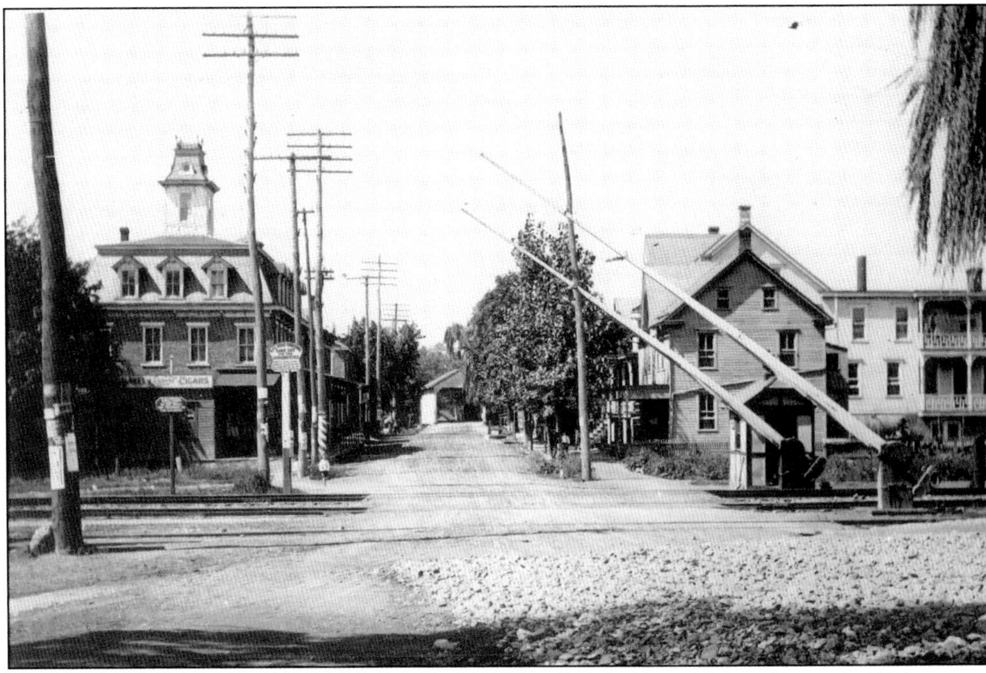

The tracks of the Central Railroad Company of New Jersey crossed Main Street in Walnutport. The Hahn and Griffith store is on the left across the tracks. In the distance, the covered bridge leading across the river to Slatington can be seen. (Courtesy of Palmerton Camera Club, Northern Lehigh Future Focus Collection.)

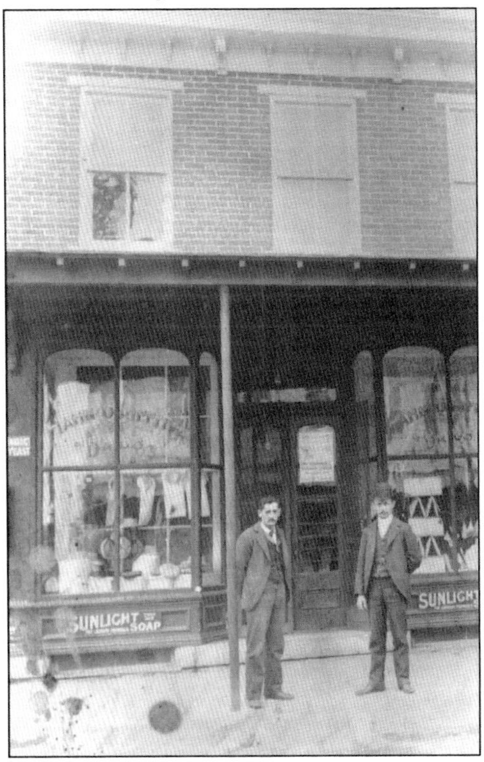

Two men stand in front of the Hahn and Griffith store in Walnutport. (Courtesy of Northern Lehigh Future Focus Collection.)

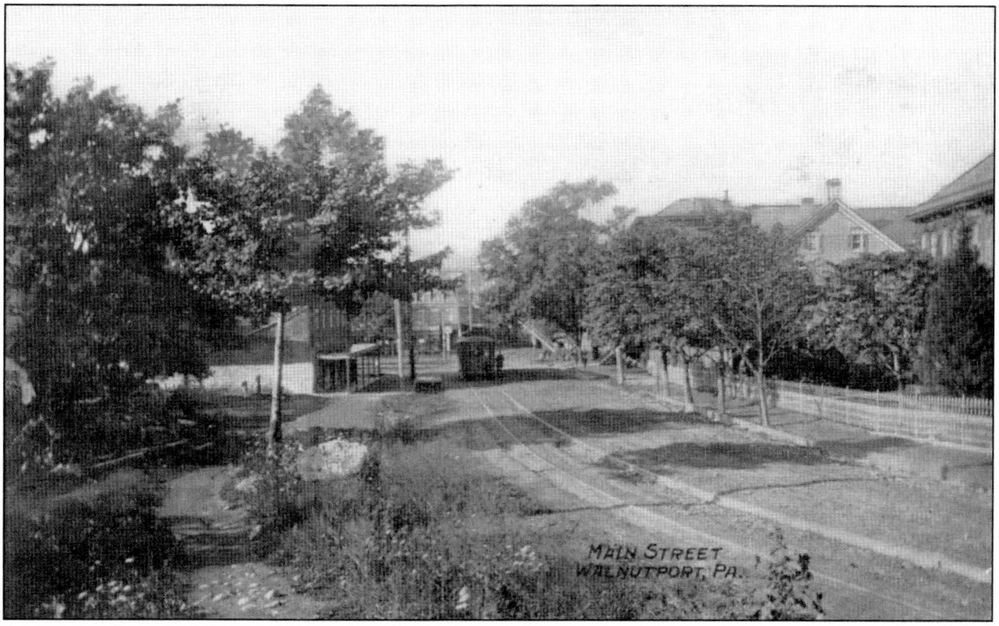

In this 1909 view of Main Street in Walnutport, looking east, the Slate Exchange Hotel is on the left. (Courtesy of Palmerton Camera Club, Northern Lehigh Future Focus Collection.)

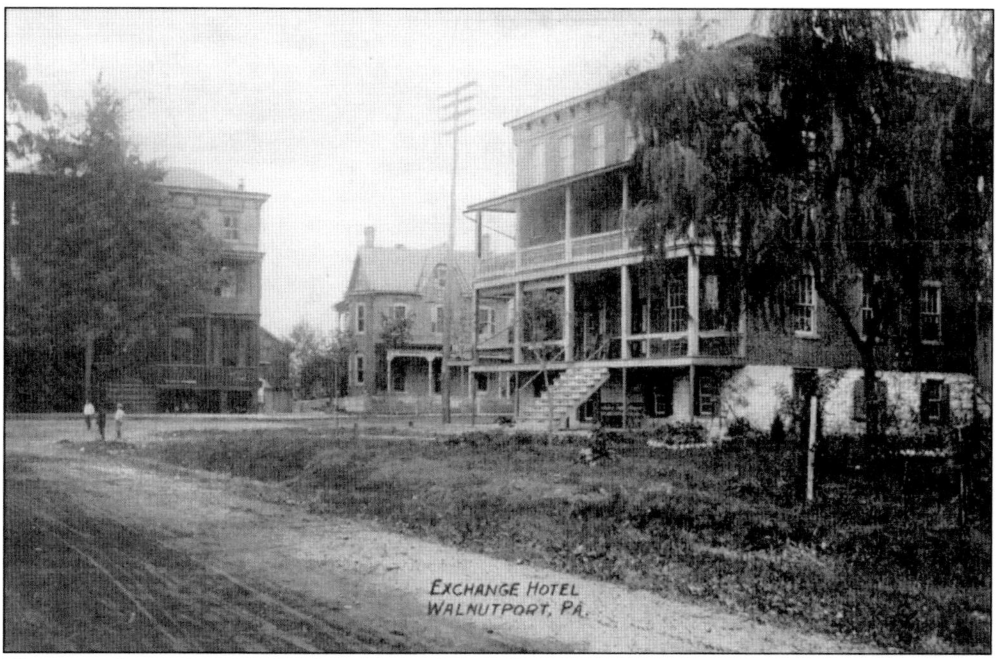

This view shows the Slate Exchange Hotel in Walnutport as it appeared around 1908. (Courtesy of Larry Hillborn.)

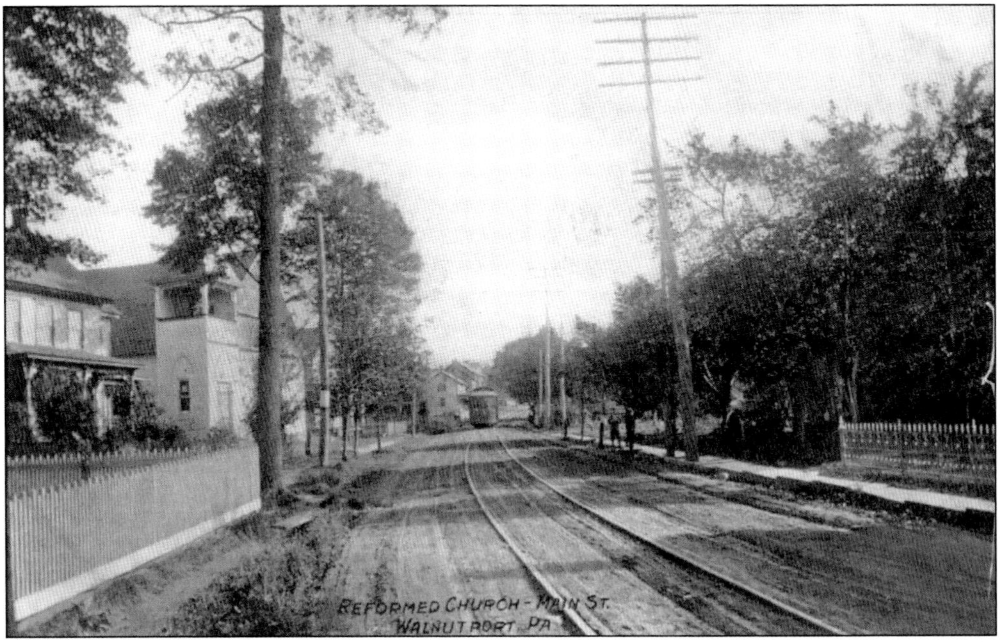

The Blue Ridge Traction trolley is seen coming up the street in this view of the Reformed church on Main Street in Walnutport.

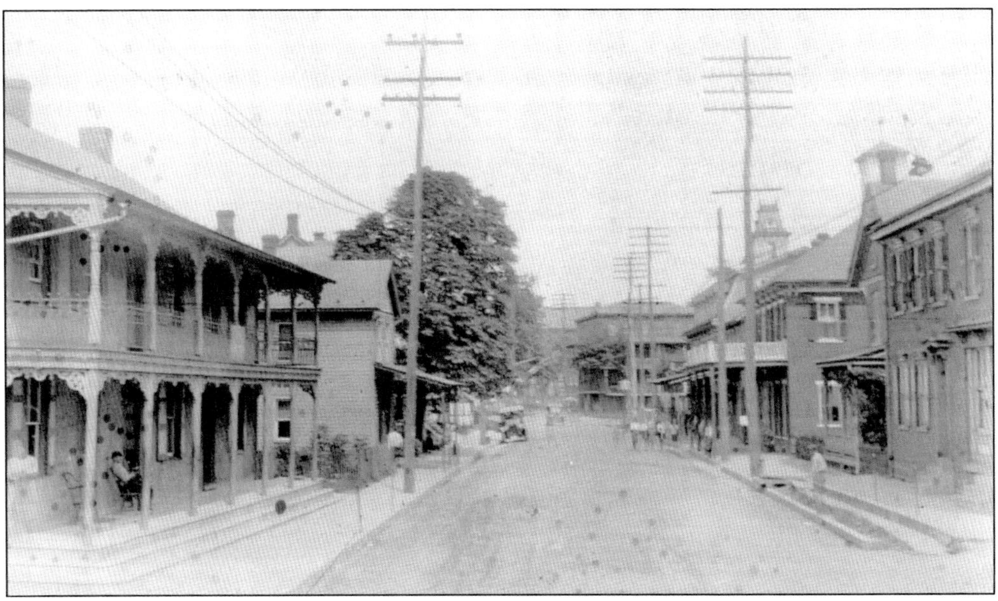
The Anchor Hotel and post office are on the left in this photograph of Main Street in Walnutport. (Courtesy of Larry Hillborn.)

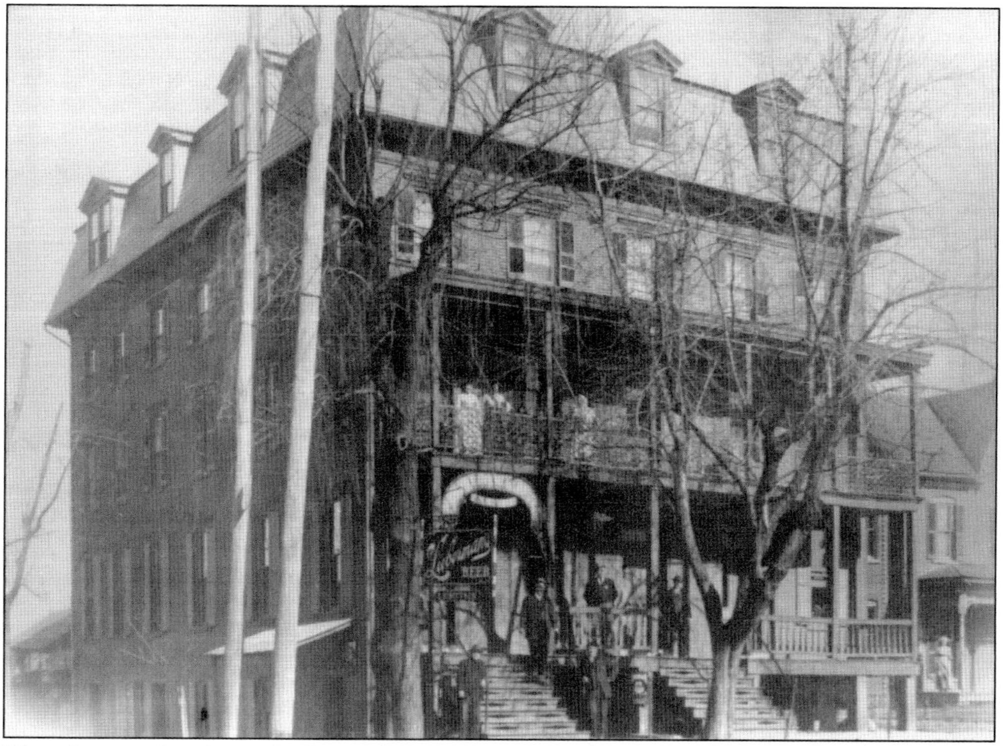

This close-up shot shows the Pennsylvania House in Walnutport as it once looked. (Courtesy of Northern Lehigh Future Focus Collection.)

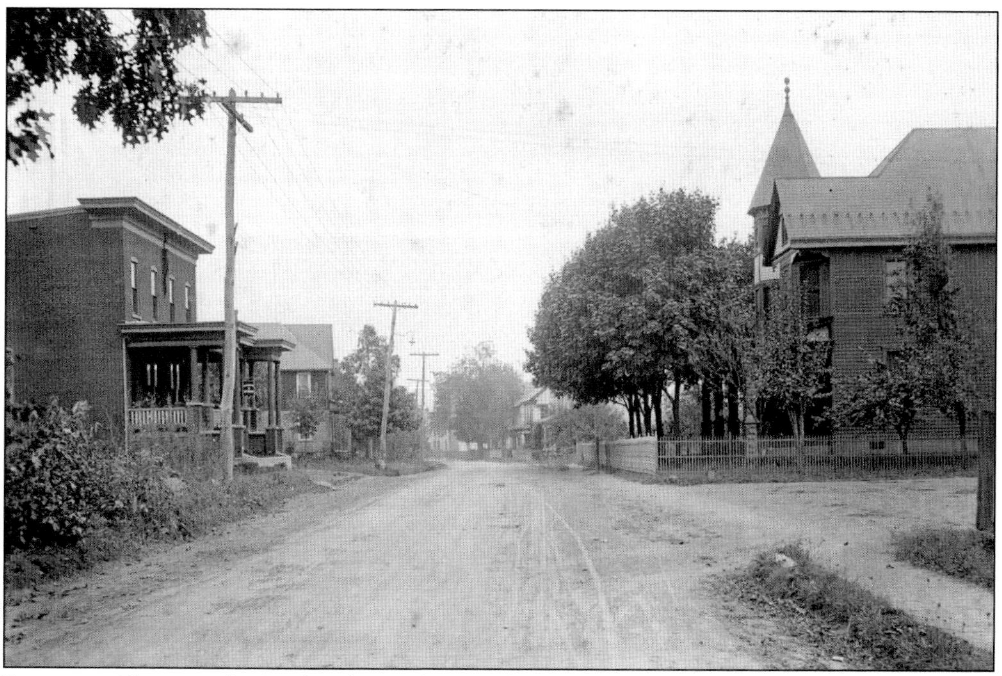

Benninger Photography Studios, located at 48 Cherry Street (left), is now a home. On the right is the former home of Granville Hahn. (Courtesy of Larry Hillborn.)

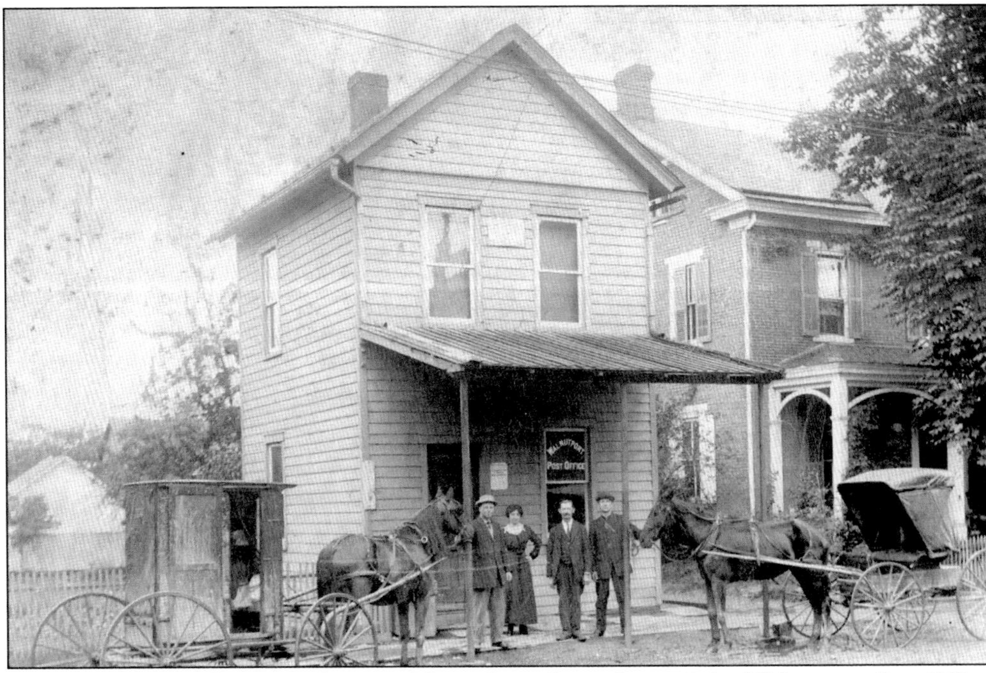

Postmaster Jim Andrews stands second from the right in front of the Walnutport Post Office. (Courtesy of Lehigh Township Historical Society.)

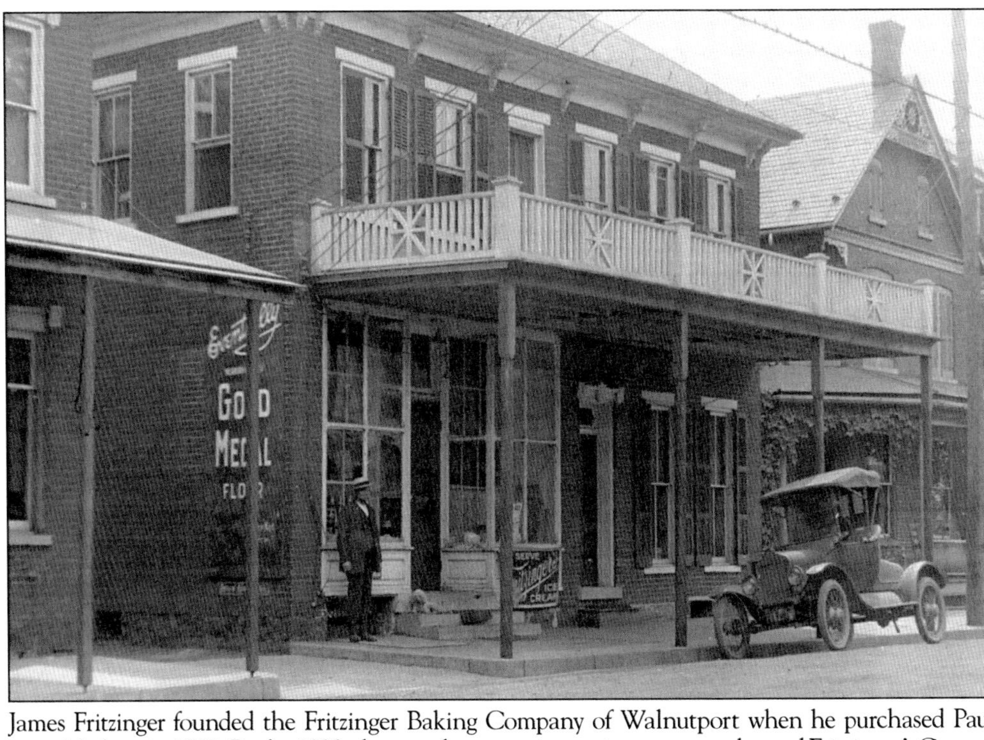

James Fritzinger founded the Fritzinger Baking Company of Walnutport when he purchased Paul Lentz's bakery in 1902. By the 1920s, he was also operating an ice-cream parlor and Fritzinger's Garage. This photograph shows his store on Main Street in Walnutport. (Courtesy of Larry Hillborn.)

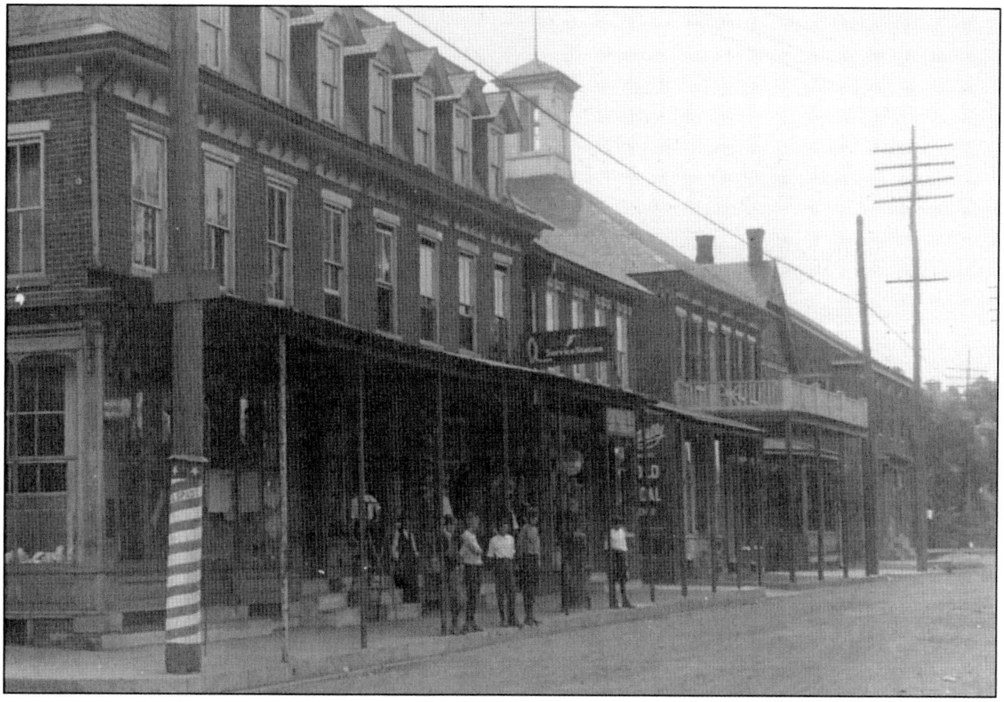

Fritzinger's store is on the right in this view of Main Street. A gas pump can be seen in front of the first building, where all the people are. (Courtesy of Larry Hillborn.)

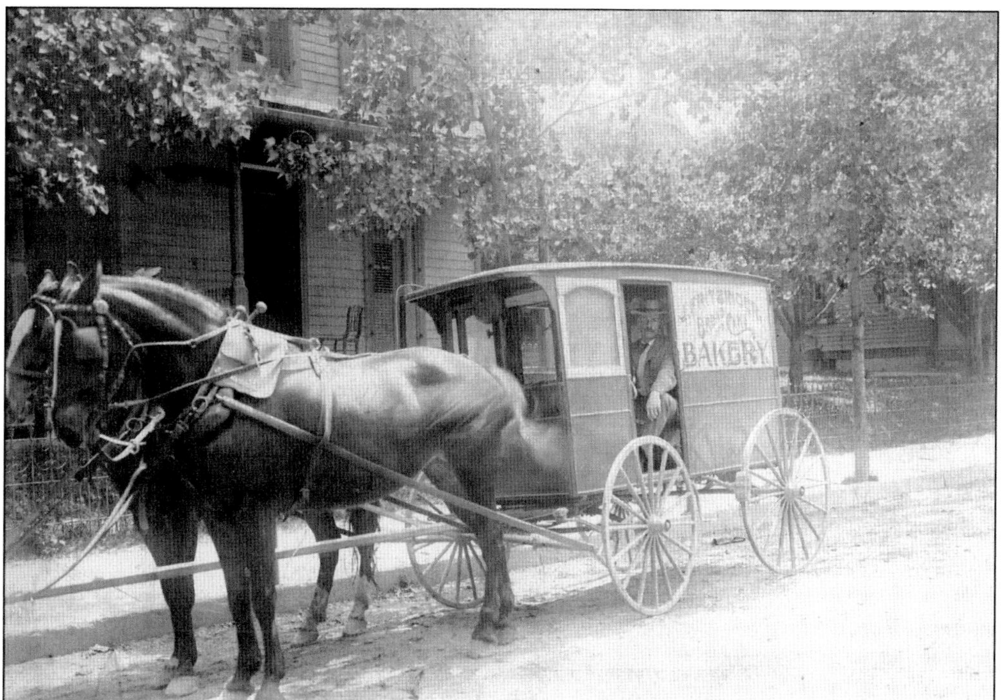

James Fritzinger peers out from the J. Fritzinger Bakery delivery wagon. The bakery was in operation until 1977. (Courtesy of Larry Hillborn.)

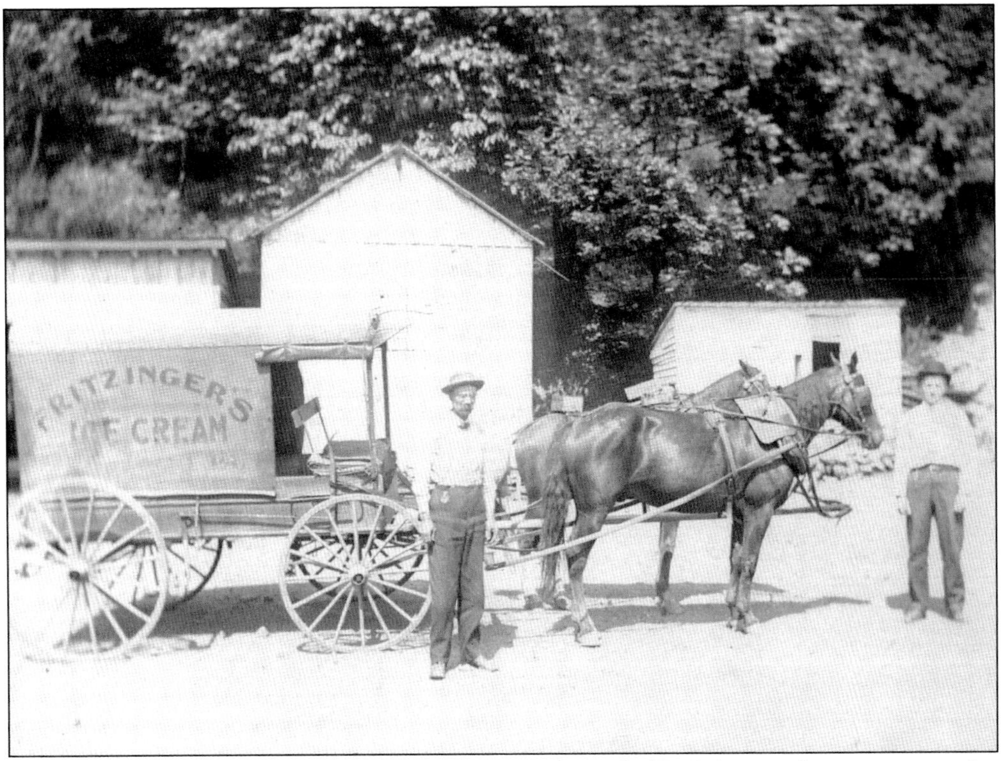

Fritzinger's Ice Cream also had a delivery wagon. At the end of Prohibition, the ice-cream parlor became the Oasis Café, a beer garden. (Courtesy of Larry Hillborn.)

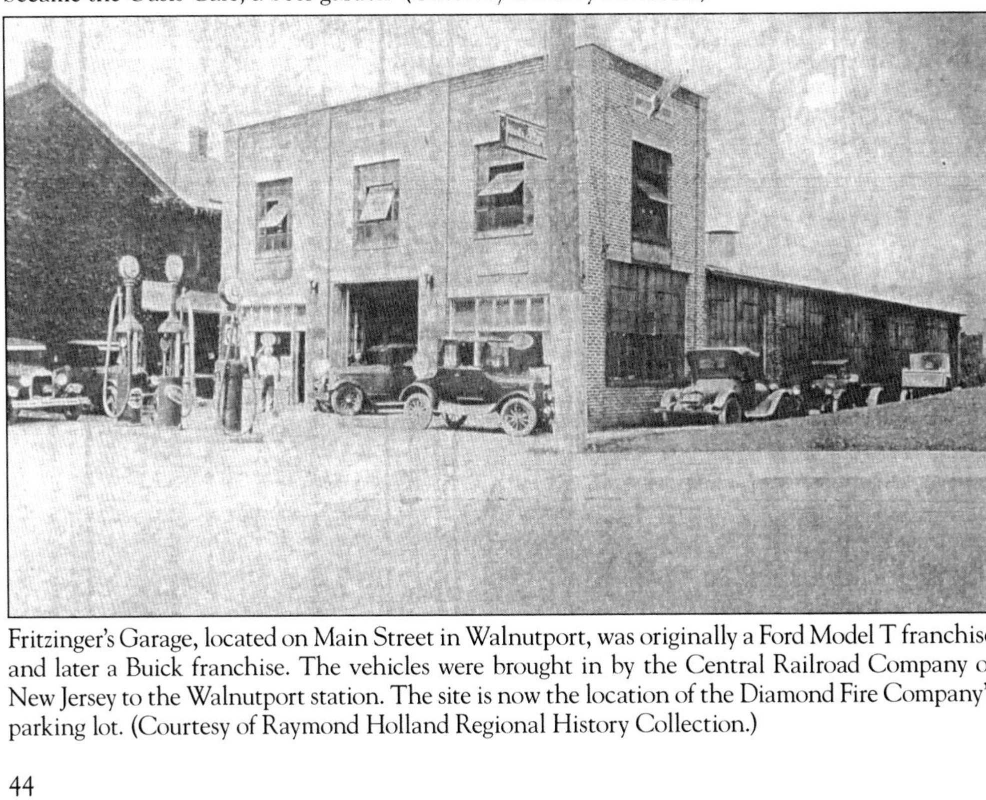

Fritzinger's Garage, located on Main Street in Walnutport, was originally a Ford Model T franchise and later a Buick franchise. The vehicles were brought in by the Central Railroad Company of New Jersey to the Walnutport station. The site is now the location of the Diamond Fire Company's parking lot. (Courtesy of Raymond Holland Regional History Collection.)

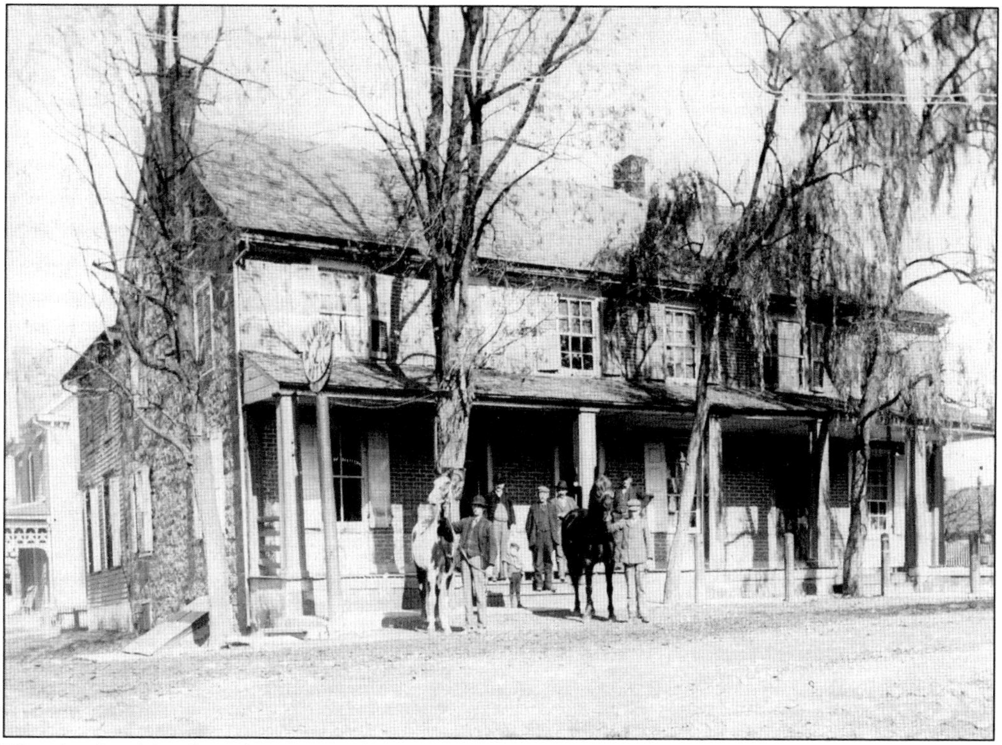

The Anchor Hotel, at the corner of Main and North Canal Streets, was a favorite stopping point for the people traveling on the Lehigh Canal. (Courtesy of Larry Hillborn.)

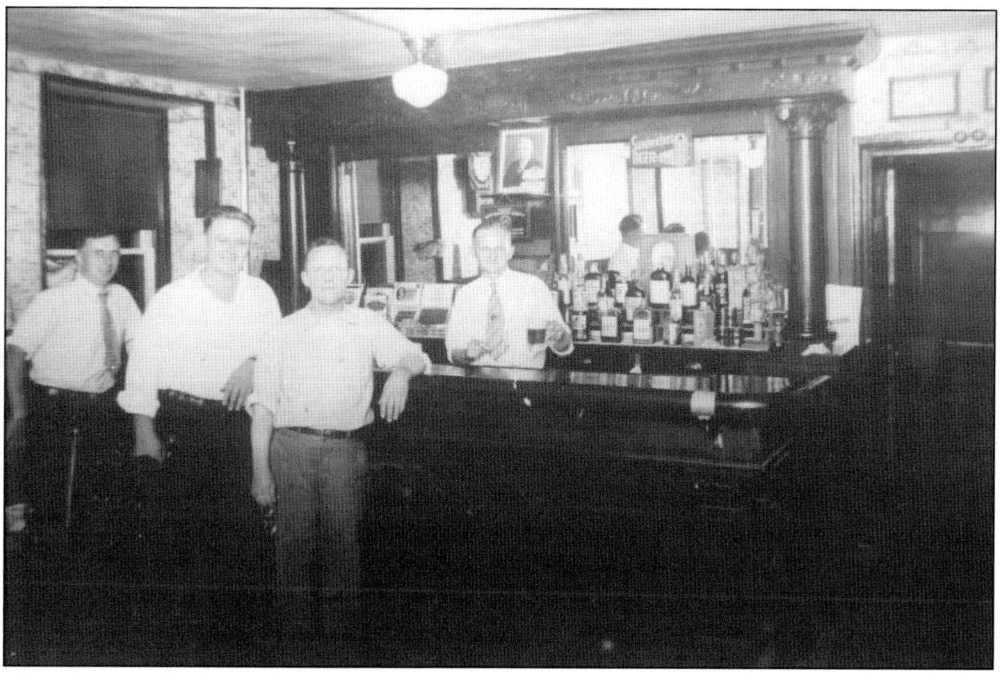

This photograph shows the bar at the Anchor Hotel. (Courtesy of Northern Lehigh Future Focus Collection.)

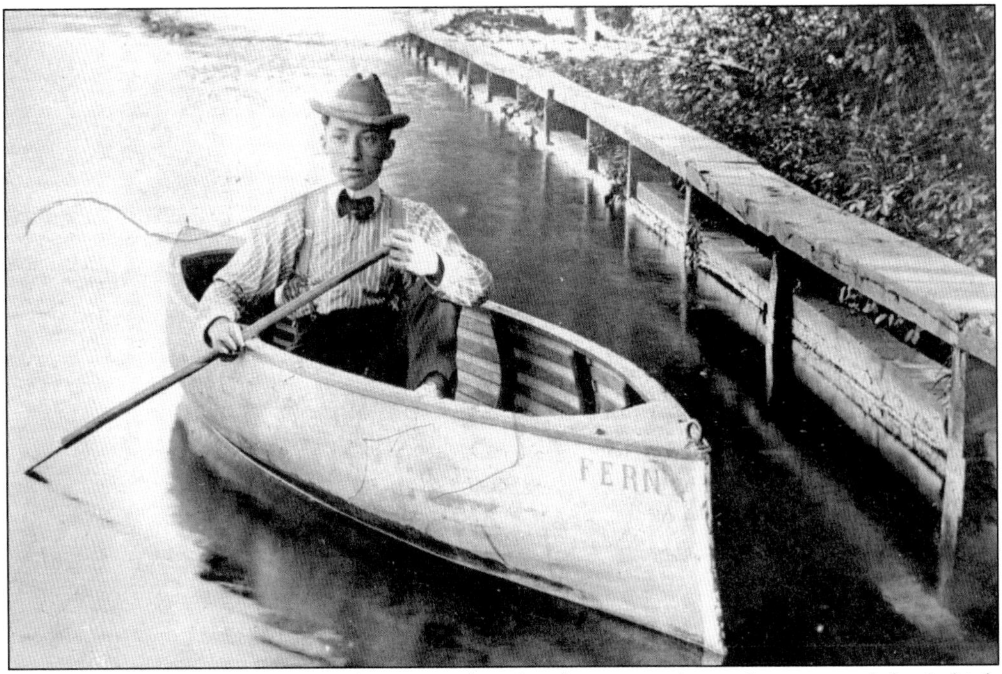

This *c.* 1900 photograph shows the *Fern*, a handmade canoe, plying the waters of the Lehigh Canal. (Courtesy of Palmerton Camera Club, Northern Lehigh Future Focus Collection.)

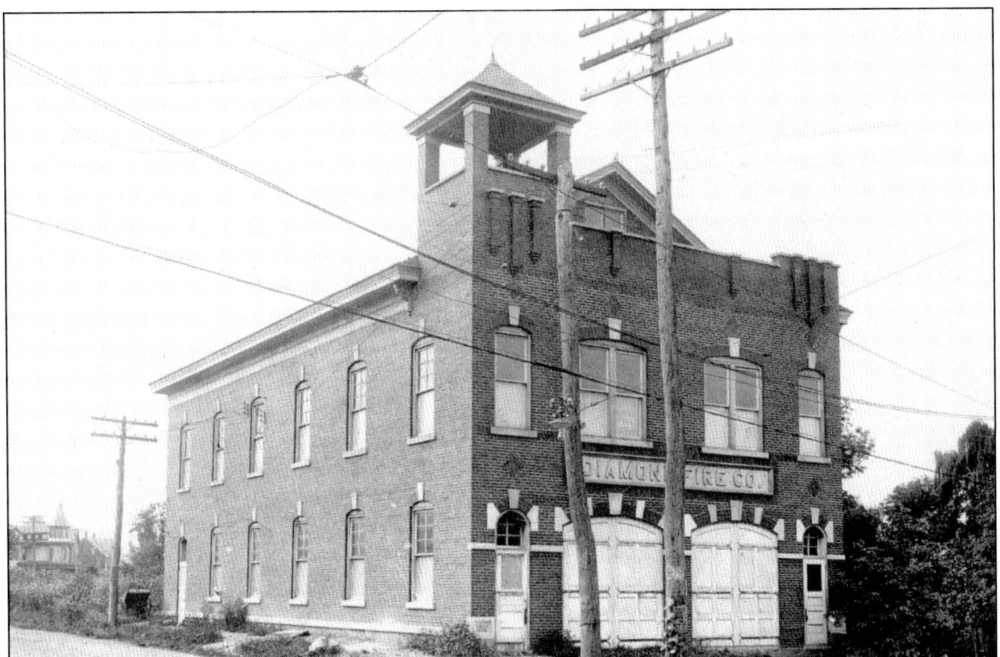

The Borough of Walnutport purchased land for the construction of Diamond Fire Company in 1902. Construction began in 1910 with lumber salvaged from the Citizen's Electric Light, Heat and Power Company. (Courtesy of Northern Lehigh Future Focus Collection.)

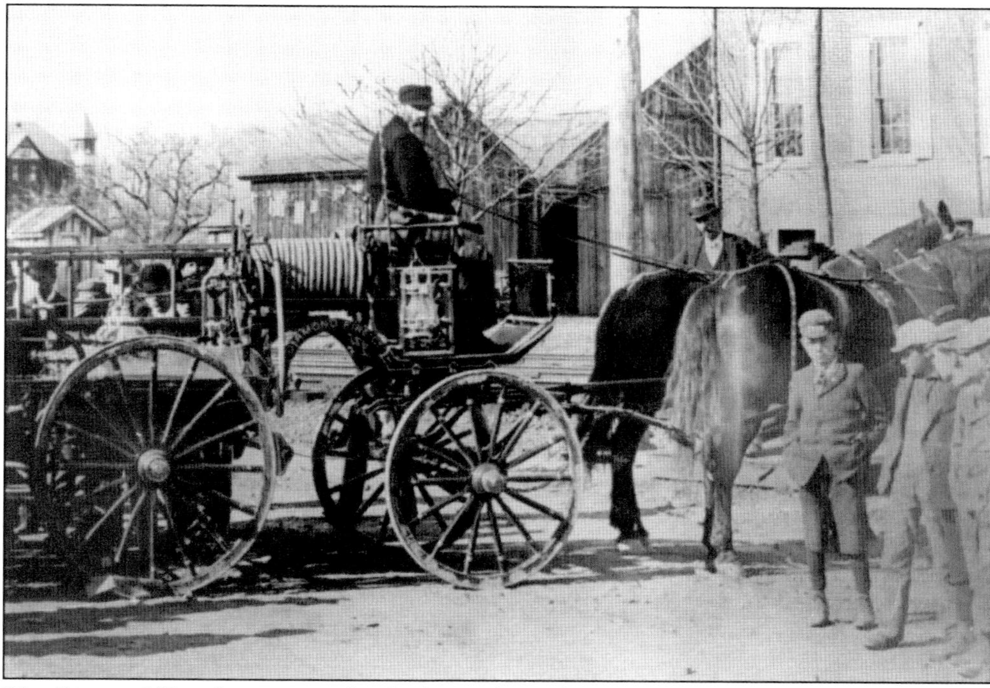

The Diamond Fire Company utilized a horse-drawn hose cart. (Courtesy of Northern Lehigh Future Focus Collection.)

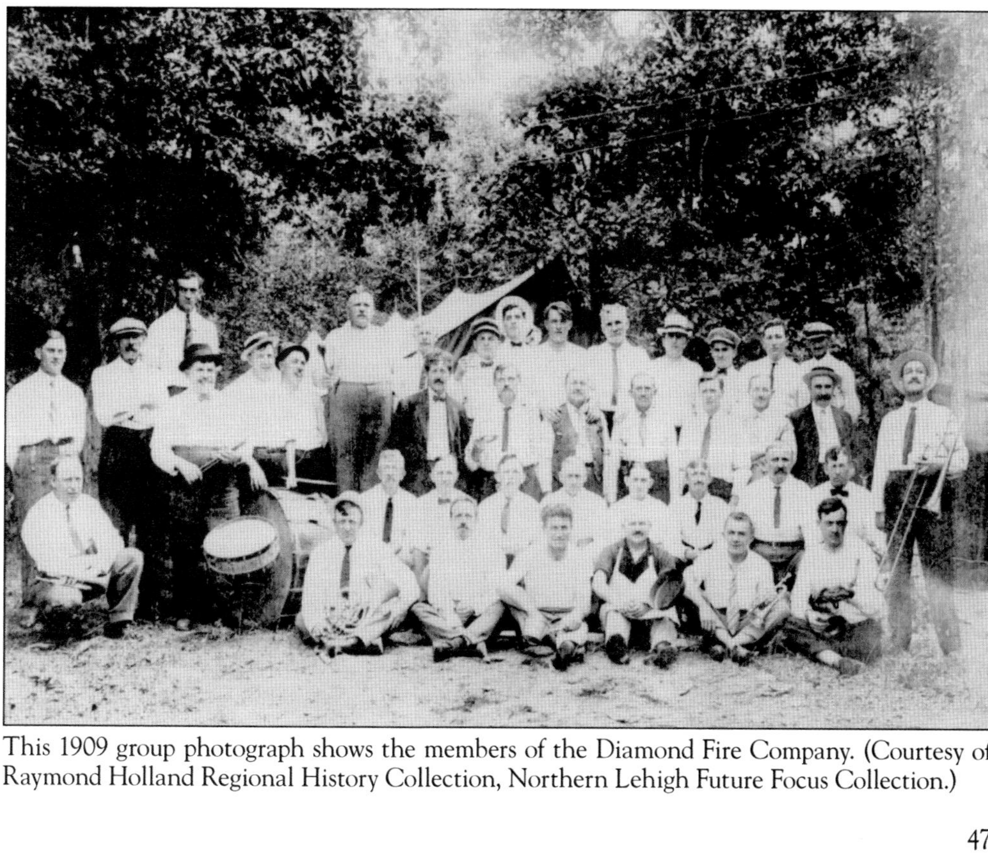

This 1909 group photograph shows the members of the Diamond Fire Company. (Courtesy of Raymond Holland Regional History Collection, Northern Lehigh Future Focus Collection.)

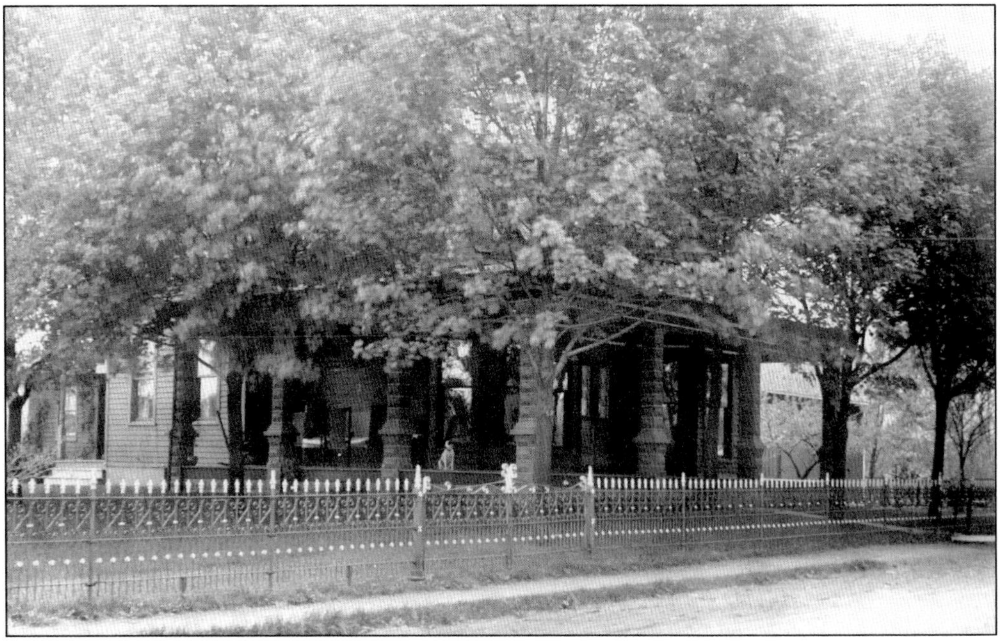

The home of Granville Hahn, business owner in Walnutport, was located on Cherry Street. (Courtesy of Larry Hillborn.)

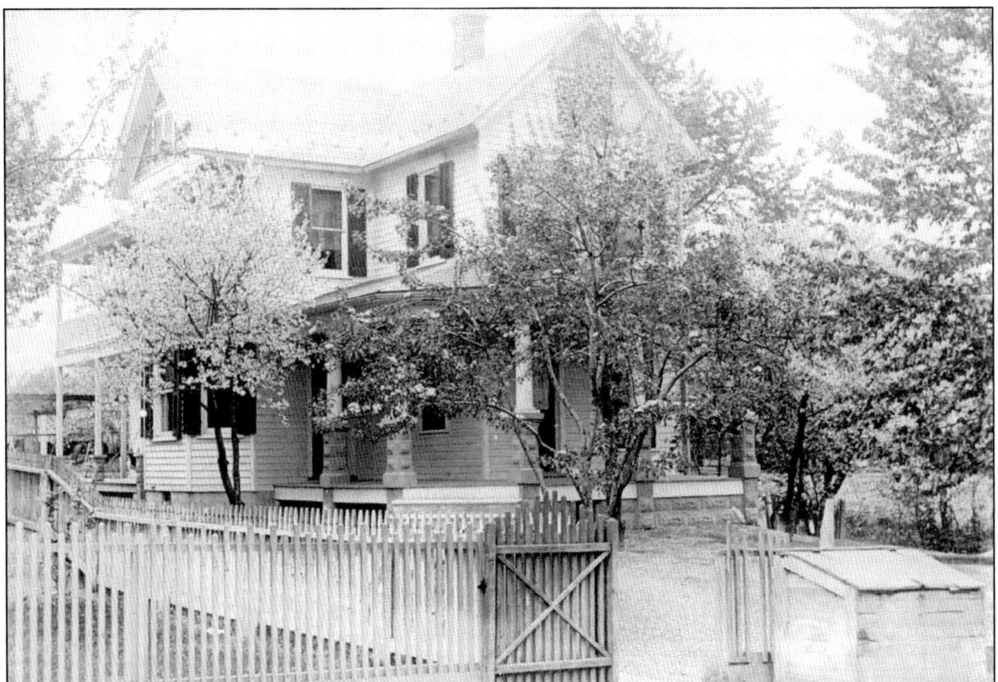

This lovely home, built around 1910, was located at 112 New Street in Walnutport. (Courtesy of Larry Hillborn.)

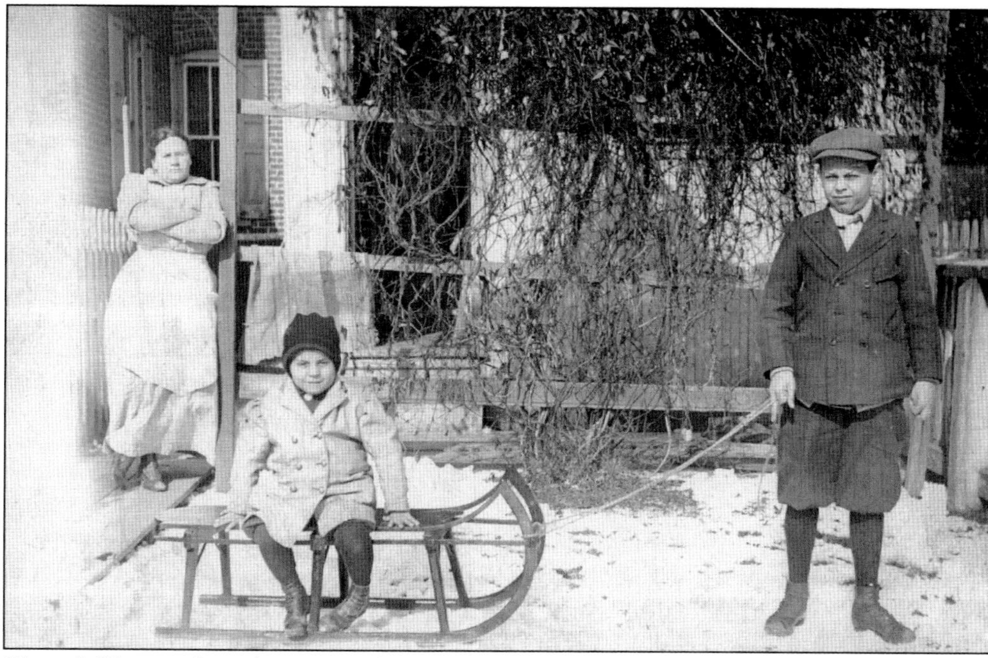

Oliver J. Kleintop Jr. is shown seated on the sled. Oliver is the son of Oliver J. Kleintop Sr. and Lydia (Hahn) Kleintop. (Courtesy of Larry Hillborn.)

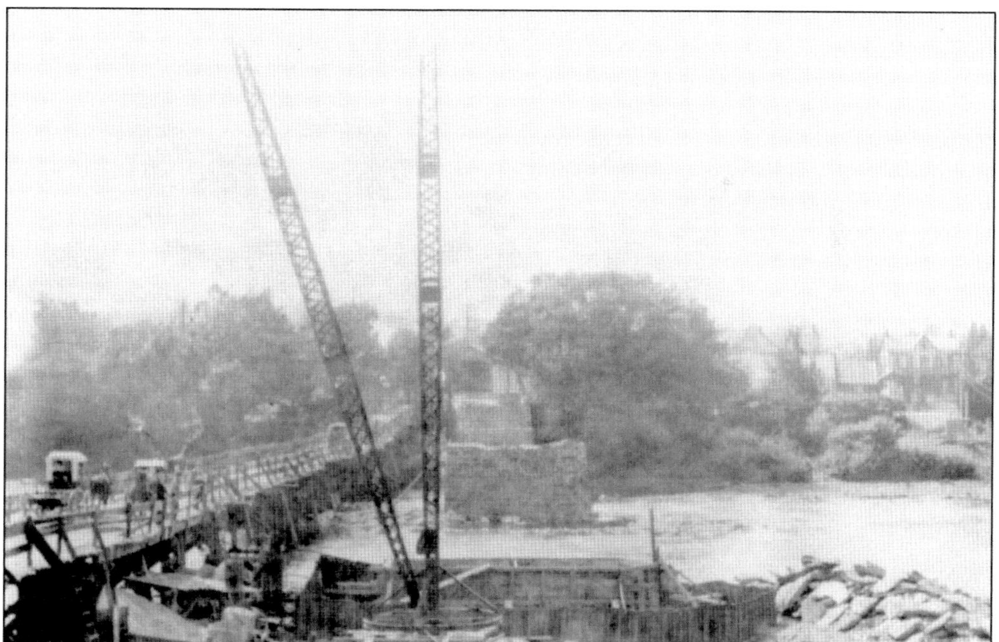

This temporary bridge was built over the Lehigh River between Walnutport and Slatington around 1911, after the covered bridge was removed. (Courtesy of Raymond Holland Regional History Collection, Northern Lehigh Future Focus Collection.)

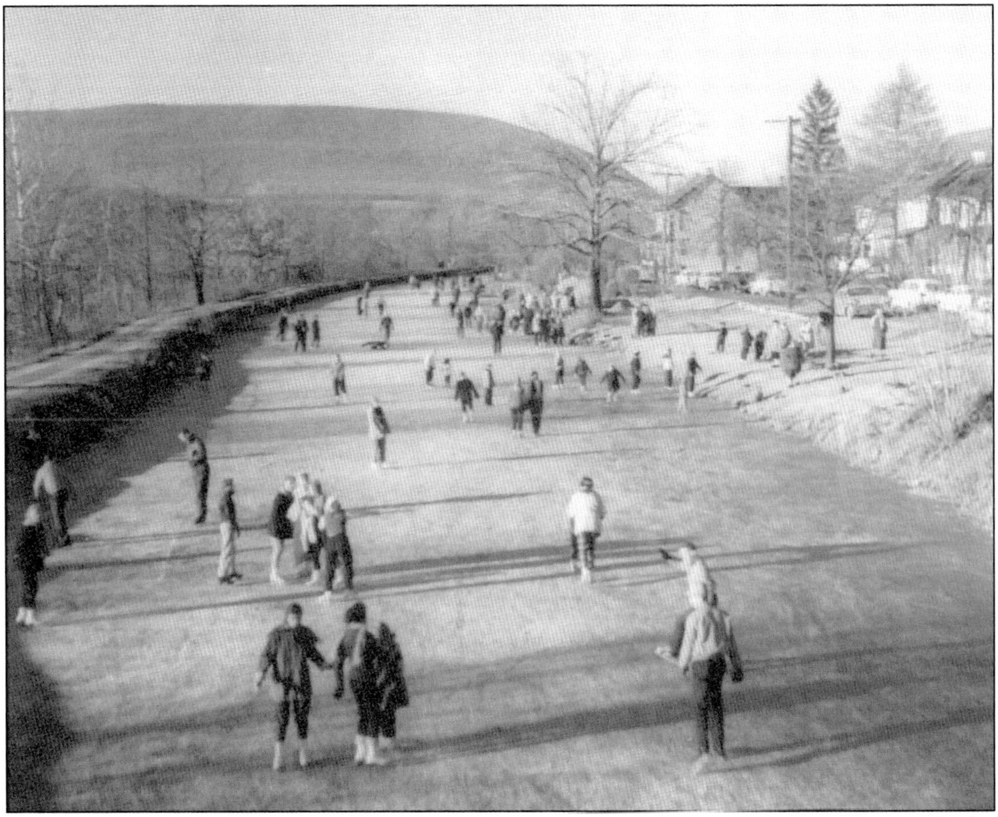

Skaters enjoy the Lehigh Canal in winter. When the canal froze, it became an ice rink the length of town. This photograph was taken by William Beck. (Courtesy of Walnutport Canal Association.)

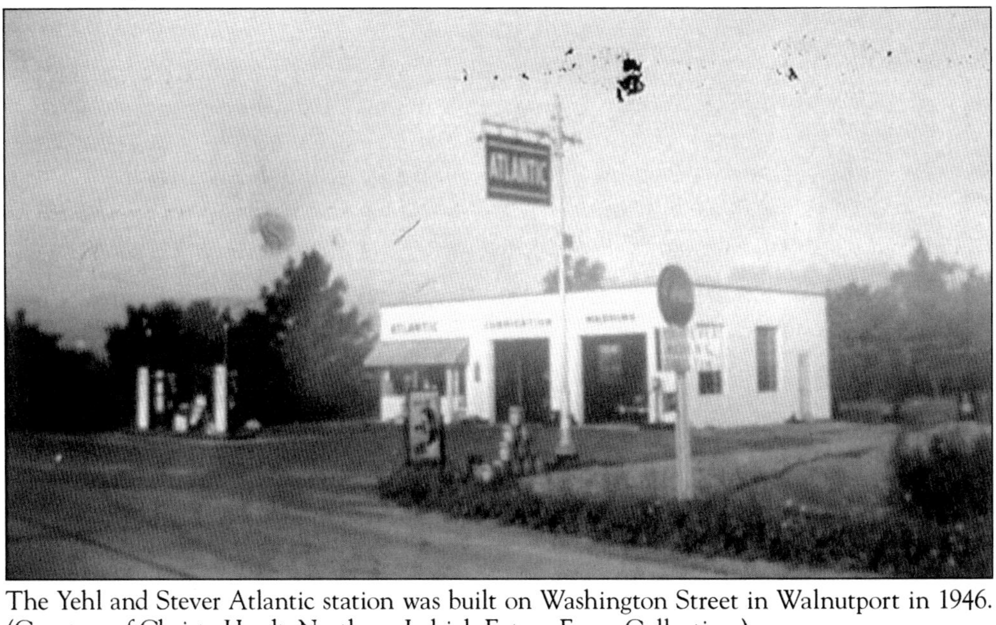

The Yehl and Stever Atlantic station was built on Washington Street in Walnutport in 1946. (Courtesy of Christy Haydt, Northern Lehigh Future Focus Collection.)

Three

Washington Township

Washington Township surrounds Slatington Borough on three sides. In 1752, it was part of Heidelberg Township, Northampton County, and then became part of the newly formed Lehigh County in 1812. The township includes the villages of Emerald, Friedens, Lehigh Furnace, and Slatedale.

Originally called Franklin, Emerald was located along the Slatedale branch of the Lehigh Valley Railroad, about one and a half miles west of Slatington. In 1885, when a post office was established, its name had to change because another town was already using the name Franklin.

Friedens, located about a mile south of Slatington, was originally called Petersburg after landowner John Peters. By 1860, the village was known as Friedensville. In 1891, the town's name changed again with the establishment of the Hoffman's post office. John Geiger became the first postmaster, followed by Francis Hoffman and Walter T. Handwerk. In 1912, the post office closed, and the village name reverted back to Friedens.

Lehigh Furnace, situated northwest of Slatedale, was named for the charcoal furnace started by Stephen Balliet and Samuel Helffrich, who purchased 25 acres from Christian Snyder and Christian Bloss in 1826. They recruited experienced workers from Shamrock in Berks County. Before the furnace closed in 1880, its owners included the Balliet family, the Cooper and Hewitt Company of New York, and Henry W. Bloss of Slatedale.

Slatedale is the largest village in Washington Township. Situated three miles west of Slatington, it was originally called LaBarsville. The Lehigh Valley Traction Company ran trolley service from Slatedale to Slatington, and the Slate Valley branch of the Lehigh Valley Railroad terminated at the village.

A bridge constructed in 1818 in Lehigh Gap was one of the earliest to cross the Lehigh River. It was destroyed by a flood. In 1826, the Lehigh Water Gap Bridge Company replaced it with a chain-link suspension bridge, but a May 1926 fire destroyed the first span. Rebuilt in June 1927, it was torn down in September 1931 following construction of the current bridge.

A covered bridge constructed in 1854 was the first to connect Walnutport and Slatington. Tolls were collected until 1893. This bridge lasted until 1911 when it was replaced by a steel-support bridge that was taken down in 1969 when the current bridge went up. A flood on May 23, 1942, damaged the tollhouse.

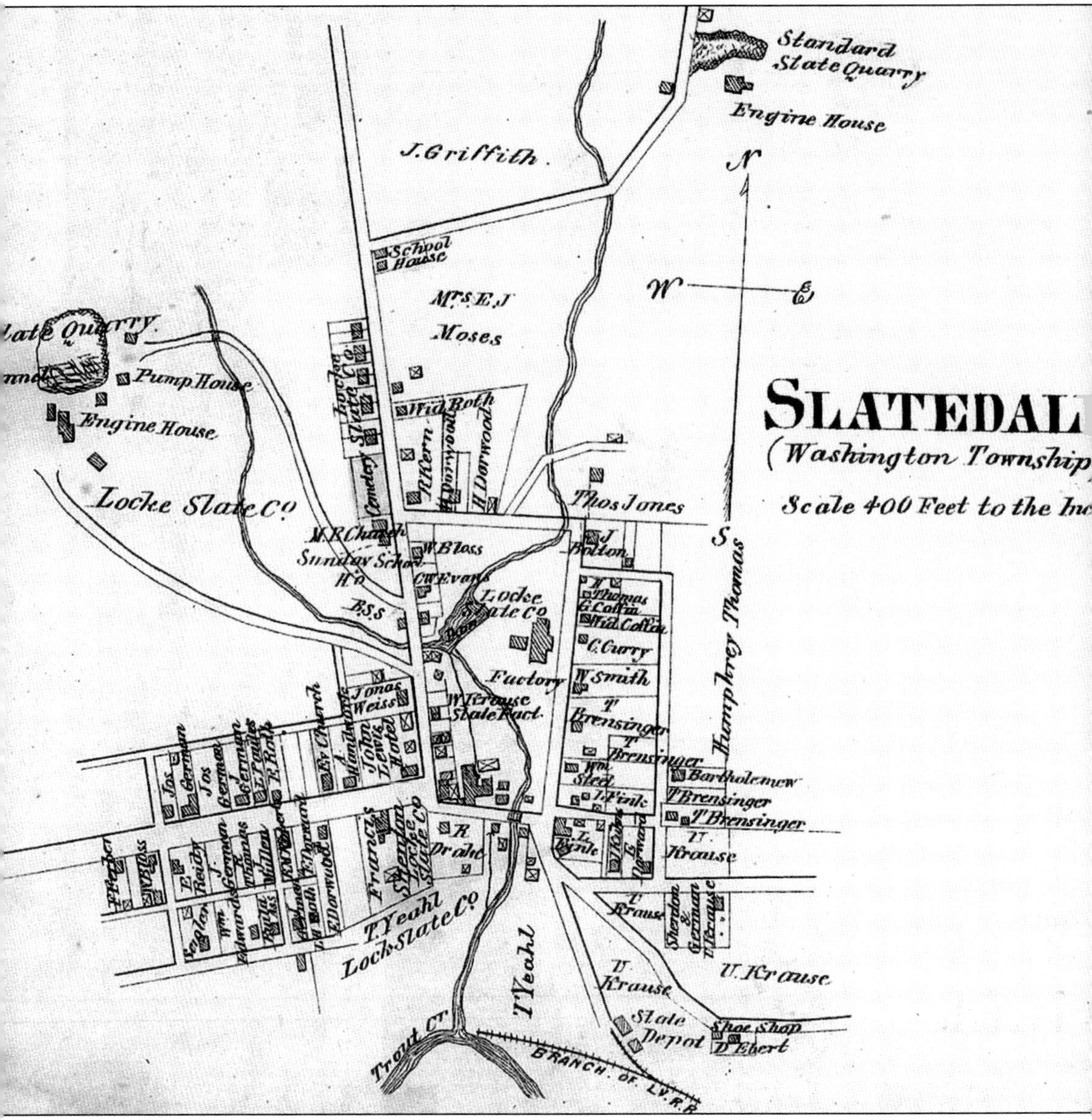

The 1876 *Centennial Atlas* also included this map of Slatedale.

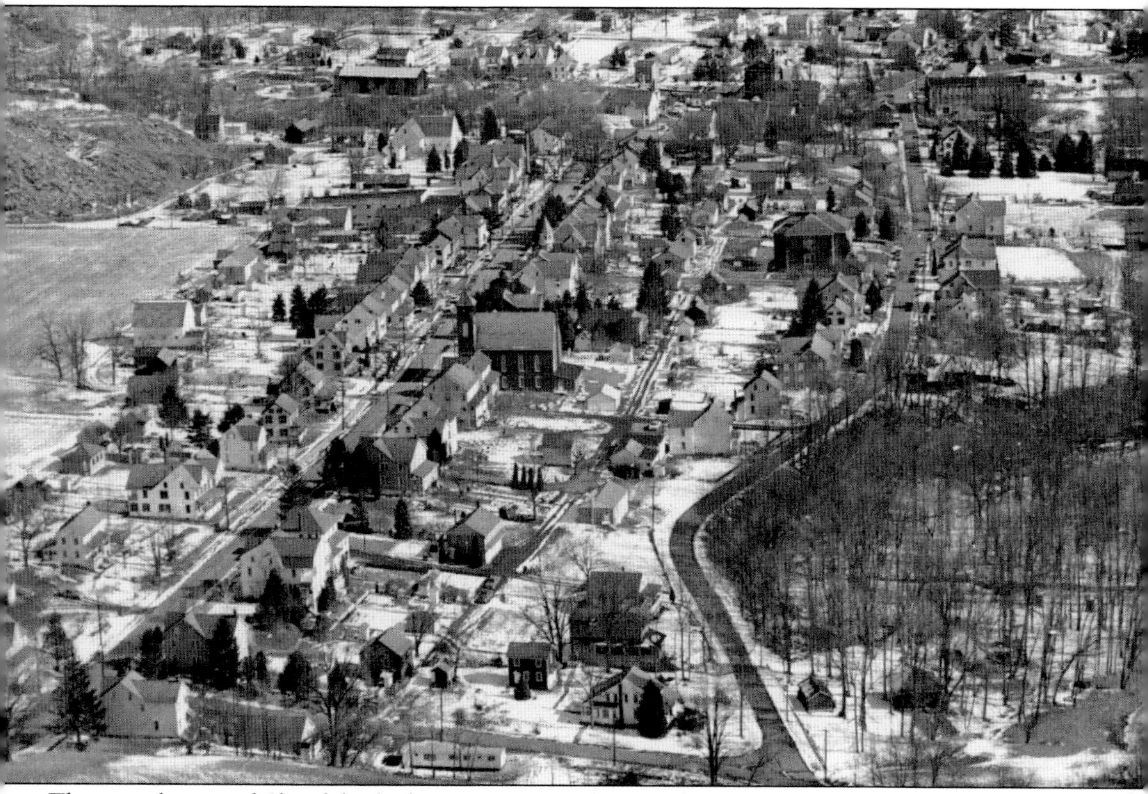

This aerial view of Slatedale, looking east, was taken in the 1960s. Holy Trinity Church is located just to the left of the center of the photograph. (Courtesy of Evelyn Haas, Northern Lehigh Future Focus Collection.)

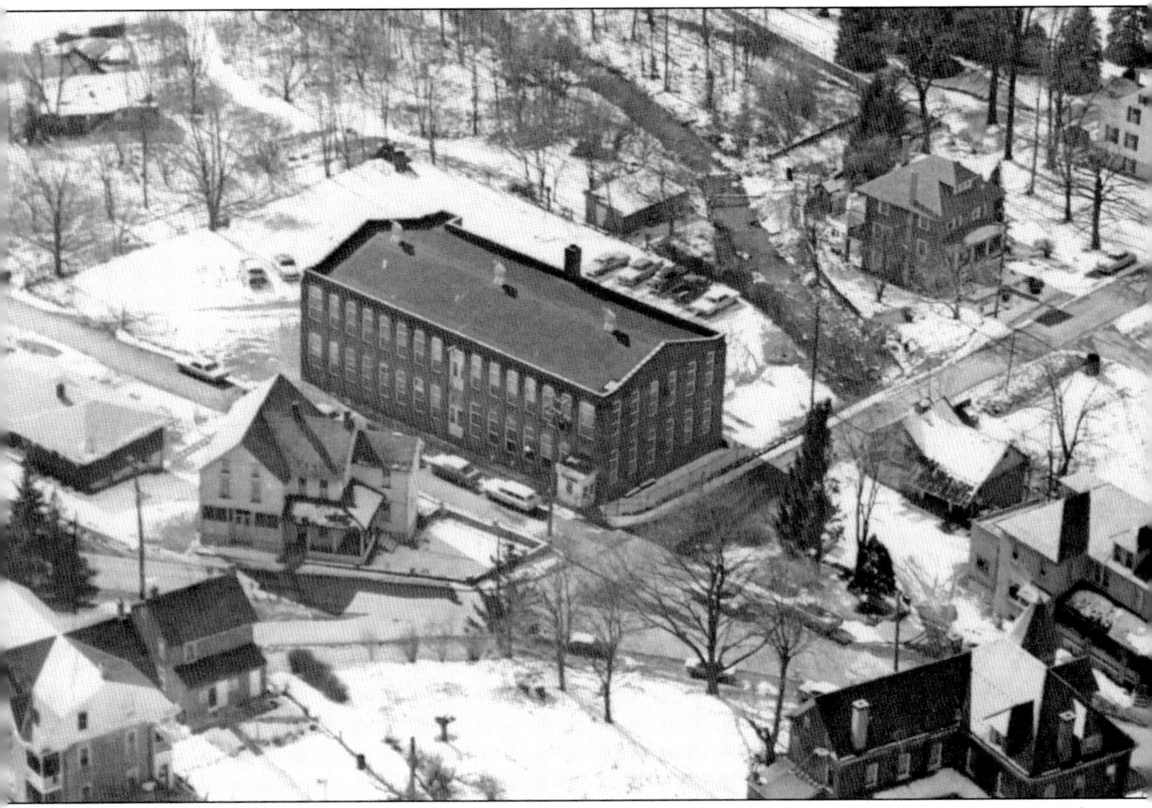

This aerial view of Slatedale is from the 1960s. The large building in the center is the Slatedale Silk Mill, which faces West Grant Street. (Courtesy of Evelyn Haas, Northern Lehigh Future Focus Collection.)

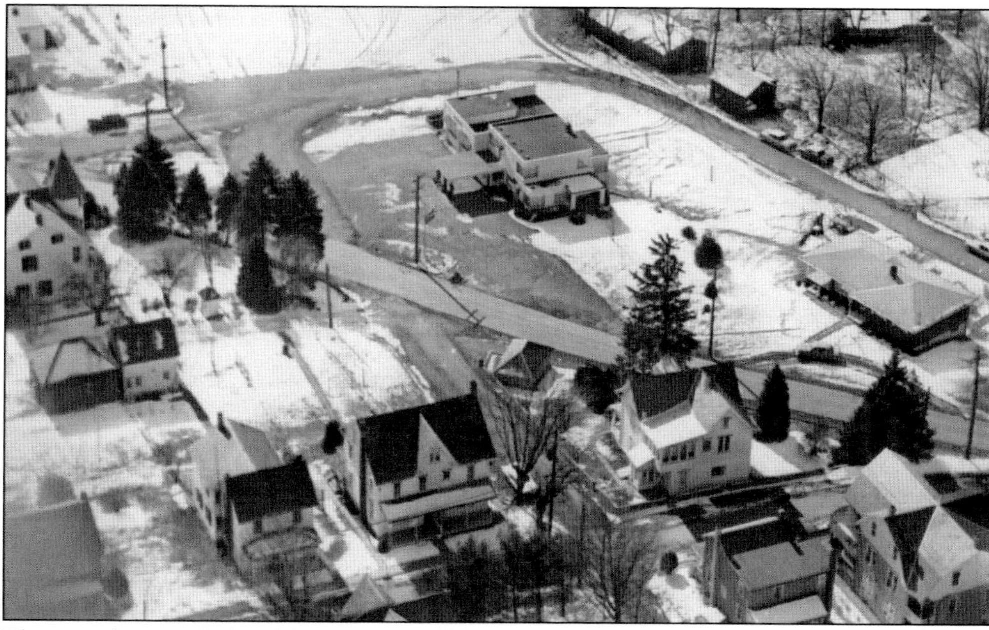

This aerial view of Slatedale from the 1960s shows Hartline Brothers General Merchandise, toward the top of the photograph. Factory Avenue runs behind the building, and Main Street is located in front of it. (Courtesy of Larry Hillborn.)

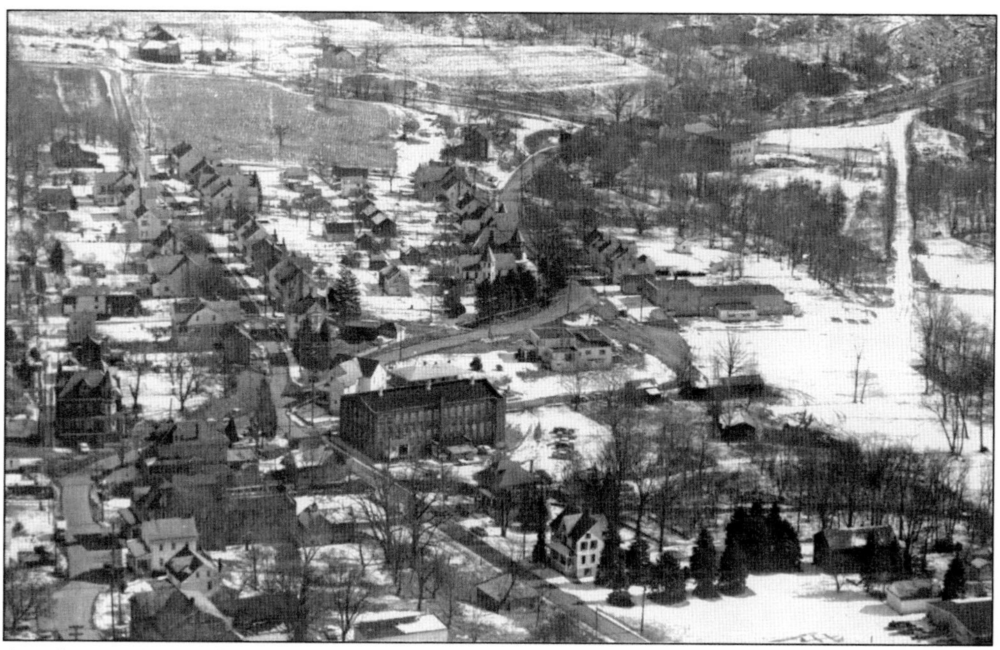

Another 1960s aerial view of Slatedale shows the Slatedale Silk Mill in the center. (Courtesy of Larry Hillborn.)

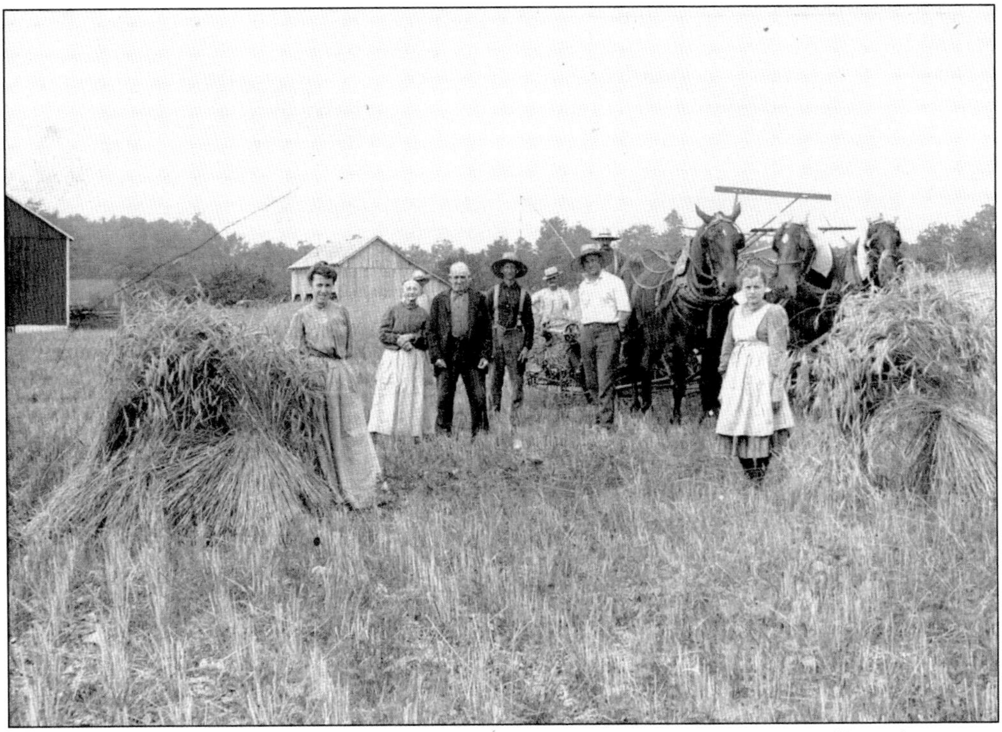

This Slatedale farm scene was taken on August 27, 1906. (Courtesy of Larry Hillborn.)

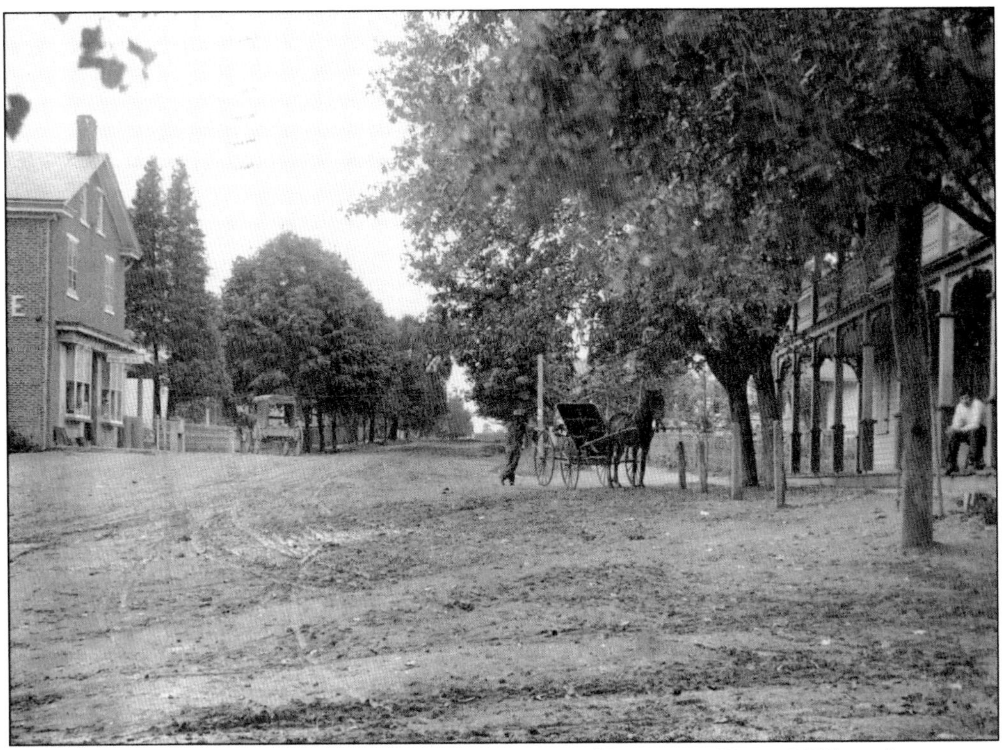

The Slatedale Hotel is on the right in this *c.* 1907 view. (Courtesy of Larry Hillborn.)

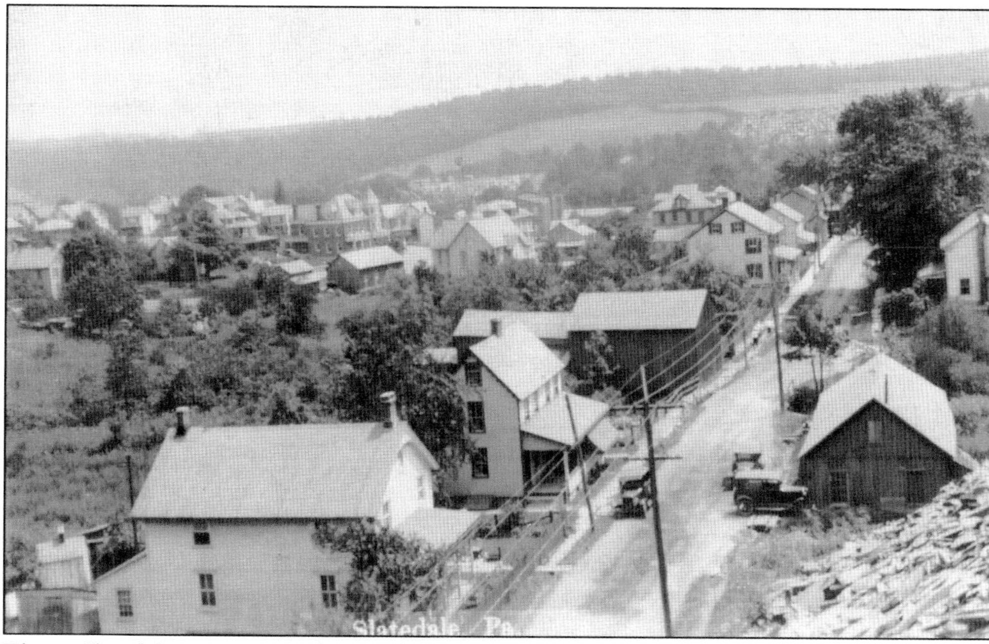

This is Slatedale as it appeared around 1936. (Courtesy of Larry Hillborn.)

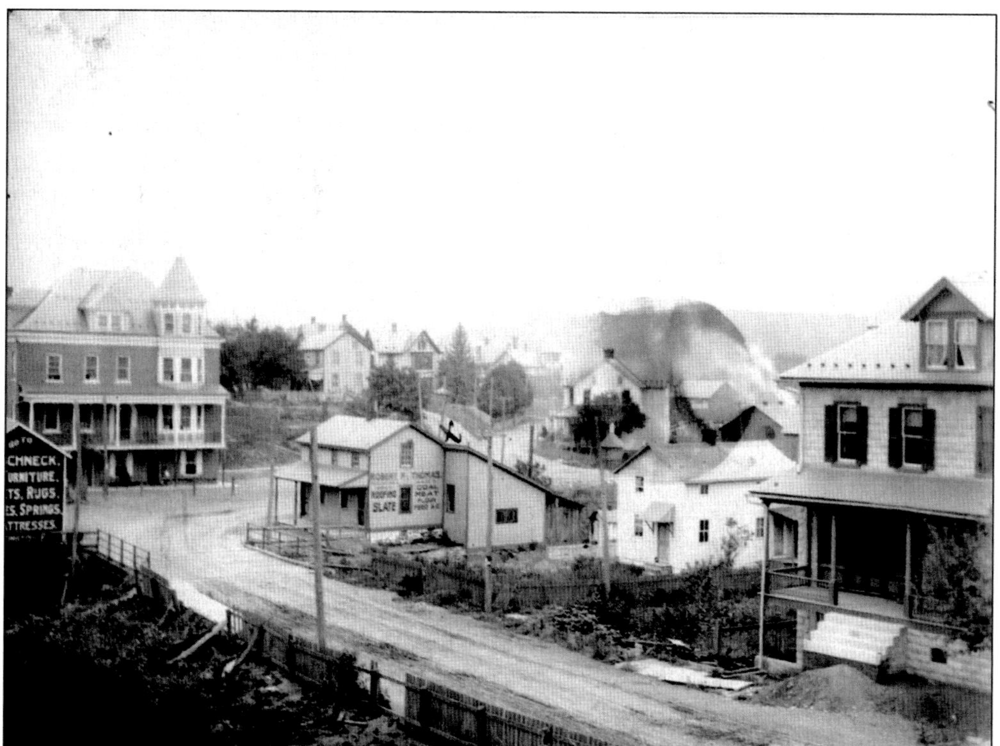

According to writing on the back of this c. 1907 photograph of Slatedale, the X marks the location of the Kuntz Bookstore. (Courtesy of Larry Hillborn.)

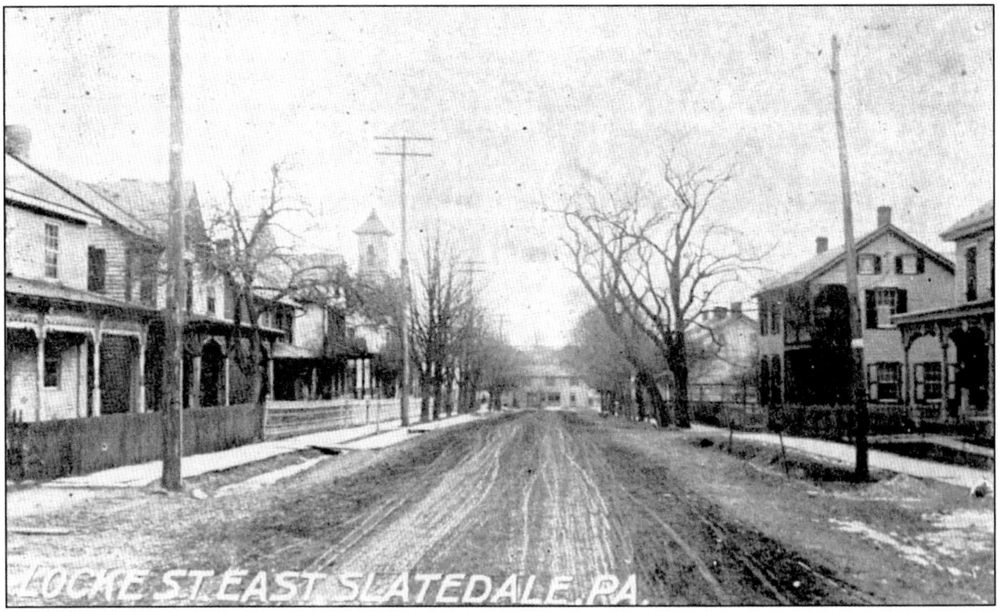

"Here the earth is full of slate and most of the people work in the slate quarries and factories. This town stands on slate," says the back of this postcard showing Locke Street. (Courtesy of Larry Hillborn.)

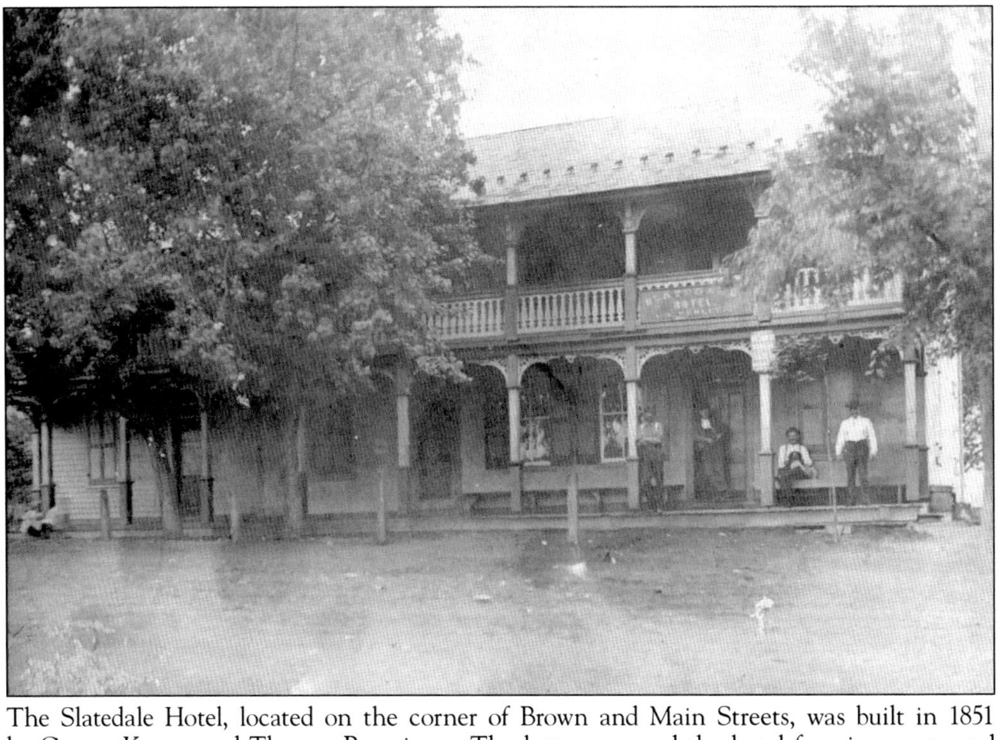

The Slatedale Hotel, located on the corner of Brown and Main Streets, was built in 1851 by George Krause and Thomas Brensinger. The latter operated the hotel for nine years, and then the Krause family took over. In 1876, John Lewis ran it under the name American Hotel. It was also owned by A. A. Werley. Today the building contains apartments. (Courtesy of Larry Hillborn.)

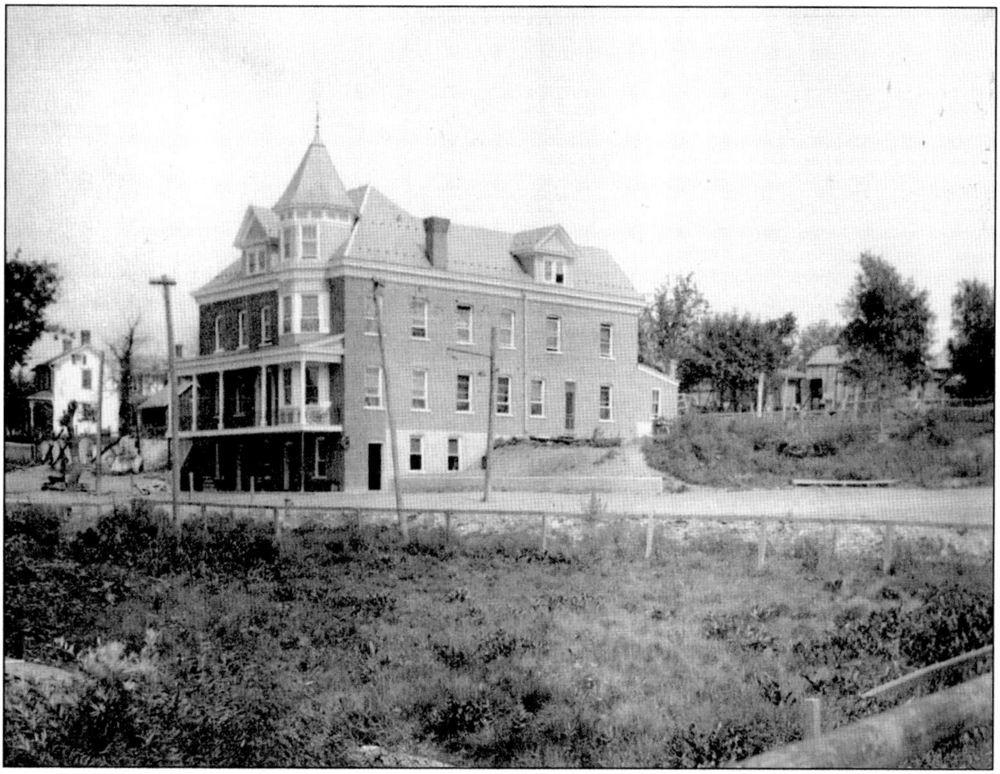

This *c.* 1907 view shows Ballier's Hotel in Slatedale. (Courtesy of Larry Hillborn.)

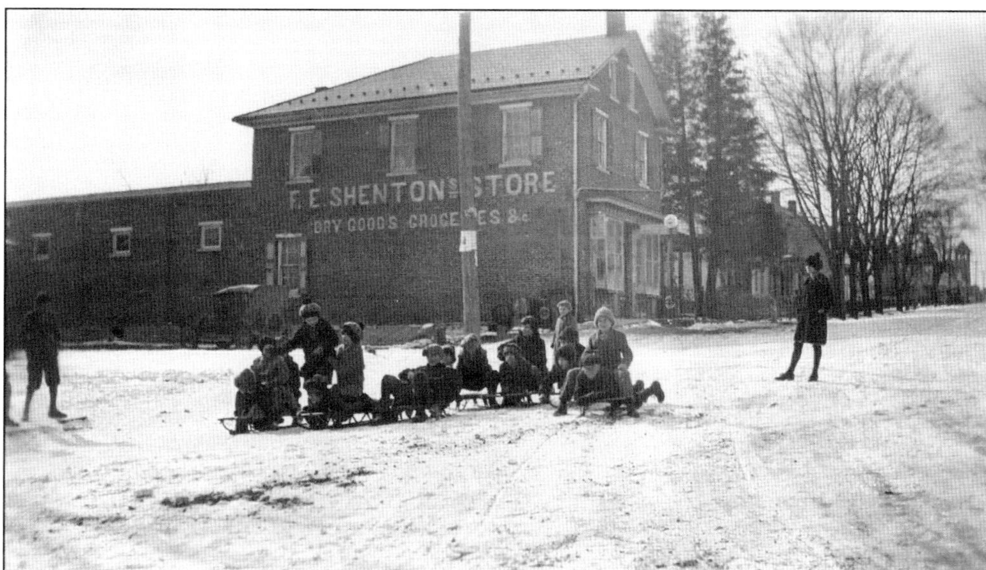

Area children enjoy sledding in this winter scene at the corner of Locke and Brown Streets. Although the building now serves as the post office, the name F. E. Shenton is still visible on the side. Locke Street was later renamed Main Street. (Courtesy of Northern Lehigh Future Focus Collection.)

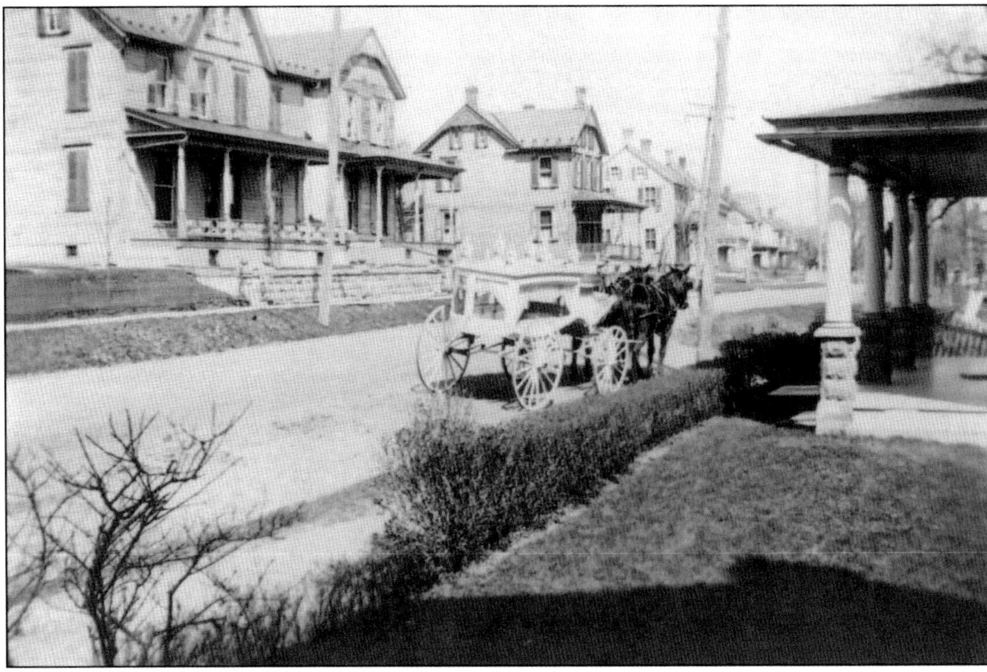

A horse-drawn hearse is parked in front of the Lewis Heintzelman Funeral Home, the first funeral home in Slatedale. Today Kevin Hunsicker runs the funeral home. (Courtesy of Northern Lehigh Future Focus Collection.)

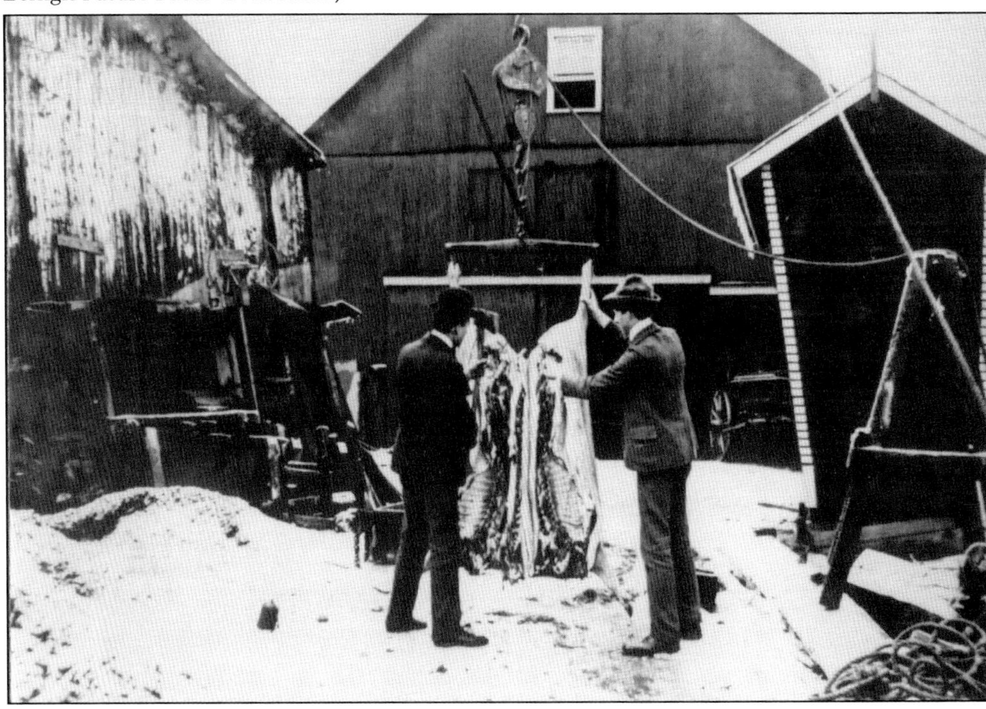

George L. Williams started his butcher shop in 1907. He delivered meats by horse and wagon throughout Slatedale. This photograph shows the slaughterhouse. (Courtesy of Northern Lehigh Future Focus Collection.)

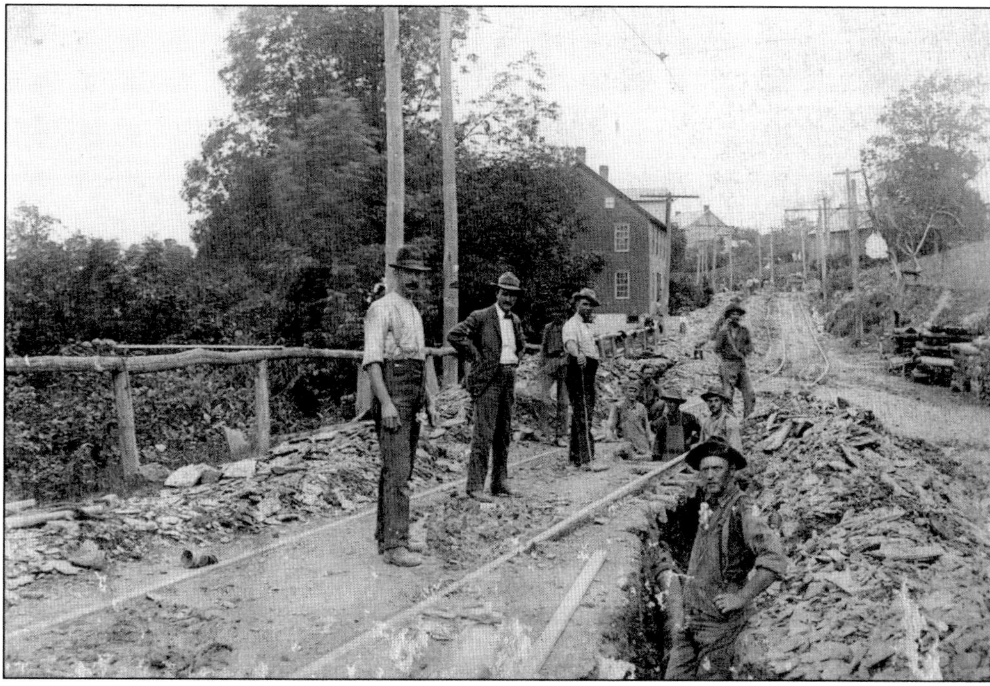

Workers take a break for the camera in this *c.* 1906 view of Slatedale. They appear to be installing a water or drain line under the trolley tracks. Lover's Lane is located to the left, out of the photograph. (Courtesy of Larry Hillborn.)

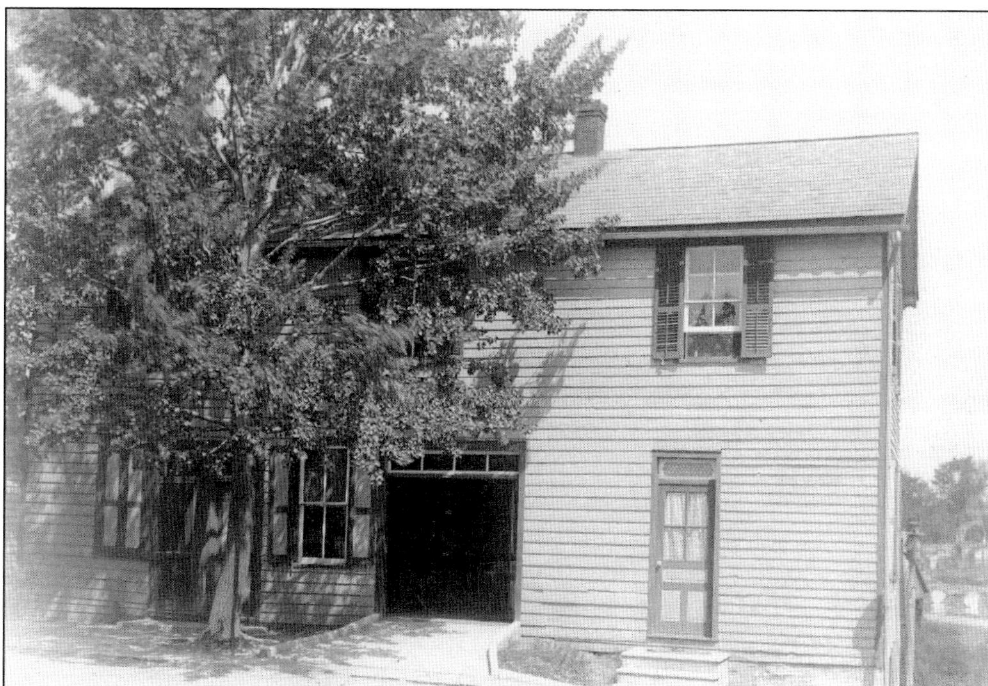

This is the original Slatedale Fire House, located at the corner of Main and Brown Streets. (Courtesy of Northern Lehigh Future Focus Collection.)

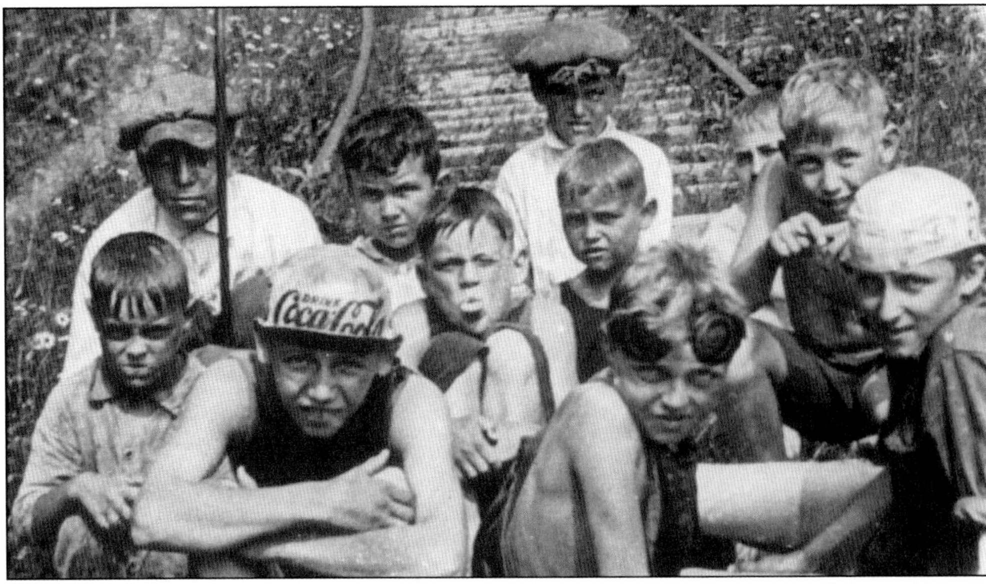

Boys gather along the railroad tracks near Slatedale. The boy with the Coca-Cola hat is Vincent Kern, and the boy with his hat on backwards is Claude Merkle. (Courtesy of W. S. Merkle, Northern Lehigh Future Focus Collection.)

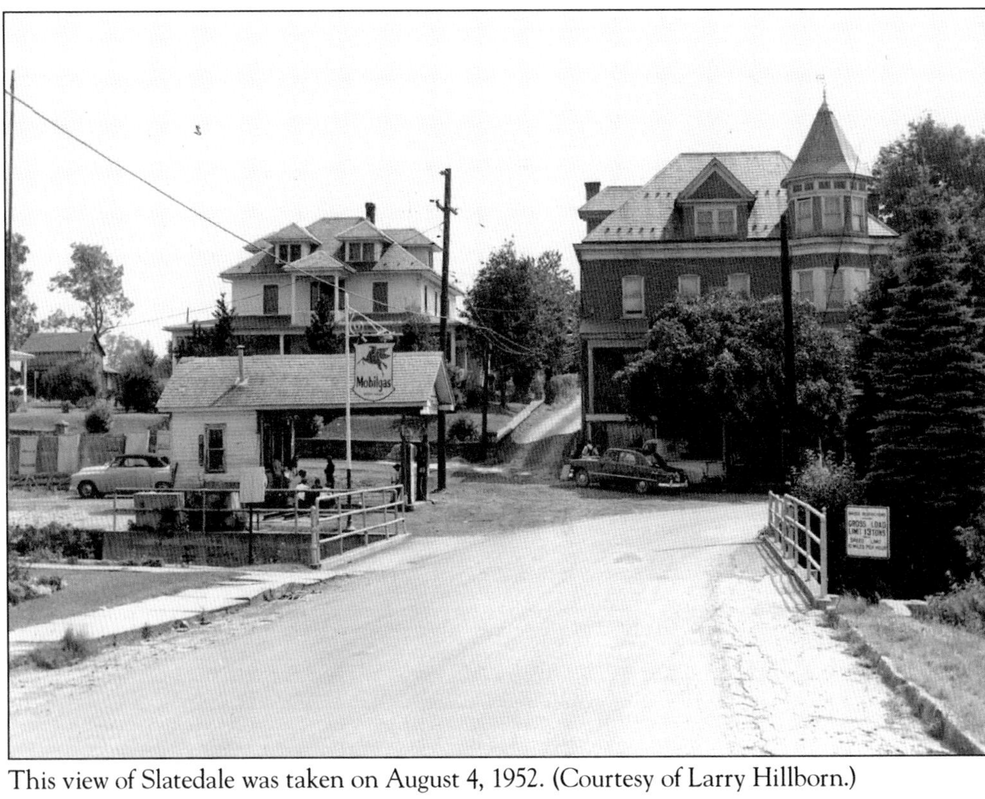

This view of Slatedale was taken on August 4, 1952. (Courtesy of Larry Hillborn.)

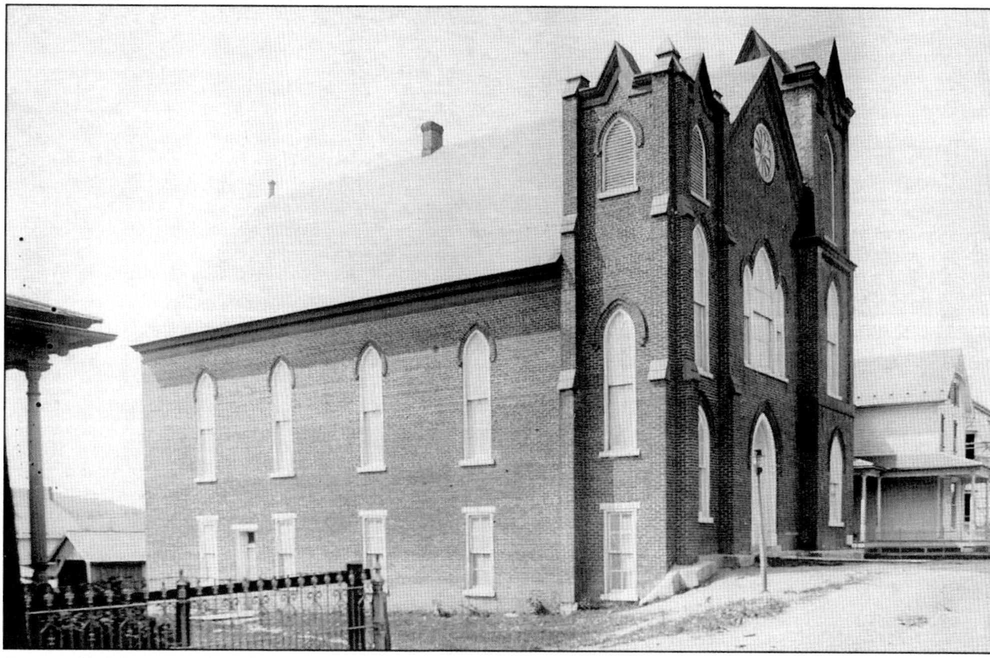

St. Paul's Union Church was organized in 1888 by Rev. J. S. Renninger, H. W. Bloss, Wilson Rex, Peter Ferber, J. H. Snyder, Henry Kern, W. B. Krause, and William Steele. The property was sold at sheriff's sale in 1889. Lafayette German and Henry Kern purchased it and sold it back to the church at a reduced price. The name was changed to Holy Trinity when the original organizers obtained possession of the church again. A clause in the deed states that only a Lutheran and Reformed church can be built on the site. (Courtesy of Northern Lehigh Future Focus Collection.)

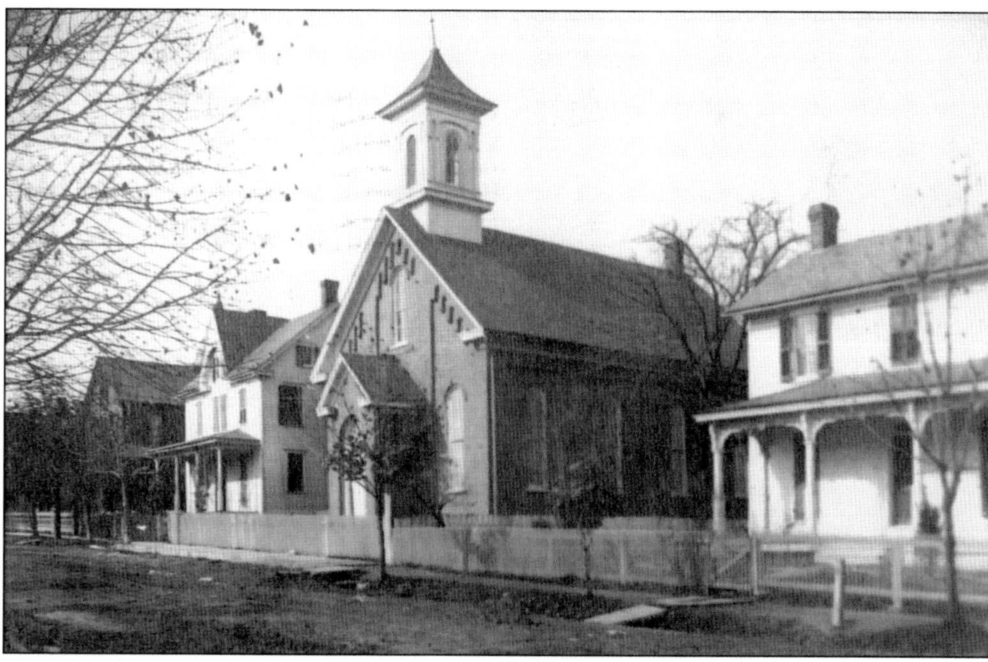

This church is part of the scene in Slatedale around 1907. (Courtesy of Larry Hillborn.)

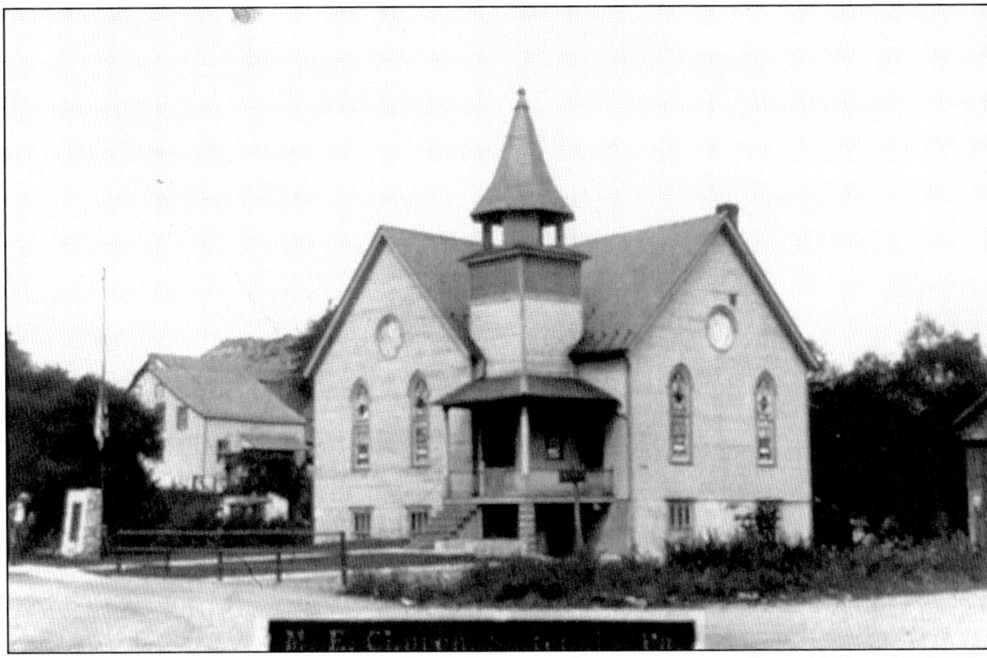

The Methodist Episcopal church in Slatedale was under construction from 1856 to 1858. The church is no longer there. A home stands in its place. (Courtesy of Everett and Marilyn Kaul, Northern Lehigh Future Focus Collection.)

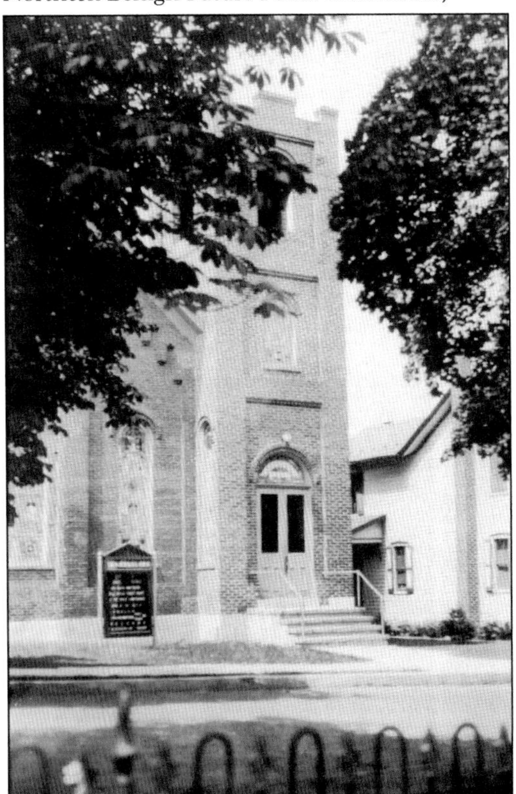

The Salem Evangelical Church in Slatedale, built in 1881, is shown here around 1942. (Courtesy of Larry Hillborn.)

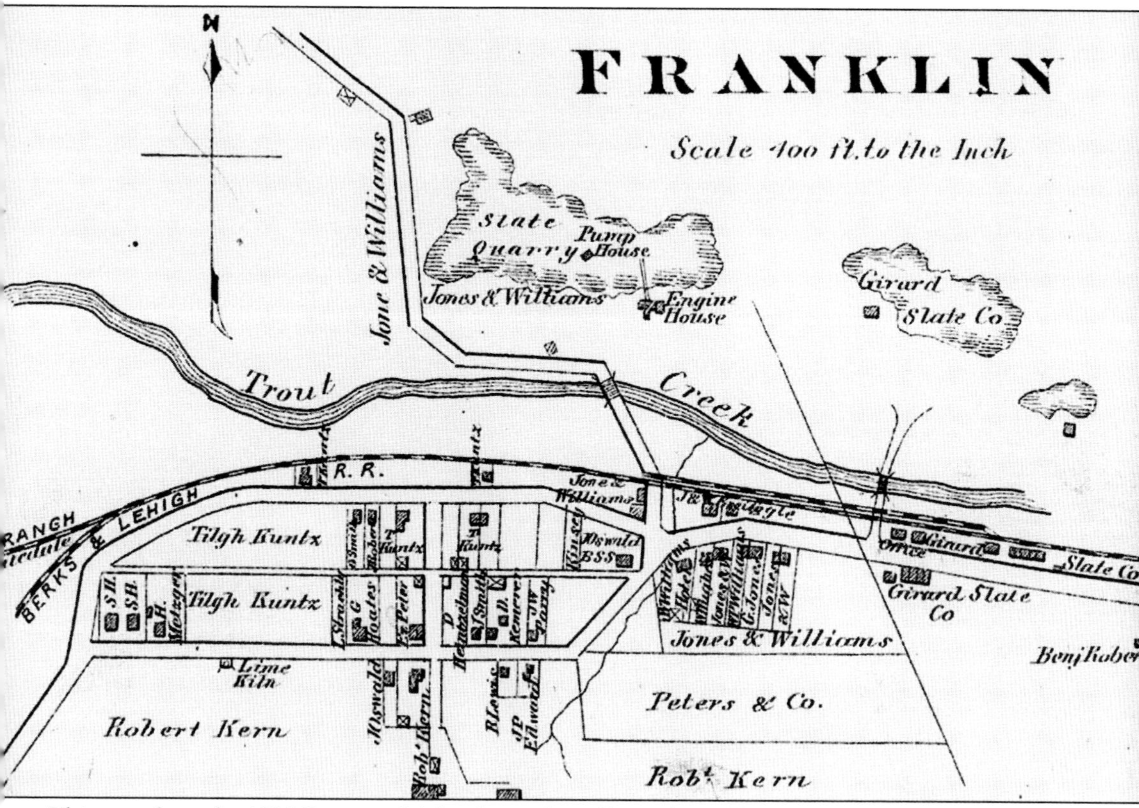

This map from the 1876 *Centennial Atlas* shows the village of Franklin, now known as Emerald.

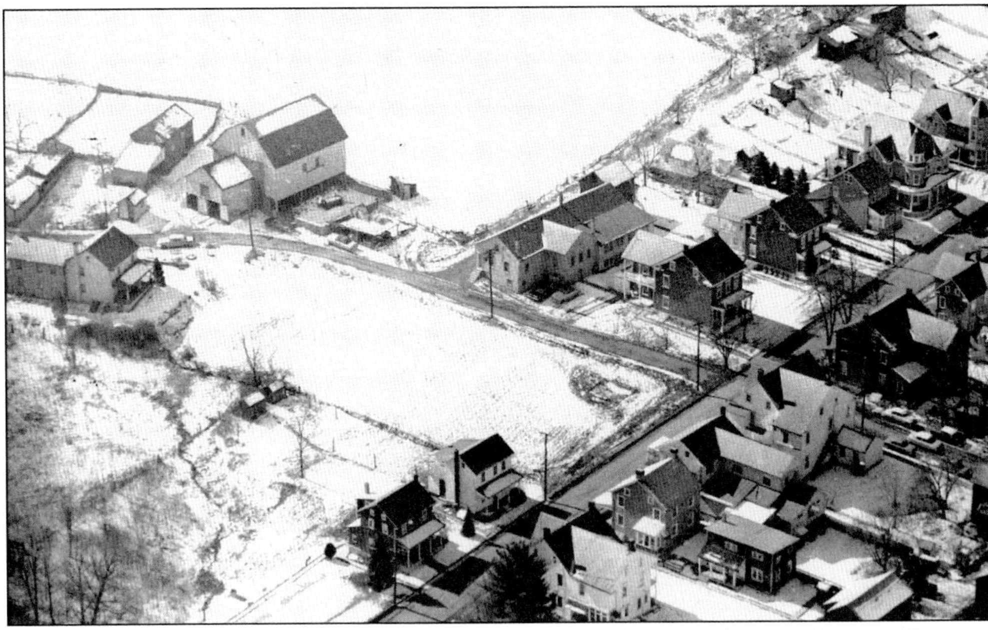

This *c.* 1960 aerial view of Emerald shows the intersection of Main and Center Streets. (Courtesy of Larry Hillborn.)

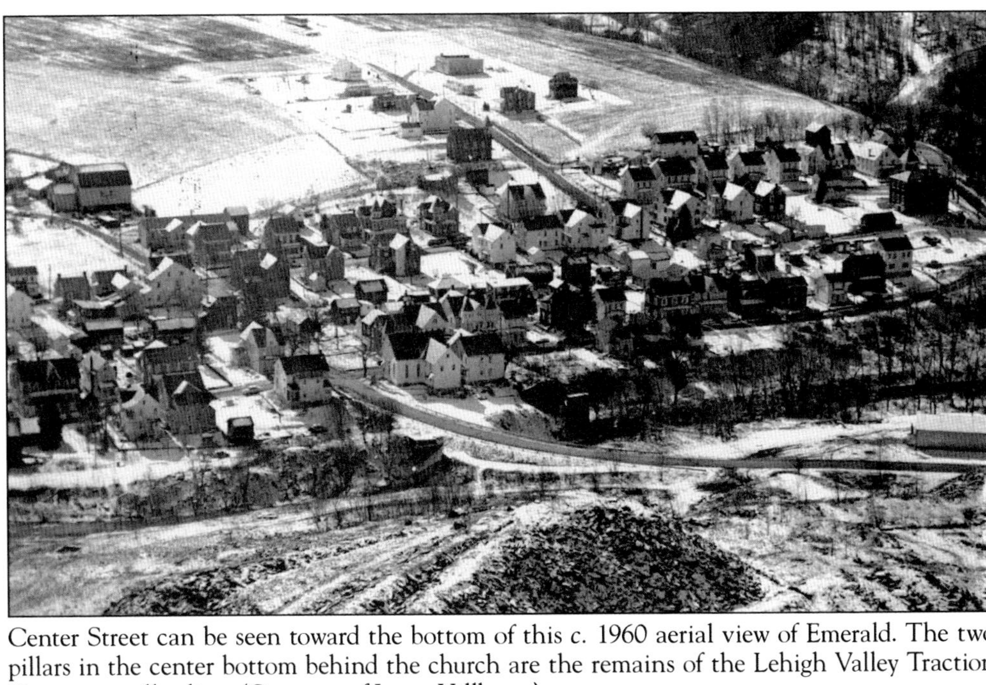

Center Street can be seen toward the bottom of this *c.* 1960 aerial view of Emerald. The two pillars in the center bottom behind the church are the remains of the Lehigh Valley Traction Company trolley line. (Courtesy of Larry Hillborn.)

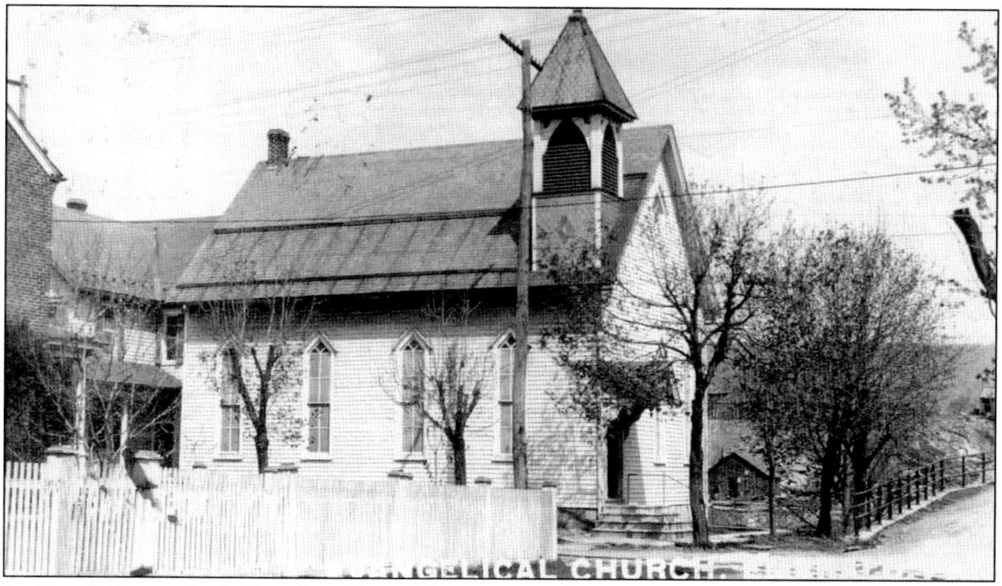

St. Peter's Evangelical Church in Emerald, constructed in 1894, is shown here around 1924. The church is located at the corner of Center and Franklin Streets. (Courtesy of Larry Hillborn.)

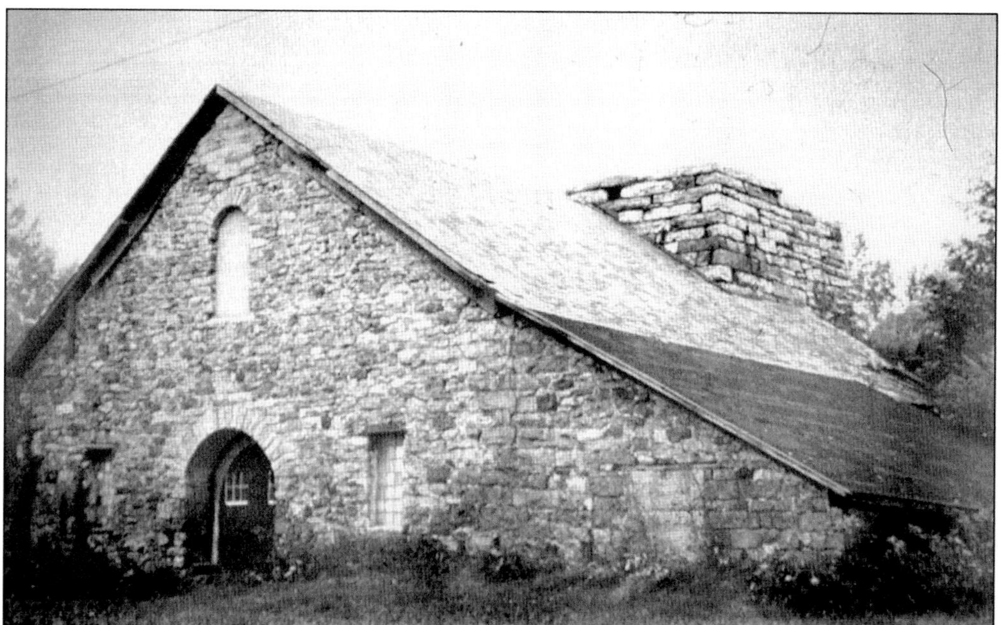

The Lehigh Furnace, shown here around 1920, was built in 1826 by Stephen Balliet and Samuel Helffrich. The furnace burned charcoal to make iron bars known as pig iron from iron brought from South Whitehall Township. The village of Lehigh Furnace still bears the name. (Courtesy of Paul Handwerk, Northern Lehigh Future Focus Collection.)

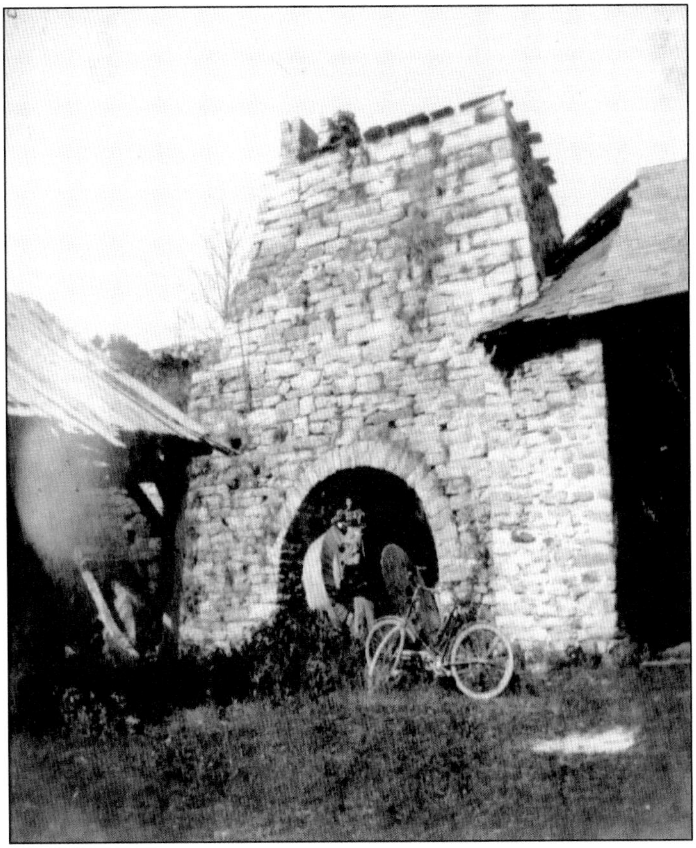

This photograph shows the Lehigh Furnace on October 10, 1897. The furnace closed around 1880. (Courtesy of Slatington Public Library, Northern Lehigh Future Focus Collection.)

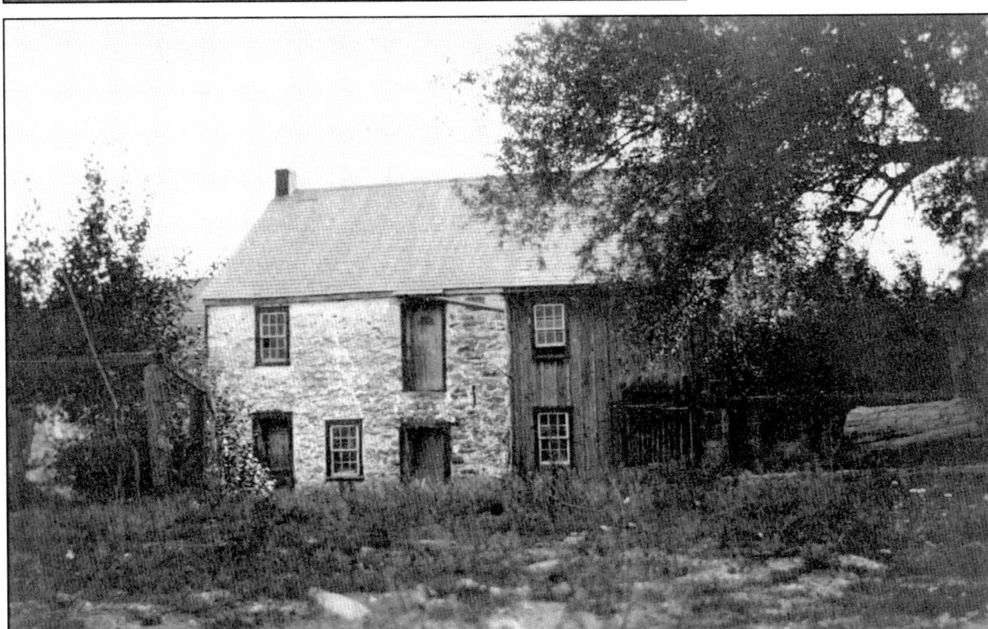

When this photograph was taken, the Bloss Homestead was called the Remaley Mill. The building was in a state of disrepair at the time of publication. (Courtesy of Larry Hillborn.)

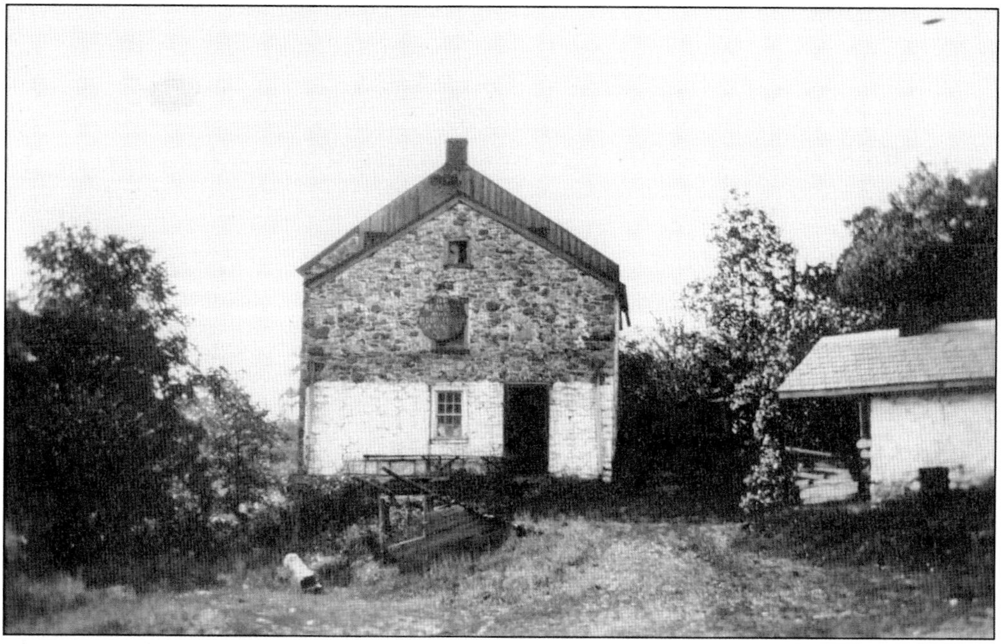

The sign on the building at the corner of Furnace and Grant Streets in Lehigh Furnace reads, "1831, Remaley Mill, Flour, Feeds, Grains."

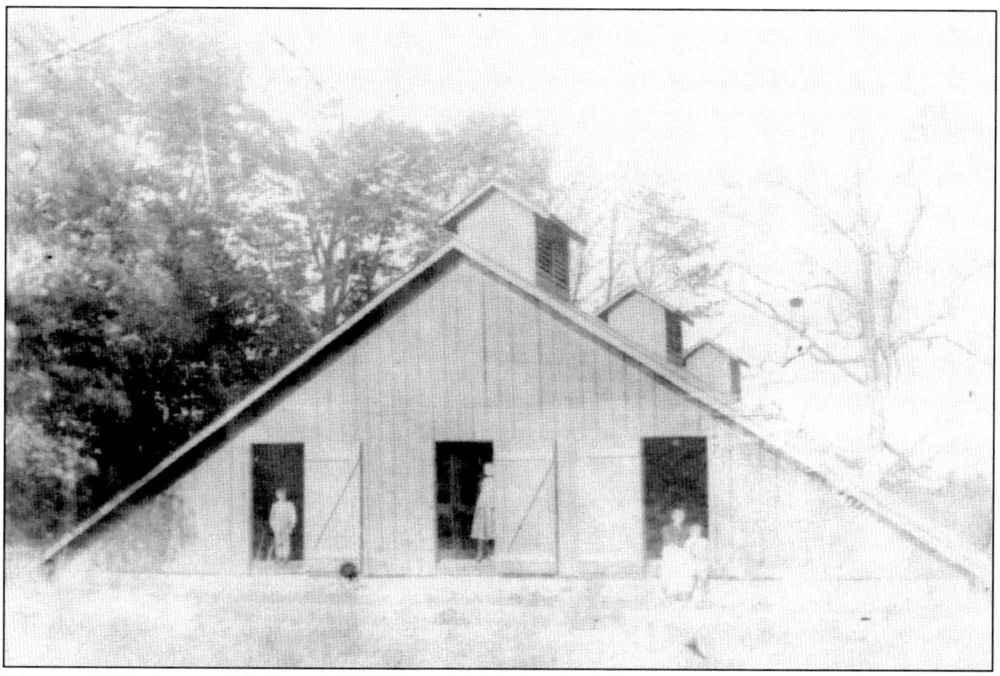

This c. 1910 photograph shows the Slatington Reservoir, located along Welshtown Road. The first building was constructed in 1891, and a second followed in 1905. (Courtesy of Raymond Holland Regional History Collection, Northern Lehigh Future Focus Collection.)

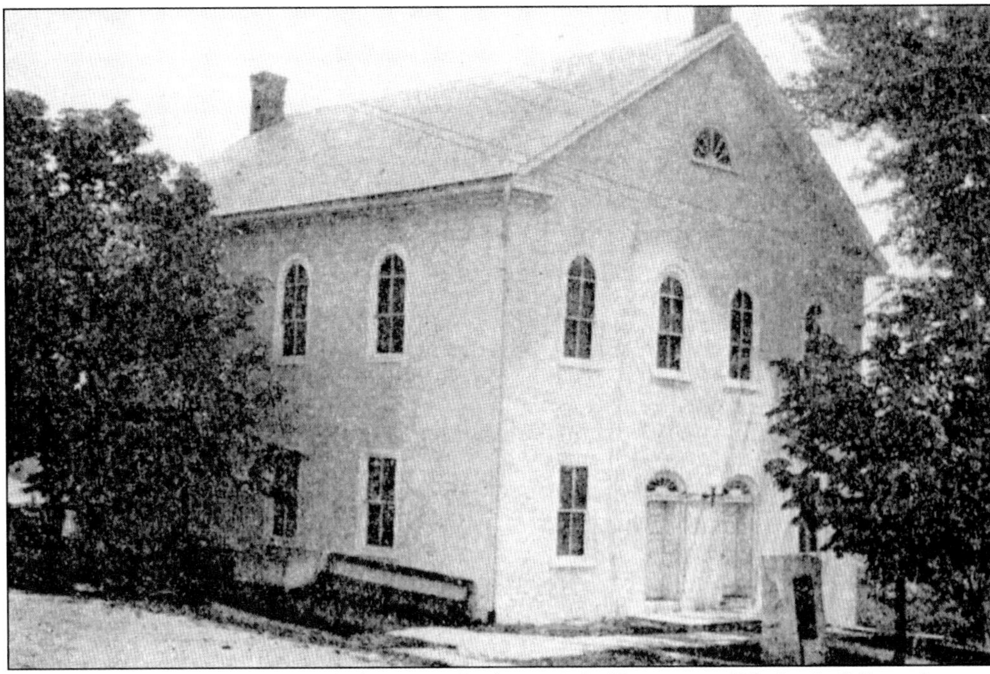

The Friedens United Church of Christ was built in 1847. (Courtesy of Kayleigh Billings.)

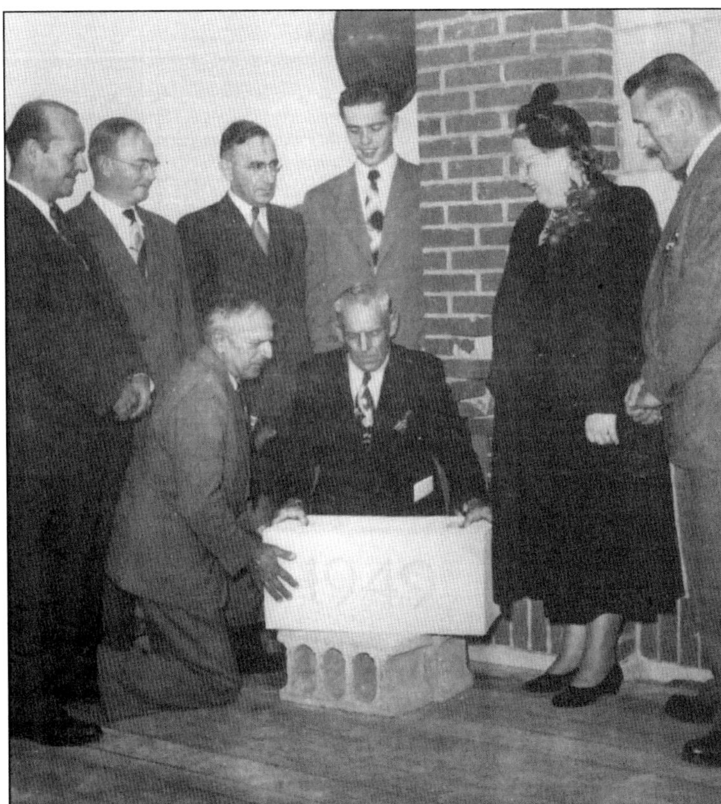

Placing the cornerstone of the Friedens Fire Company in 1949 are Walter T. Handwerk (left) and Victor Deibert. Standing are, from left to right, Charles W. Deichman, Harry Deibert, Judge James F. Henninger, William Hunsicker, Mildred Lentz, and Martin Deibert. (Courtesy of Kayleigh Billings.)

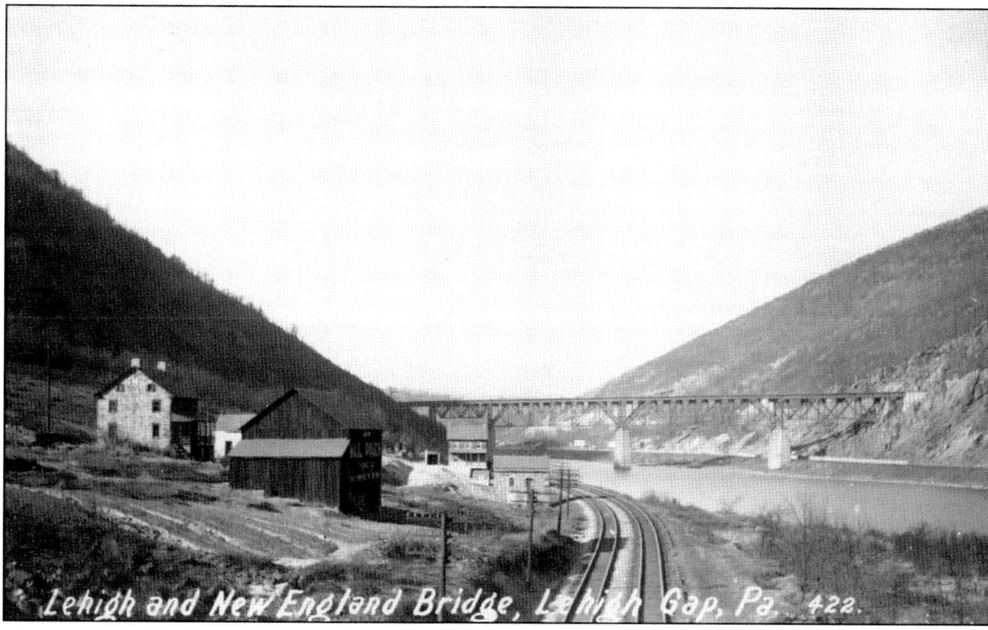

The Lehigh and New England Railroad Bridge stands in the background of this c. 1949 photograph of Lehigh Gap. (Courtesy of Larry Hillborn.)

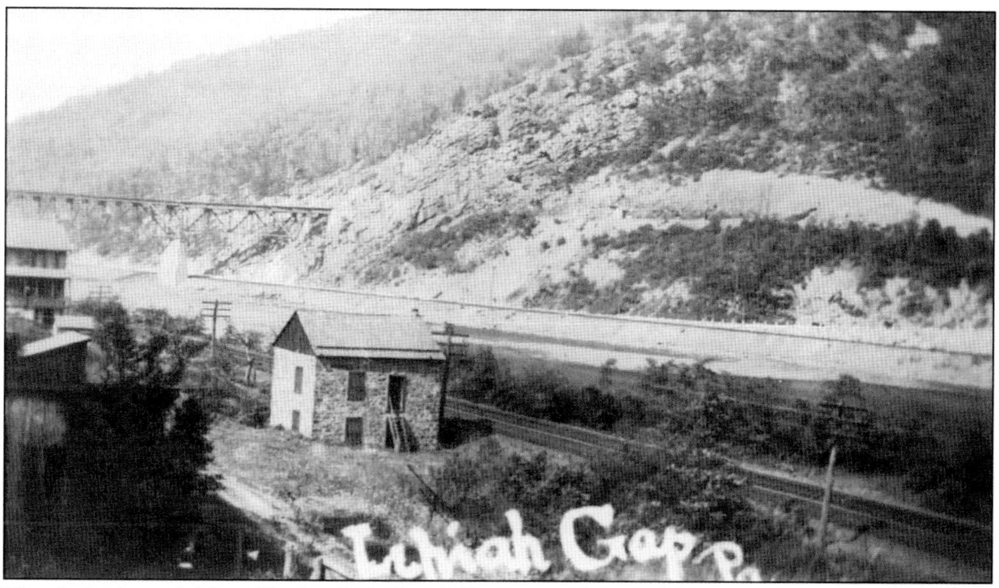

The Lehigh and New England Railroad Bridge is also visible in the background of this photograph. The building in the center, which was once a tannery, still stands today. (Courtesy of Larry Hillborn.)

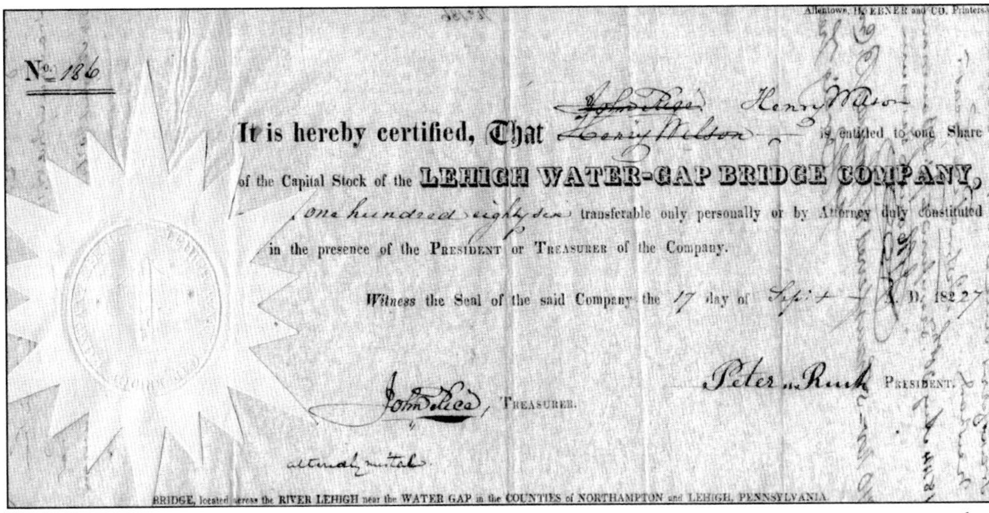

Allentown, HUEBNER and CO. Printers.

No. 186

It is hereby certified, That Henry Wilson is entitled to one Share of the Capital Stock of the LEHIGH WATER-GAP BRIDGE COMPANY, one hundred eighty six transferable only personally or by Attorney duly constituted in the presence of the PRESIDENT or TREASURER of the Company.

Witness the Seal of the said Company the 17 day of Sept A. D. 1827

PRESIDENT.

TREASURER.

BRIDGE, located across the RIVER LEHIGH near the WATER GAP in the COUNTIES of NORTHAMPTON and LEHIGH, PENNSYLVANIA.

This original stock certificate for the Lehigh Water-Gap Bridge Company is No. 186, issued to Henry Wilson on September 17, 1827. (Courtesy of Larry Hillborn.)

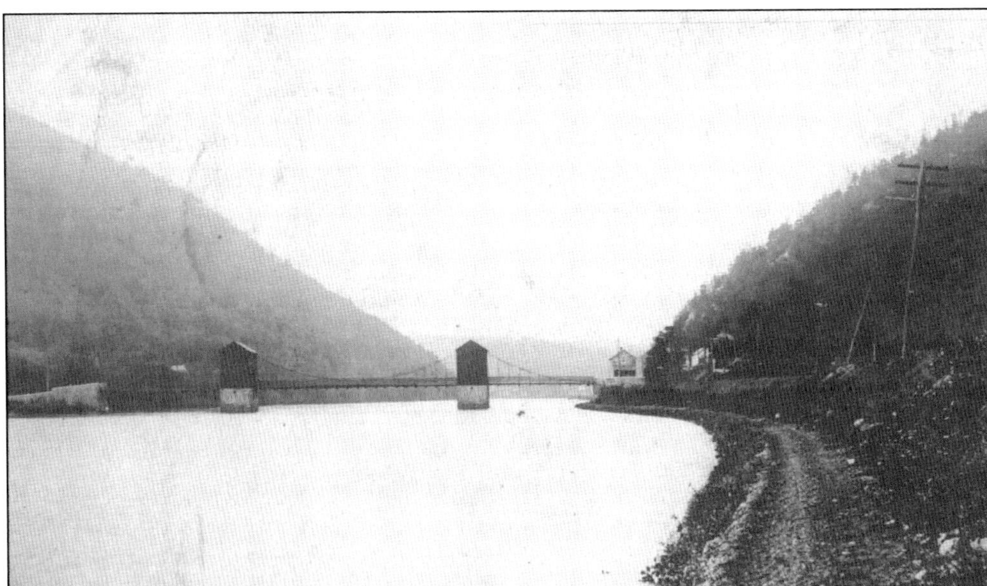

Lehigh Gap is visible in the distance in this photograph of the chain bridge. The toll taker's house stands on the right in this c. 1905 photograph. The towpath is in front of it, along the right side of the water. (Courtesy of Larry Hillborn.)

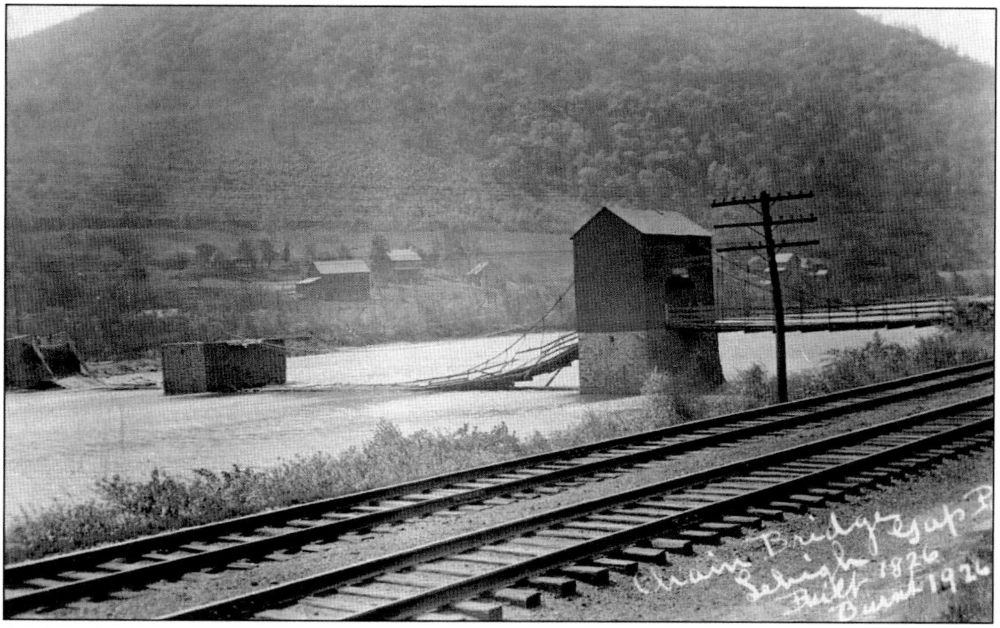

A chain bridge was erected in 1826 at a cost of $1,200. In 1925, it was partially destroyed by fire, as shown here. It was reopened in 1927 and removed in 1933 when the present-day Route 873 bridge opened. (Courtesy of Larry Hillborn.)

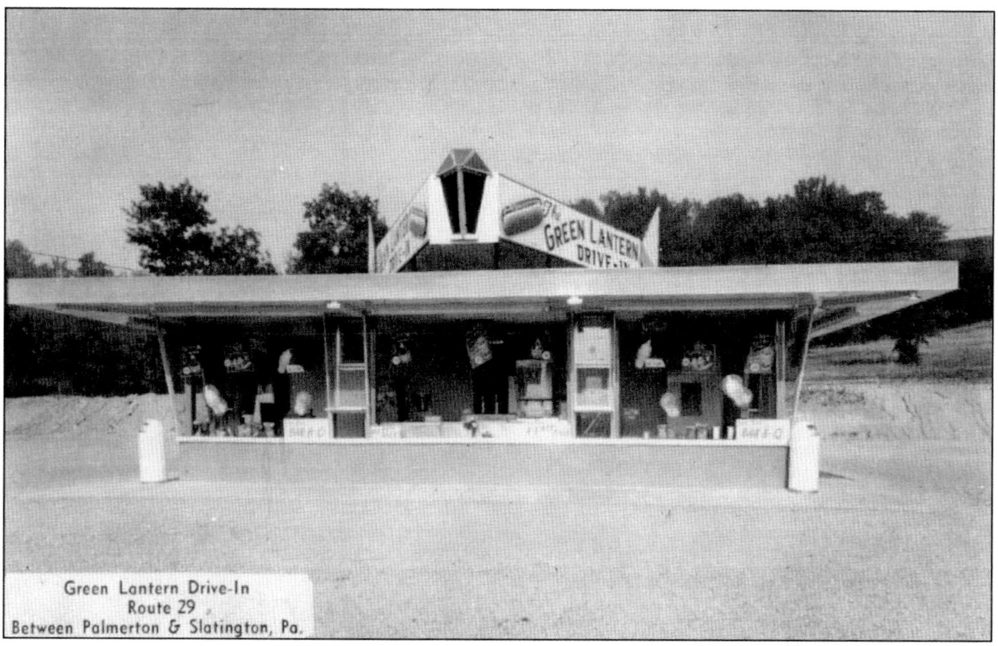

The Green Lantern Drive-In operated in Washington Township, just outside of Slatington on Route 29 (now Route 873). This photograph is from about 1955. (Courtesy of Evelyn Haas, Northern Lehigh Future Focus Collection.)

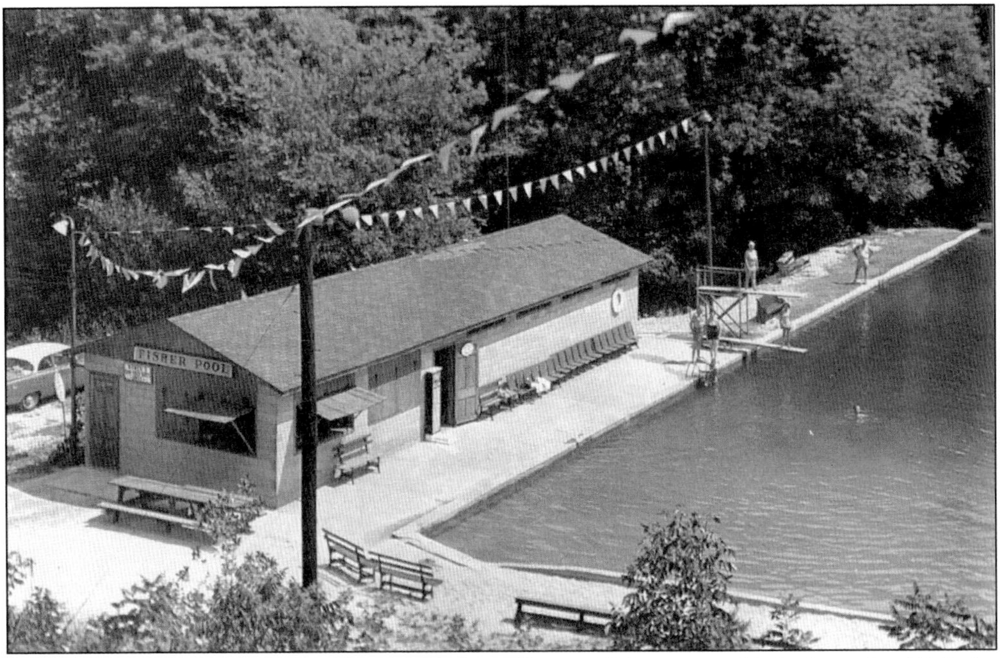

The Fisher Pool, located along Route 29 (now Route 873), was established in the 1920s by friends Howard Yehl and John Evans. It was originally named Caronell Park for their wives, Carolyn Evans and Nellie Yehl. It was later operated by the Maranatha Settlement Association of Philadelphia. The group hosted underprivileged children for nine weeks of camping during the summer. (Courtesy of Larry Hillborn.)

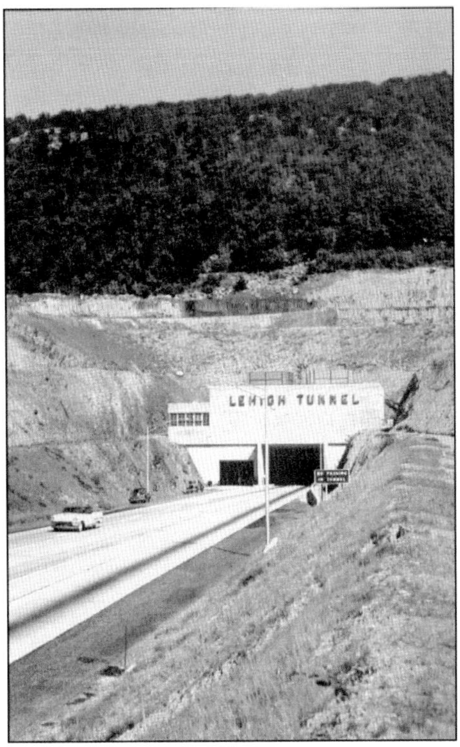

The southern portal of the Lehigh Tunnel on the Northeast Extension of the Pennsylvania Turnpike calls Washington Township home. In 1991, a second portal was added to alleviate traffic congestion. (Courtesy of Larry Hillborn.)

Four

RAILROADS, TROLLEYS, AND THE LEHIGH CANAL

The Lehigh Canal follows the Lehigh River from Mauch Chunk (present-day Jim Thorpe) to Easton. It was the brainchild of Josiah White, who, with his partner Erskine Hazard, formed the Lehigh Coal Company as a means of getting fuel for their Philadelphia area forges during the War of 1812. The canal was completed in 1829. Walnutport Borough currently owns the 146 acres from Lehigh Gap through Walnutport to the Bertsch Creek. The Walnutport Canal Association has converted the parcel into a park.

Many locks were known by the name of their last locktender. Lock 22 is known as "Frantz's Lock." Lock 23 is named after Frank Kelchner. Lock 24 is "Schaffer's Lock," and Lock 25 was named for Charles W. Sheckler.

The Lehigh and Susquehanna Railroad was founded in 1837 to transport coal from the Wyoming Valley. In 1862, the railroad was extended along the river to Easton. The Central Railroad Company of New Jersey eventually bought the Lehigh and Susquehanna, and Conrail took it over in 1976.

The Pennsylvania, Slatington, and New England Railroad grew from a consolidation of the Delaware and Slatington and the Pennsylvania and New England in 1882, but work ceased in 1885 when the company filed for receivership. The Pennsylvania, Poughkeepsie, and Boston Railroad bought this company in 1887 but was in receivership by 1891. The Lehigh and New England (L&NE) then bought the Pennsylvania, Poughkeepsie, and Boston in 1894.

In 1934, the railroad asked permission to abandon the Slatington branch from Slate Junction near Danielsville to Slatington, a distance of six miles. In 1961, the L&NE abandoned operations, and the bridge across the Lehigh River at Lehigh Gap was removed from 1967 to 1968.

Lehigh Valley Railroad was formed in 1853 from the Delaware, Lehigh, Schuylkill and Susquehanna Railroad Company and ran along the river through Slatington. It too became part of Conrail in 1976. The Lehigh Valley also had a spur track from Slatington to the Saegersville Quarries, through Slatedale and Emerald, along Trout Creek. This branch is currently being turned into a rail trail.

The Blue Ridge Traction Company, chartered by the Hower family in 1902, was a small trolley line that ran from Danielsville to Walnutport with four stops: Danielsville, Edgemont Park, Berlinsville, and Walnutport. The trolley line was abandoned on May 30, 1924.

The Allentown and Slatington Street Railway Company began trolley service from Allentown to Slatington in 1900, and a branch from Slatington to Slatedale started in 1902. The Lehigh Valley Traction Company took over the firm in 1905. The Slatedale branch was abandoned in 1929, and the trolley from Allentown stopped coming to Slatington in 1931.

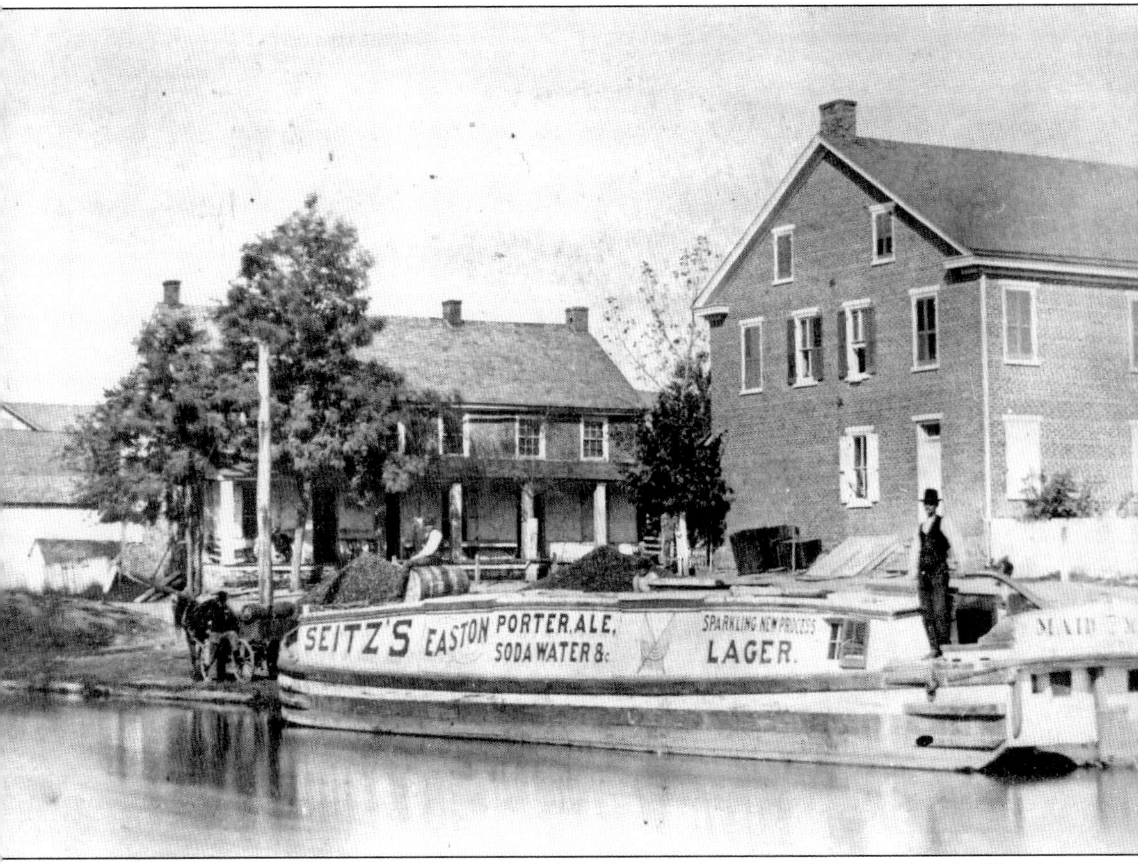

Seitz's Brewery had two boats that traveled the Lehigh, Delaware, and Morris Canals. This barge is stopped in front of the Anchor Hotel in Walnutport. (Courtesy of Palmerton Camera Club, Northern Lehigh Future Focus Collection.)

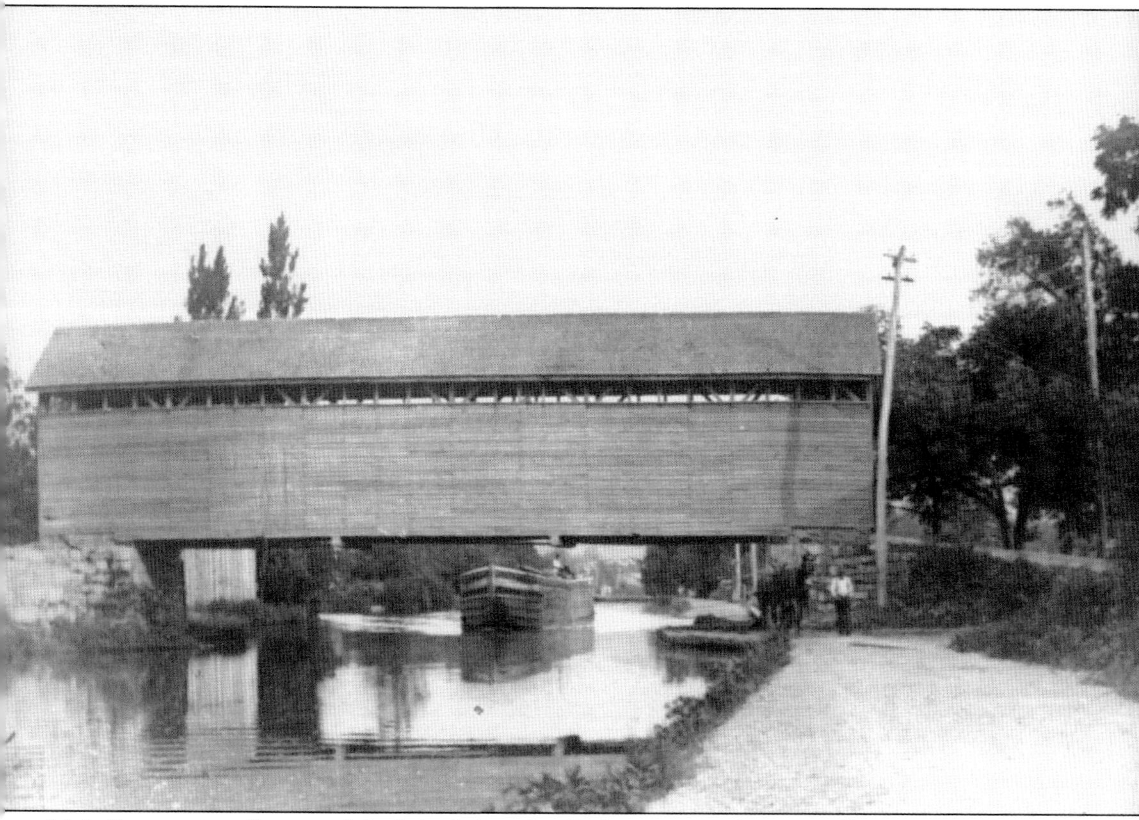

Main Street originally crossed the Lehigh Canal in Walnutport via the covered bridge shown here, looking south toward the locktender's house. (Courtesy of Walnutport Canal Association.)

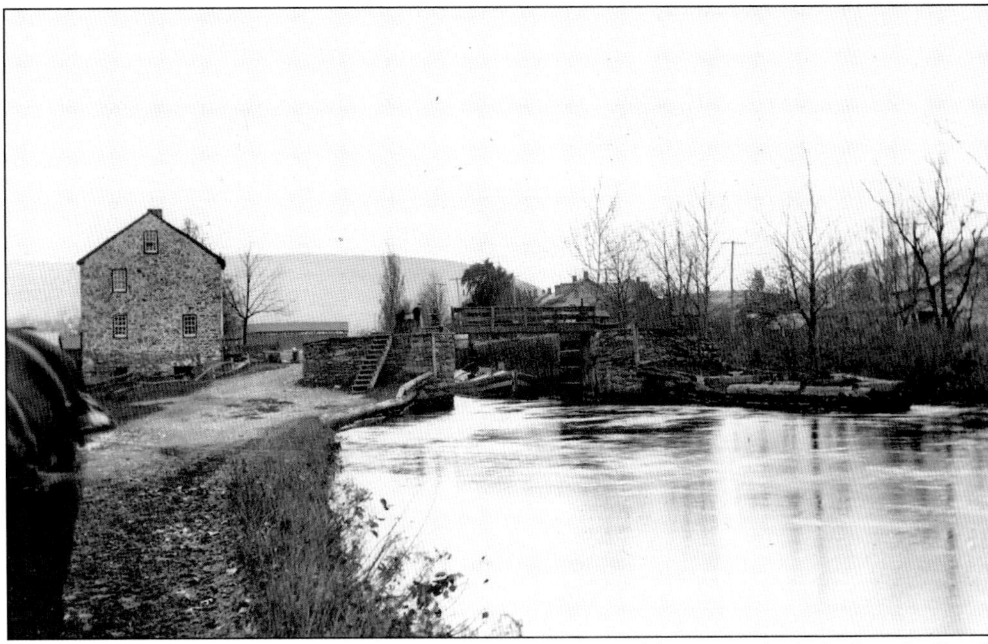

A loaded canal boat comes through Lock No. 23, known as "Kelchner's Lock" for locktender Frank Kelchner. (Courtesy of Palmerton Camera Club, Northern Lehigh Future Focus Collection.)

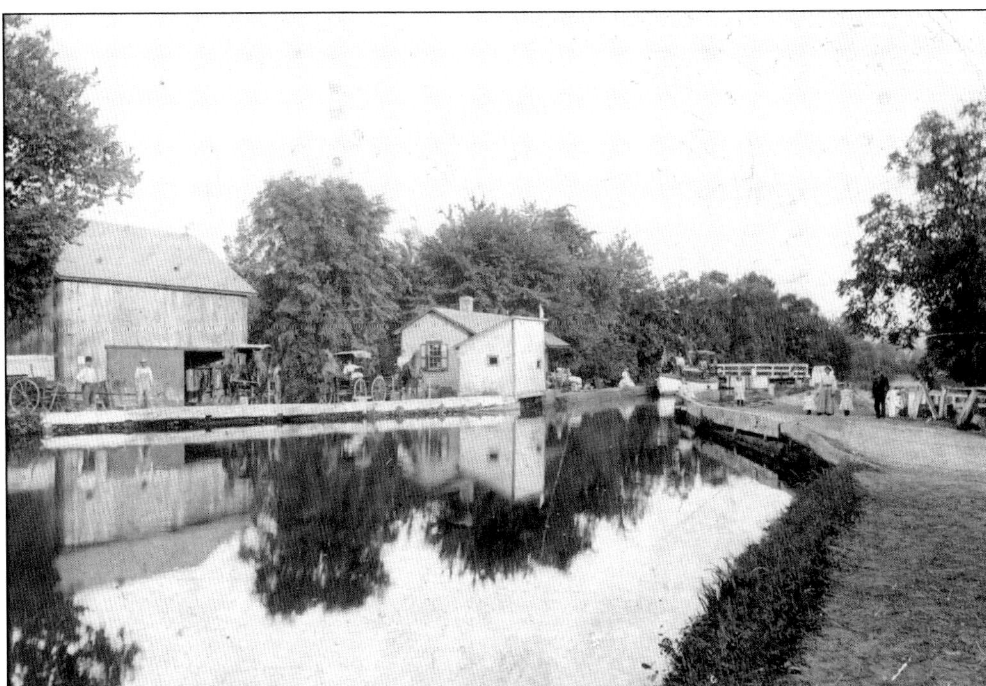

This photograph also shows Kelchner's Lock, No. 23, on the Lehigh Canal. (Courtesy of Palmerton Camera Club, Northern Lehigh Future Focus Collection.)

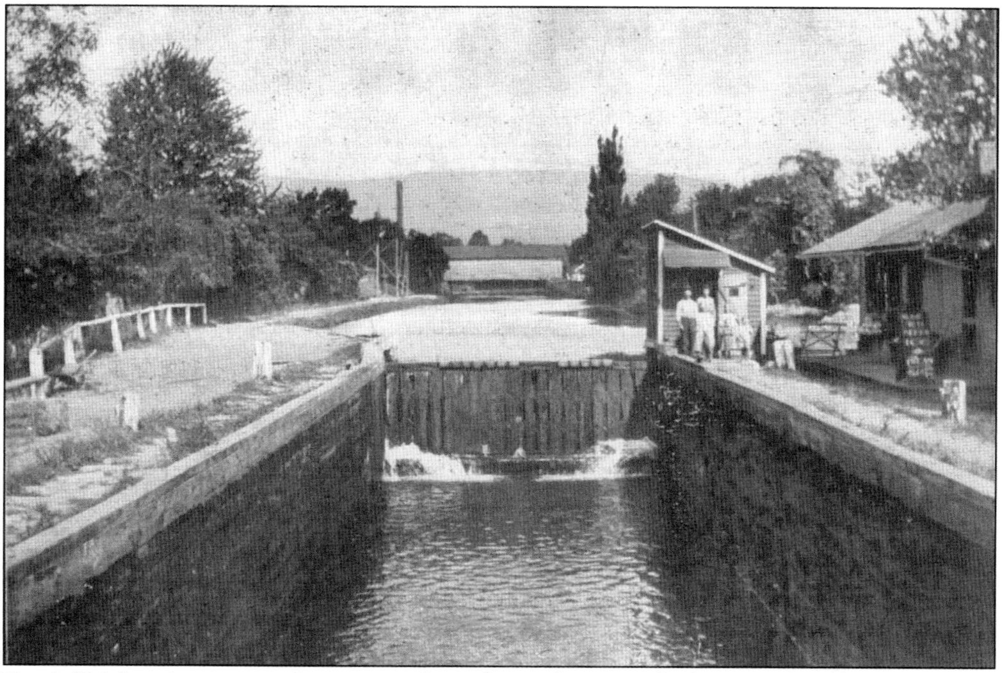

Frank Kelchner's store can be seen to the right in this view, looking north from the lock. In the distance, one can see the covered bridge over the Lehigh Canal and the Citizen's electric company smokestack, situated to the left of the bridge. (Courtesy of Larry Hillborn.)

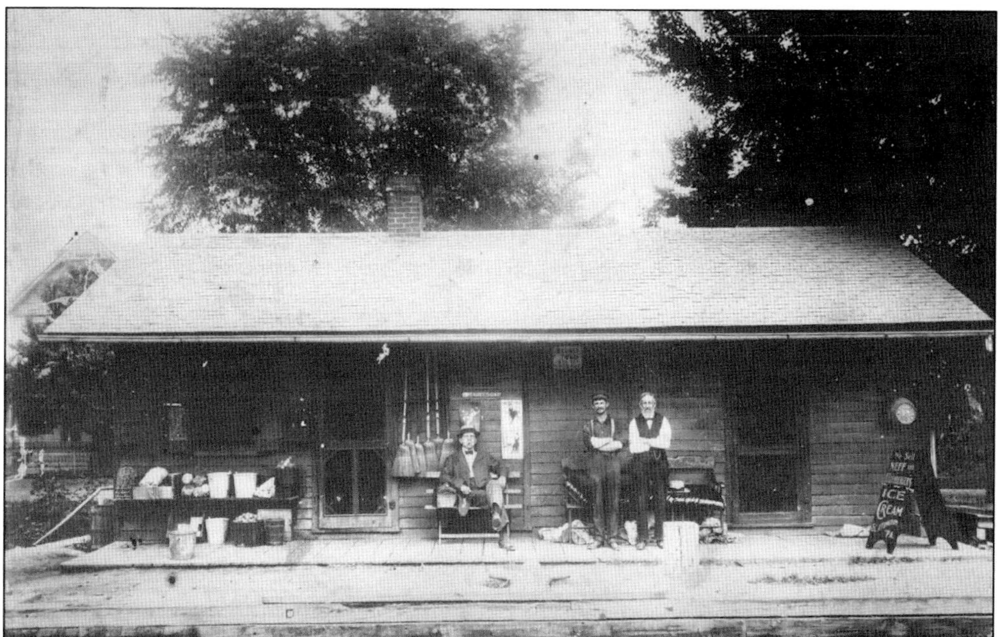

Frank Kelchner can be seen wearing suspenders in the center of this *c.* 1900 photograph of his general store. The sign to the right advertises Neff and Fritzinger's ice cream. (Courtesy of Raymond Holland Regional History Collection, Northern Lehigh Future Focus Collection.)

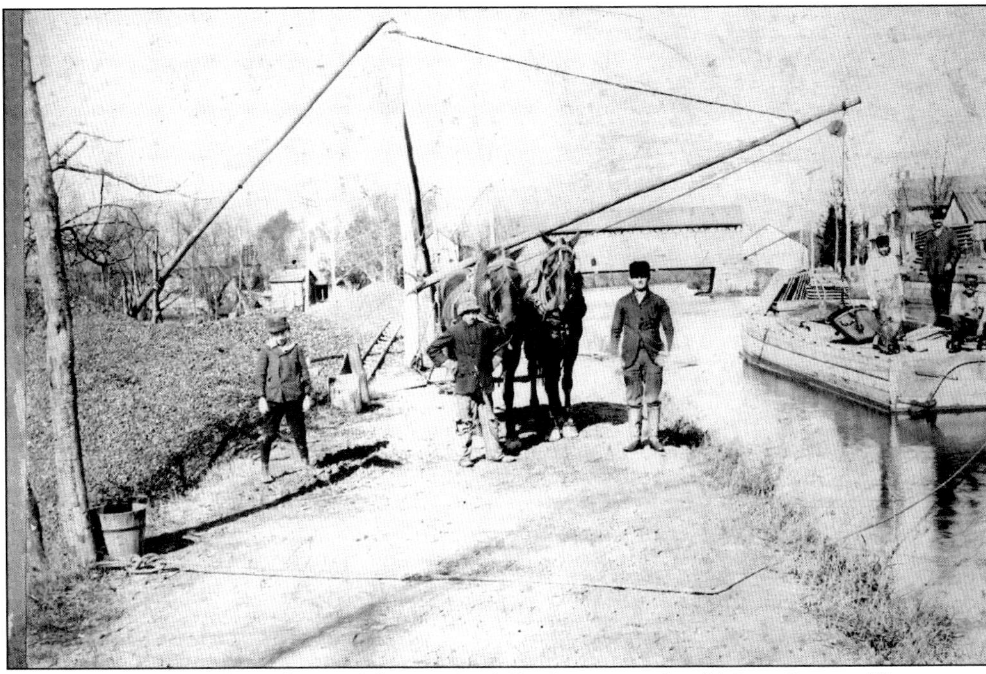

A canal boat unloads coal at Kelchner's Coal Yard, just south of Main Street. (Courtesy of Walnutport Canal Association.)

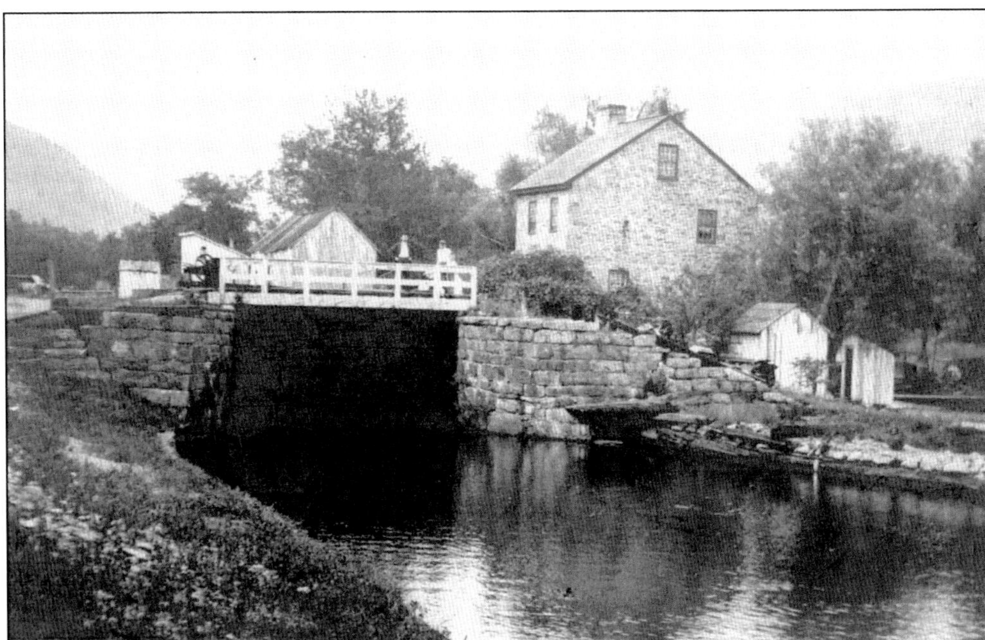

Frantz's Lock, No. 22, is situated along the Lehigh Canal, going north out of Walnutport. (Courtesy of Larry Hillborn.)

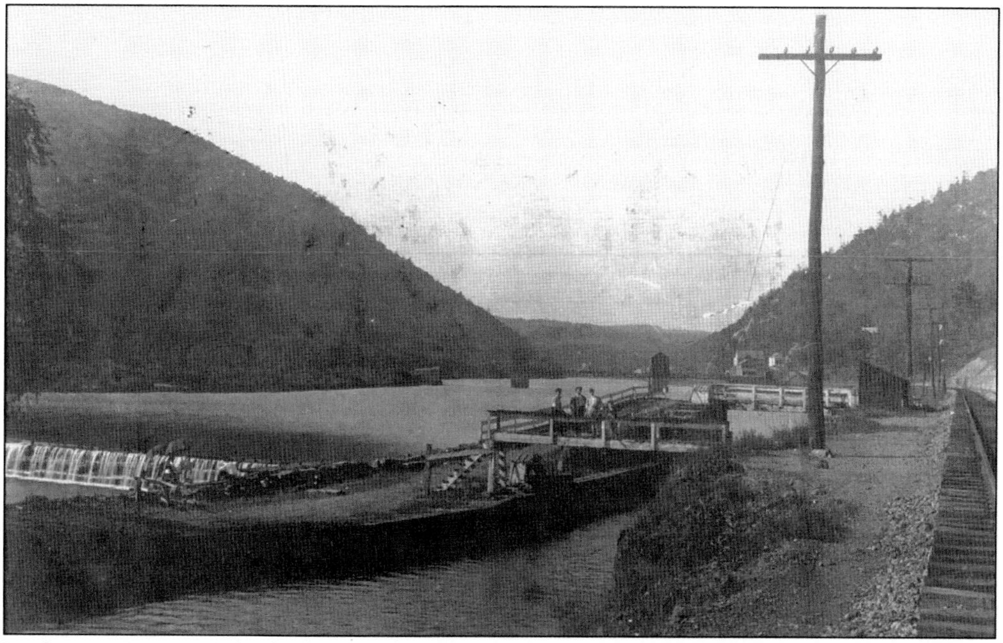

In this c. 1908 view of Lehigh Gap, the chain bridge is seen in the distance. In the foreground are Dam No. 3 and the guard lock, through which boats entered the Lehigh Canal. (Courtesy of Larry Hillborn.)

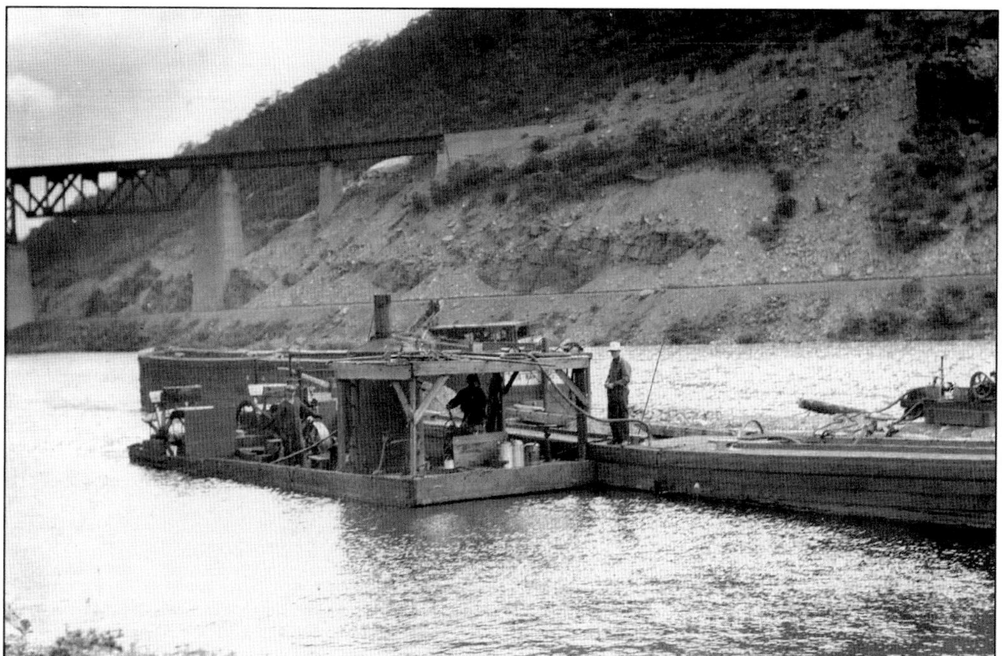

After more than 100 years, the bottom of the river became littered with coal from hauling operations. A number of people made a living dredging it back up and selling it. Here they work on the Lehigh River, north of Dam No. 3. (Courtesy of Palmerton Camera Club, Northern Lehigh Future Focus Collection.)

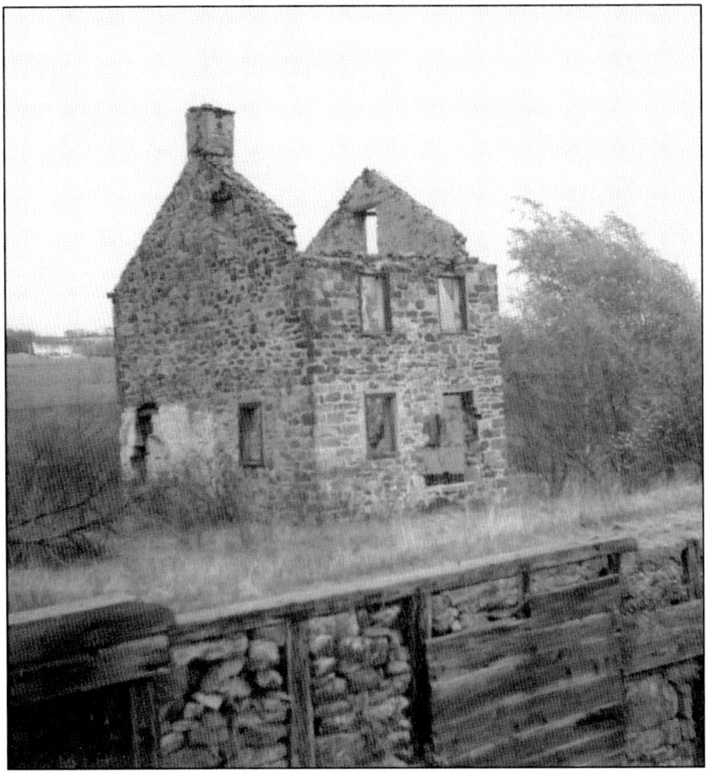

This photograph shows the remains of the lockhouse at Frantz's Lock, No. 22, following a fire that destroyed it. (Courtesy of Walnutport Canal Association.)

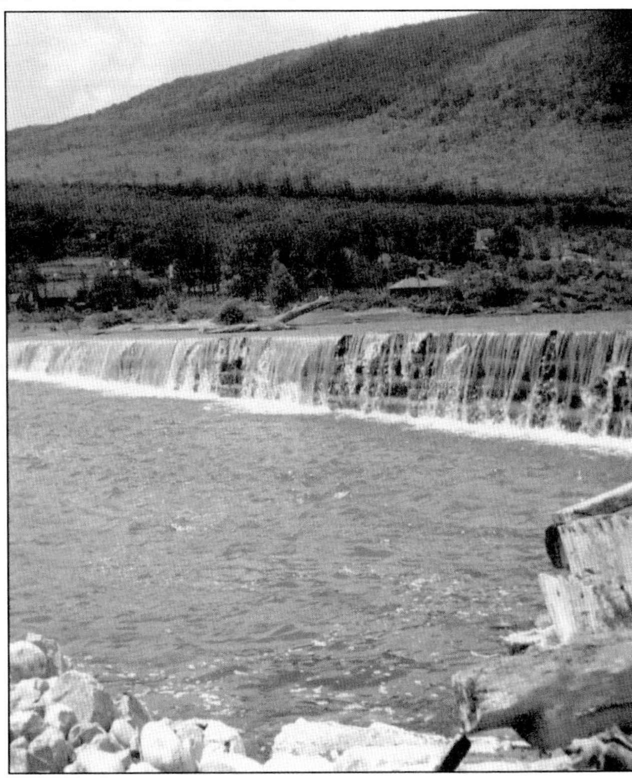

This 1950s view of Dam No. 3 was taken by Pennsylvania Fish Commission photographer Johnny Nicklas. The Lehigh Valley Railroad station at Lehigh Gap appears across the river. (Courtesy of Walnutport Canal Association.)

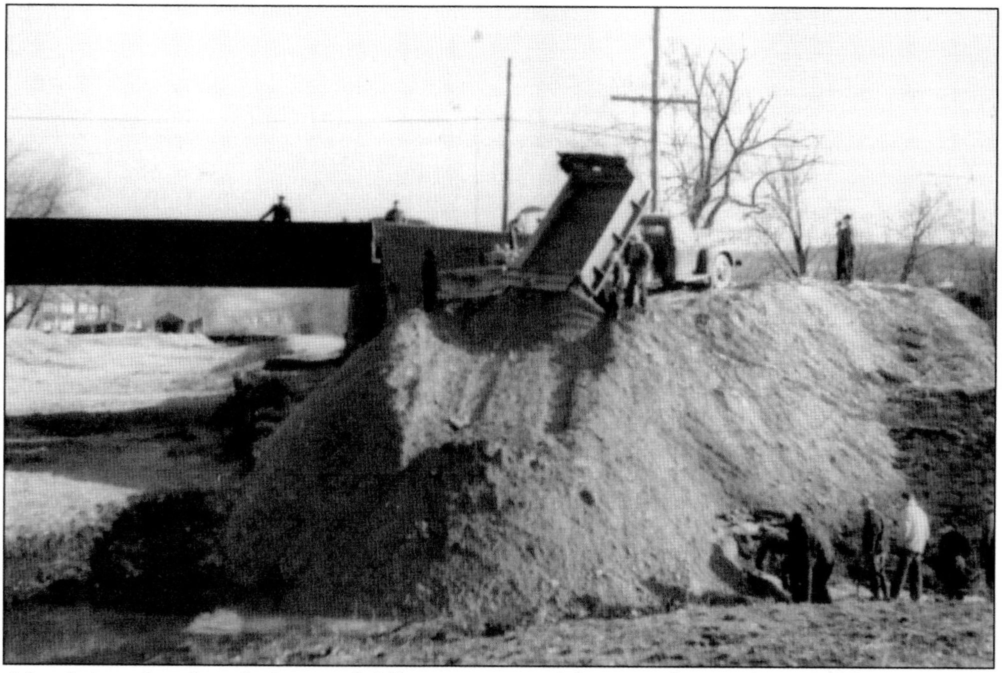

After being abandoned, the canal fell into a state of disrepair, having been hard-hit by floods and hurricanes. This 1953 photograph shows work being done to repair a towpath break north of Main Street. (Courtesy of Walnutport Canal Association.)

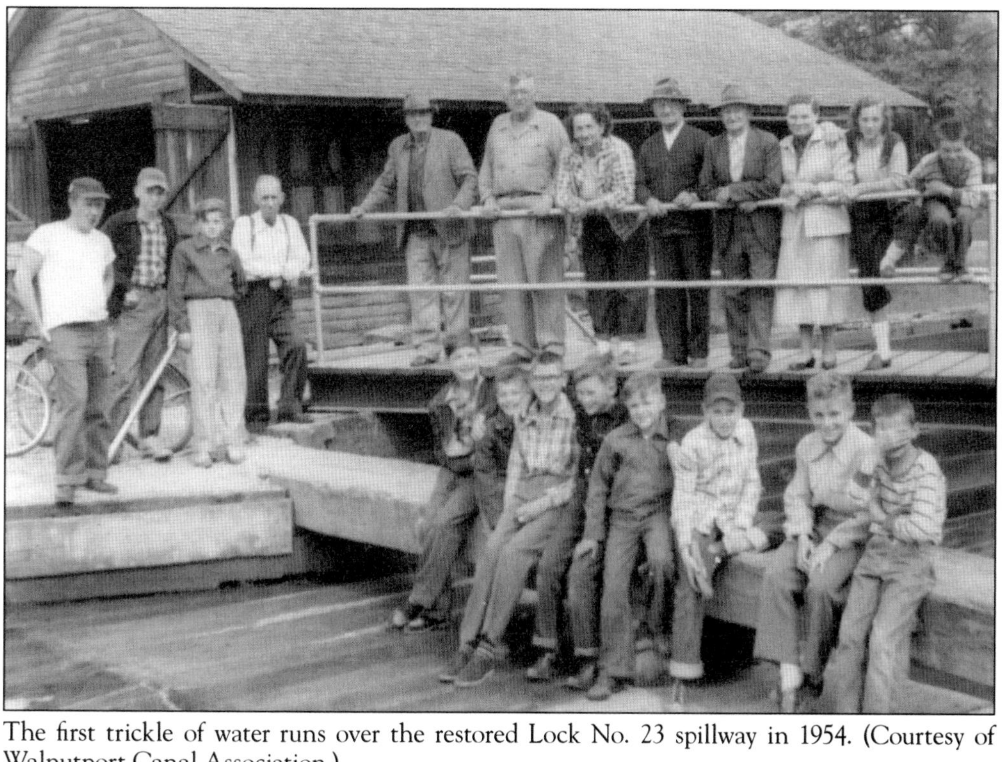

The first trickle of water runs over the restored Lock No. 23 spillway in 1954. (Courtesy of Walnutport Canal Association.)

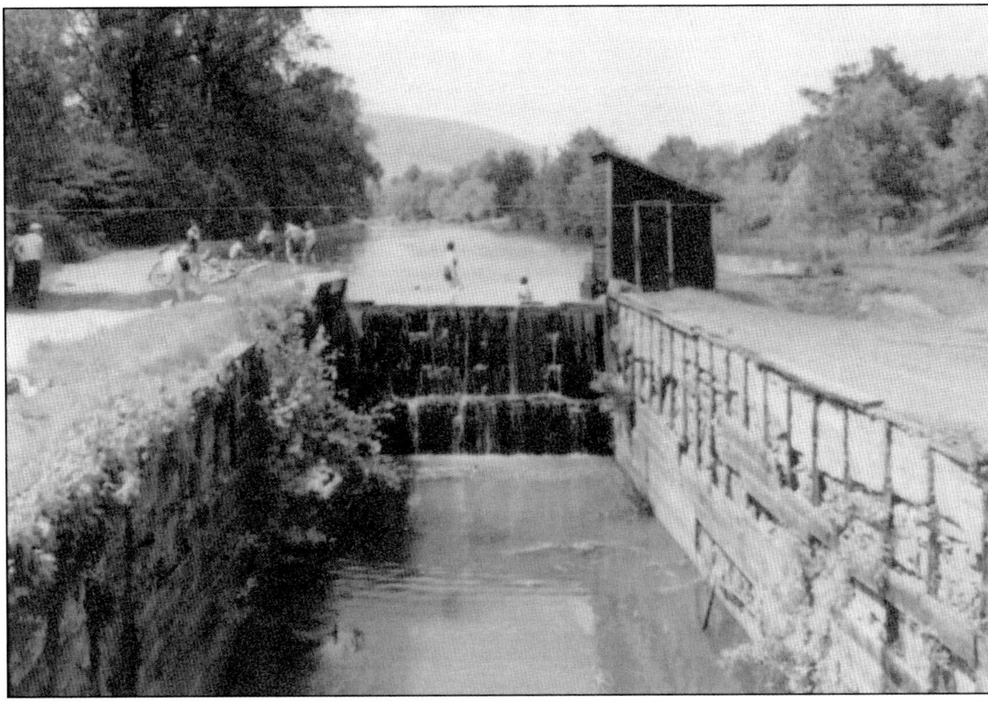

Swimmers enjoy the water at Schaffer's Lock, No. 24, south of Walnutport, in this photograph, taken on June 28, 1954. (Courtesy of Walnutport Canal Association.)

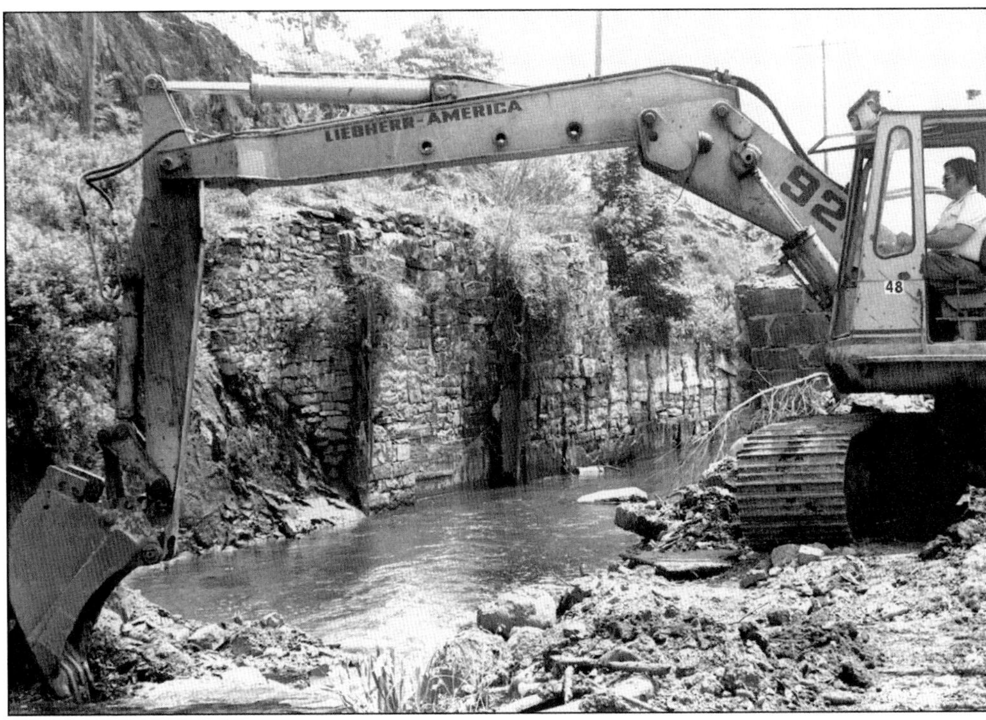

A man operating a piece of equipment works to repair Guard Lock No. 3 at Lehigh Gap. (Courtesy of Walnutport Canal Association.)

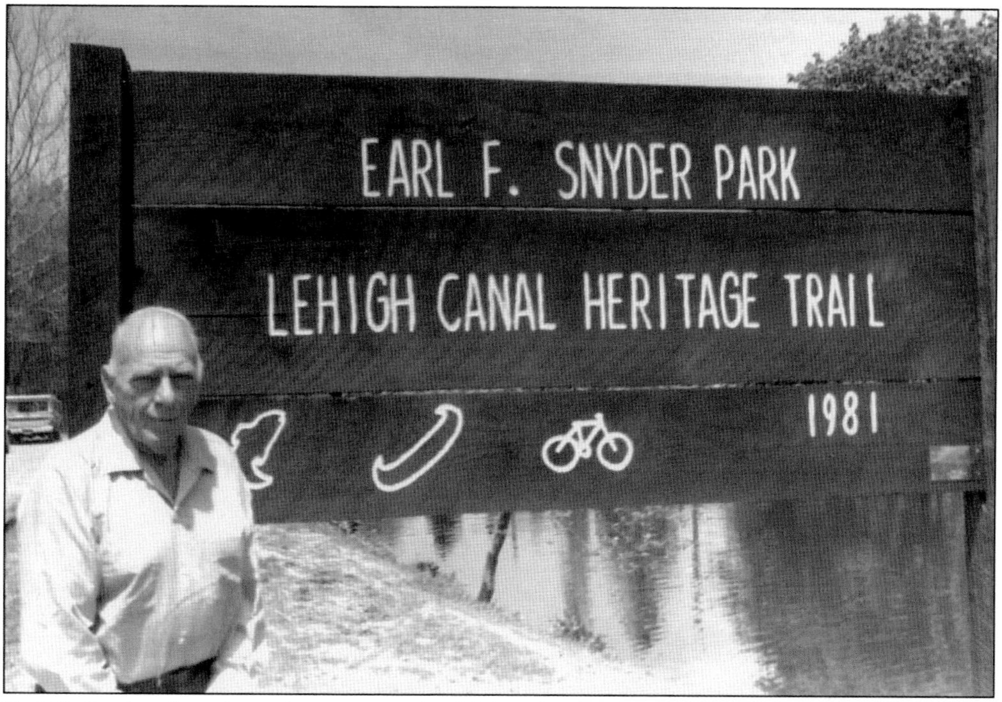

Earl F. Snyder, for whom the area north of Main Street is named, is responsible for much of the restored Lehigh Canal. This photograph was taken in 1981 by William Beck. (Courtesy of Walnutport Canal Association.)

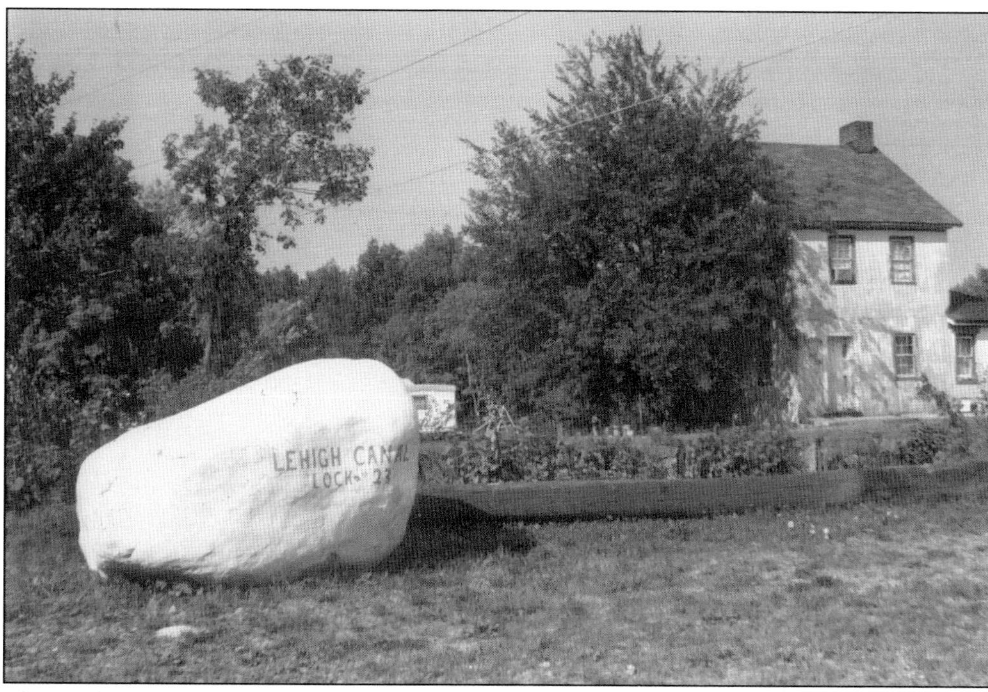

This is what the locktender's house at Lock No. 23 looked like on September 8, 1980. (Courtesy of Walnutport Canal Association.)

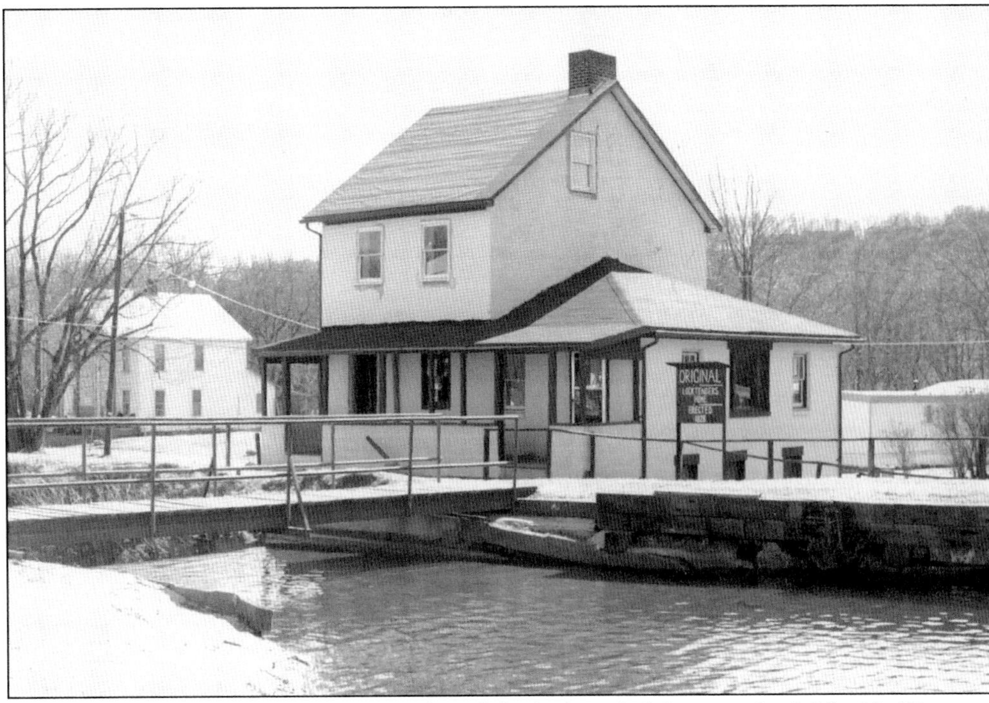

The Walnutport Canal Association purchased the locktender's house at Lock No. 23. (Courtesy of Walnutport Canal Association.)

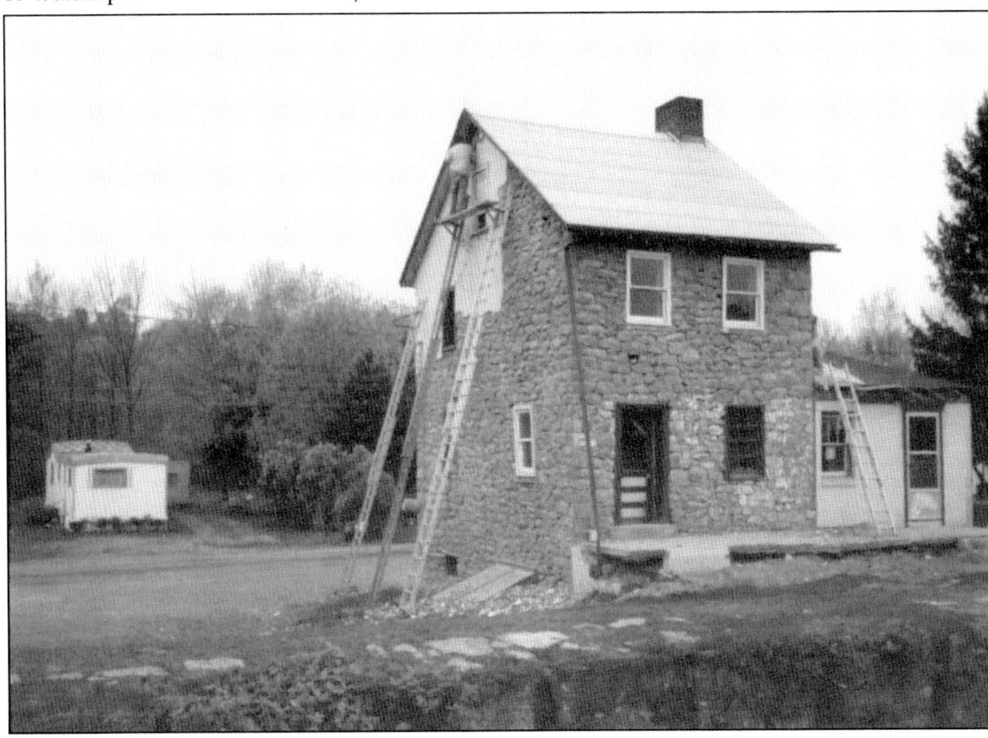

Restoration work begins at the locktender's house at Lock No. 23. (Courtesy of Walnutport Canal Association.)

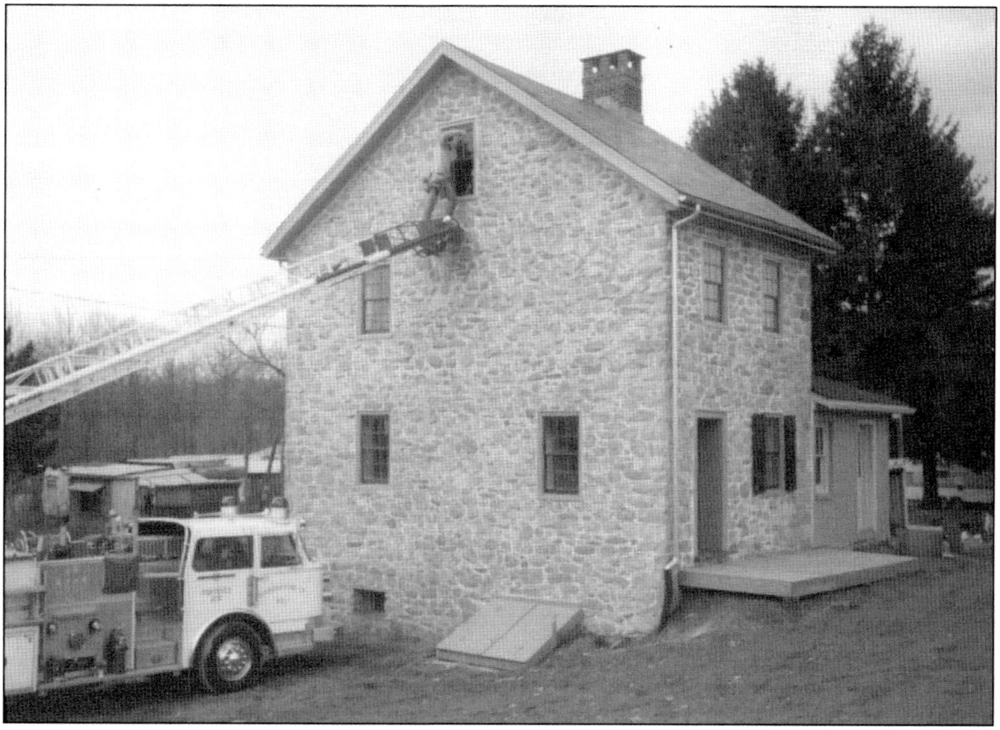

After the stone has been repointed, the outside of the locktender's house is starting to look complete. (Courtesy of Walnutport Canal Association.)

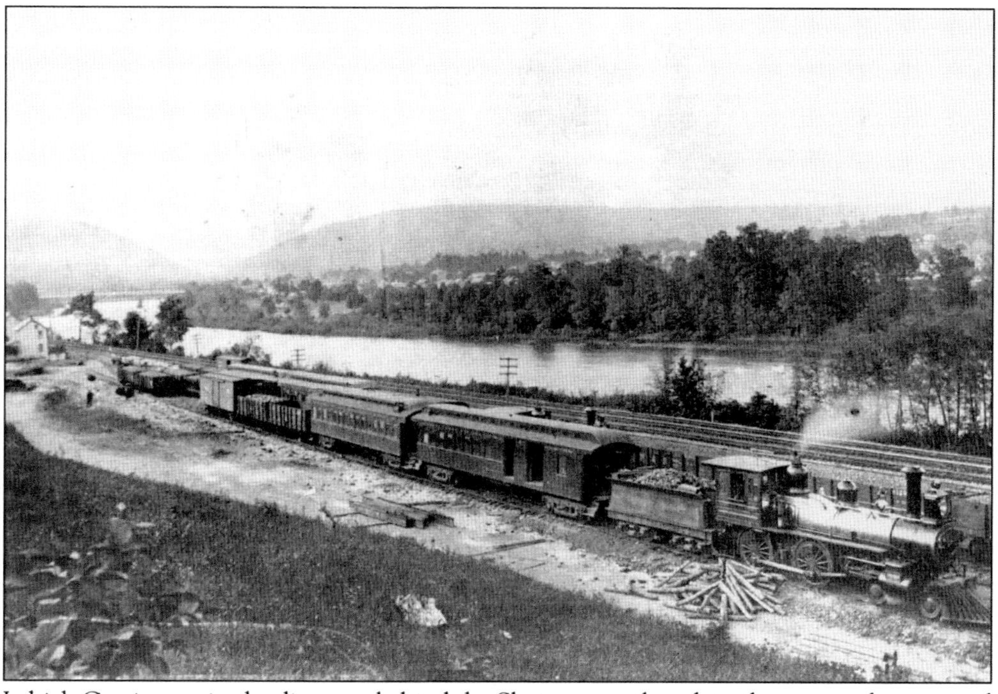

Lehigh Gap is seen in the distance, behind the Slatington rail yard, in this picture from around 1880. (Courtesy of Northern Lehigh Future Focus Collection.)

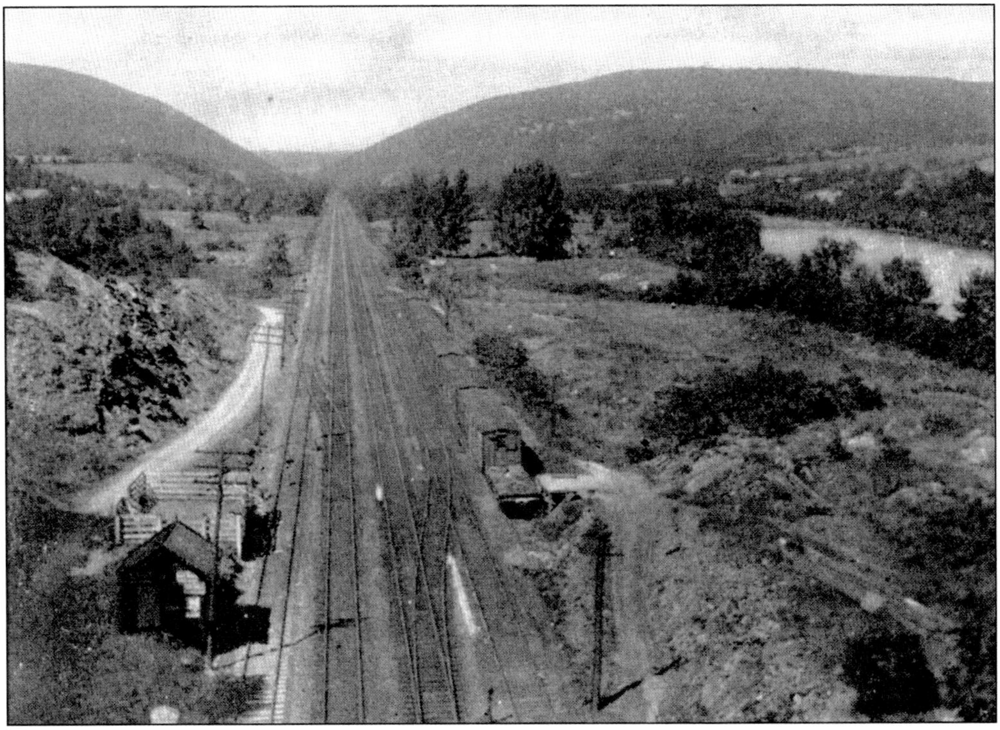

This photograph features the Lehigh Valley Railroad rail yard in Slatington. (Courtesy of Larry Hillborn.)

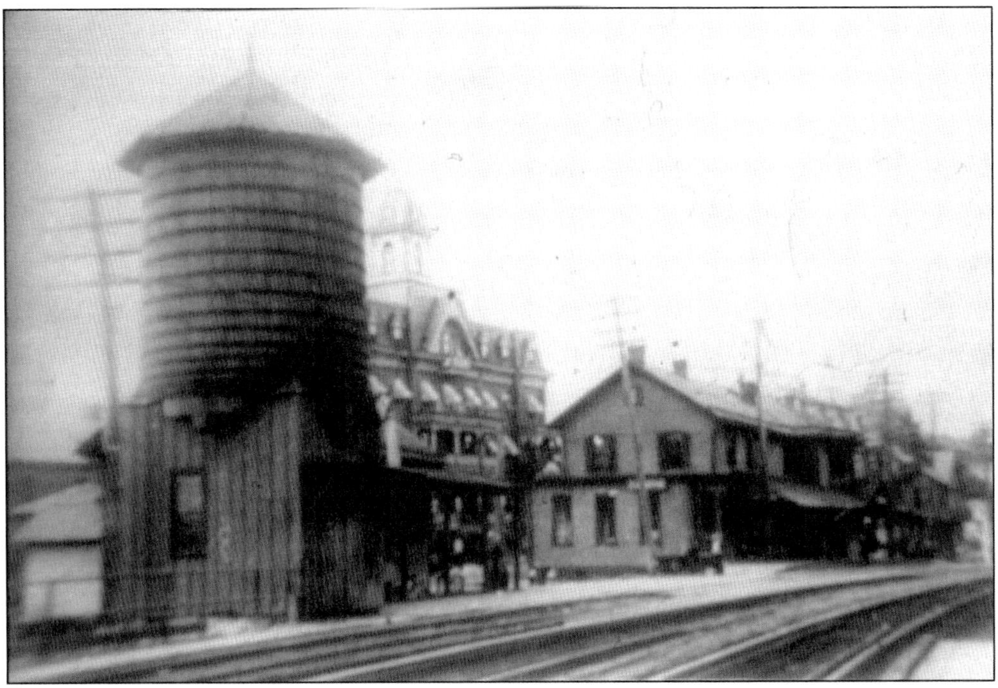

The water tower stands next to the Lehigh Valley Railroad station in Slatington. The Bittner House stands to the rear of the station. (Courtesy of Northern Lehigh Future Focus Collection.)

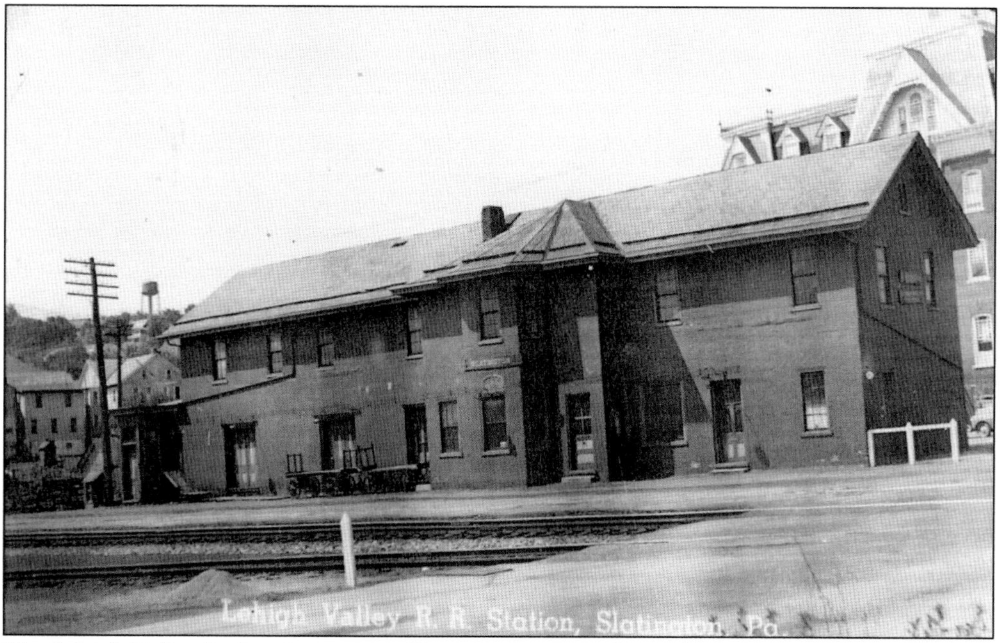

The Lehigh Valley Railroad station in Slatington was razed on February 1, 1969, after a derailed freight train damaged it. The station was built in 1862 and closed in 1961. The Reading Railroad shared use of the station when it was operating. (Courtesy of Northern Lehigh Future Focus Collection.)

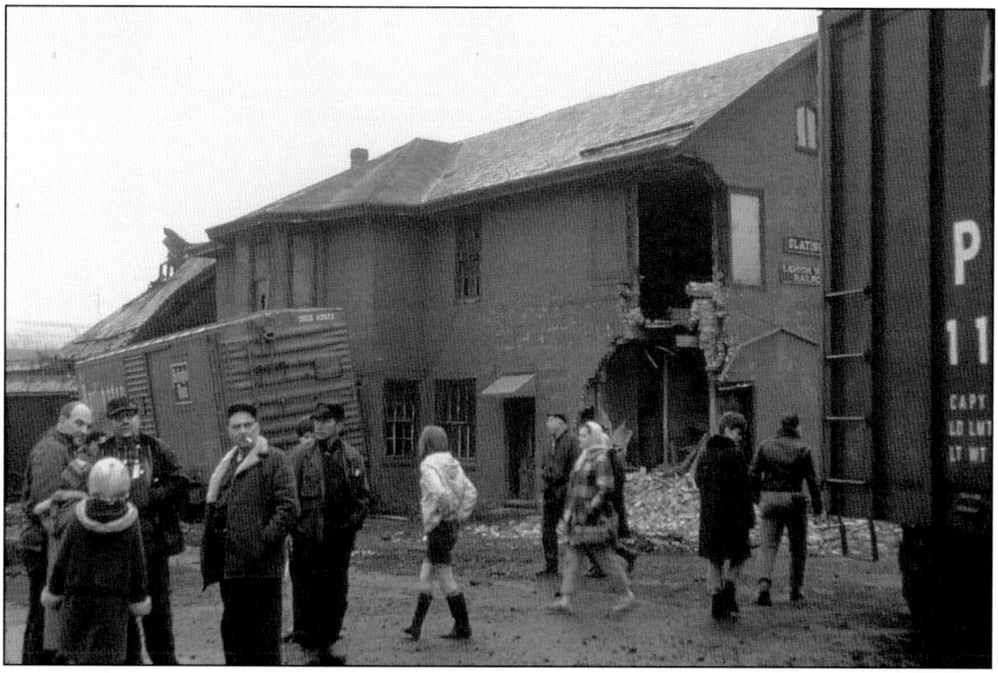

People mill about on February 1, 1969, after the derailing of a Lehigh Valley Railroad freight train en route to Buffalo, New York, from Newark, New Jersey. Thirty-one of the 58 cars left the tracks. The damaged station was razed shortly afterward. (Courtesy of Neil Kuntz, Northern Lehigh Future Focus Collection.)

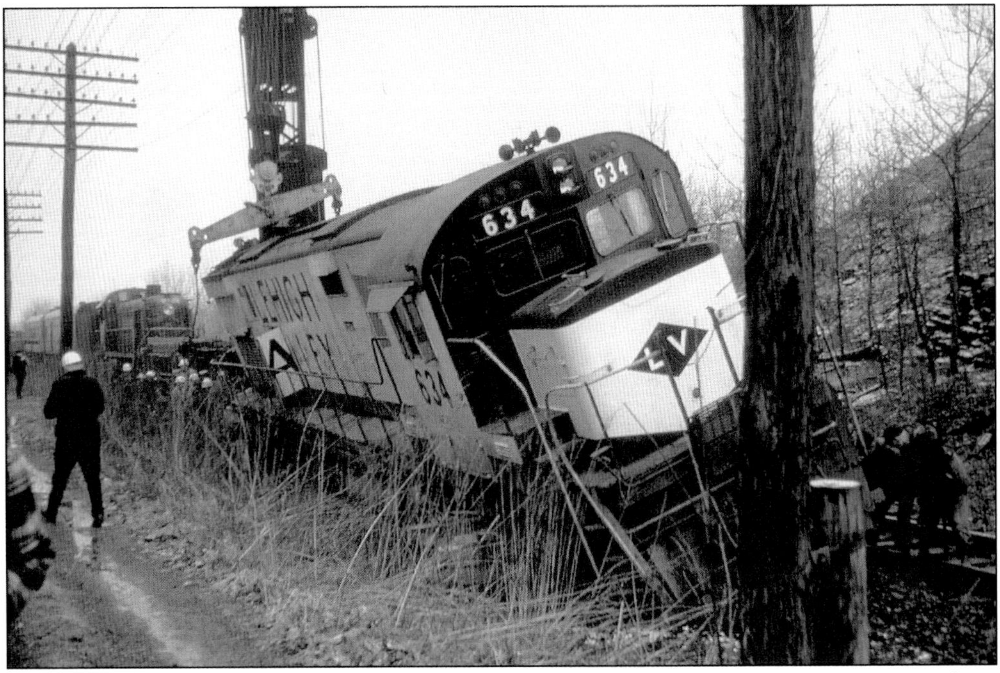

The derailed Lehigh Valley locomotive sits in the weeds after the February 1, 1969, accident. (Courtesy of Neil Kuntz, Northern Lehigh Future Focus Collection.)

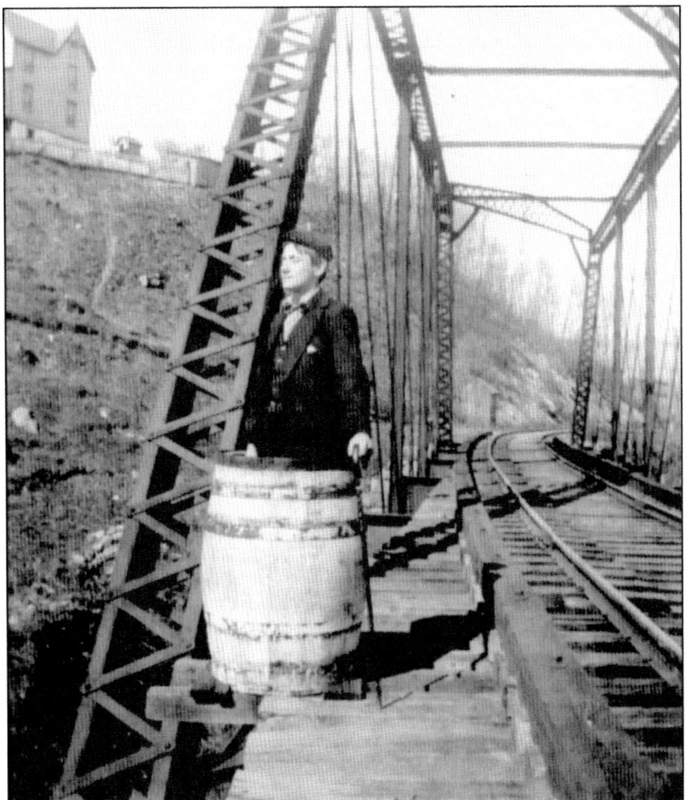

J. Anthony stands on the trestle over Trout Creek on March 6, 1898. (Courtesy of Slatington Public Library, Northern Lehigh Future Focus Collection.)

Locomotive No. 1054 in Walnutport is shown in this *c.* 1910 photograph. (Courtesy of Raymond Holland Regional History Collection, Northern Lehigh Future Focus Collection.)

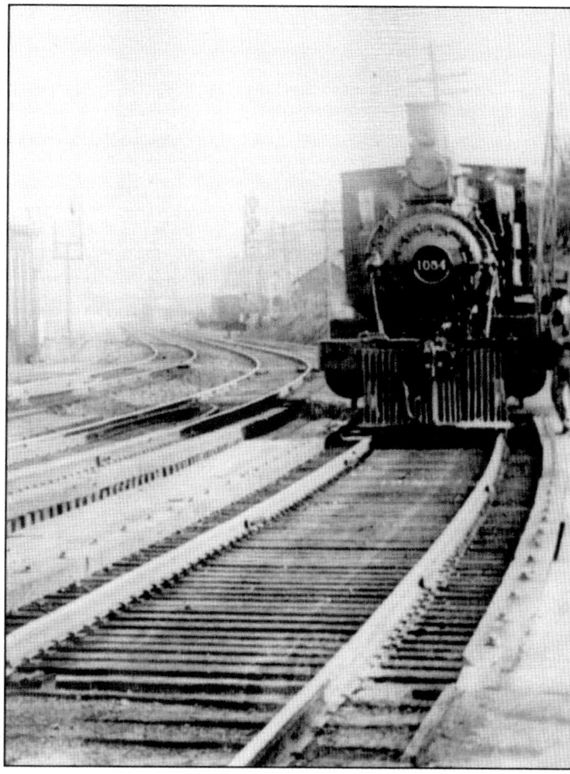

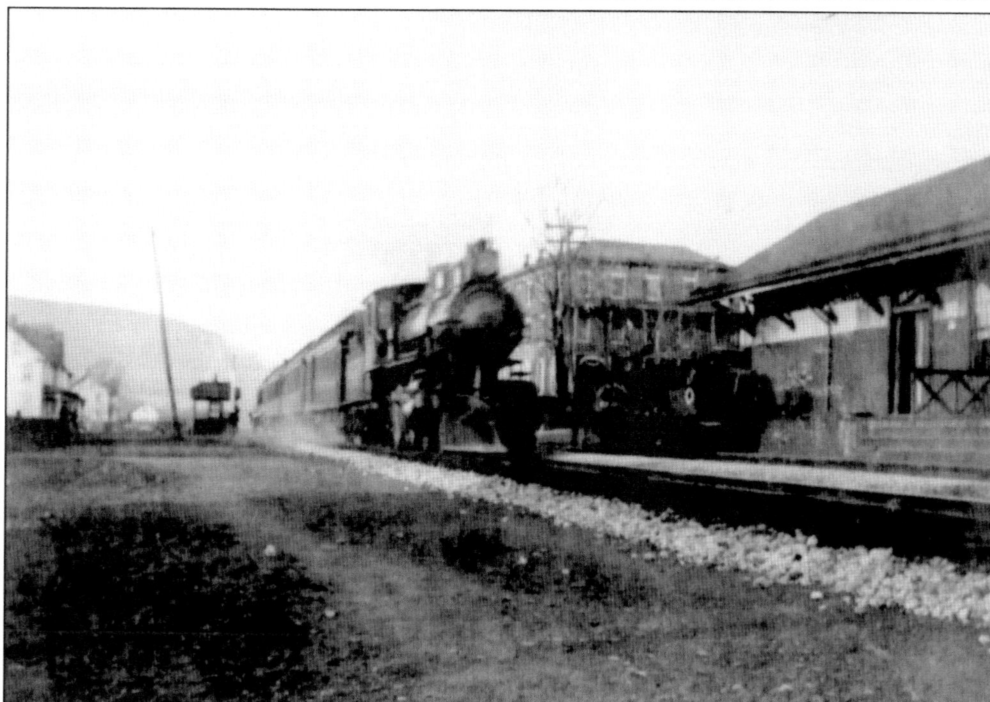

This December 18, 1897, photograph shows the Central Railroad Company of New Jersey *Flyer* in Walnutport. (Courtesy of Slatington Public Library, Northern Lehigh Future Focus Collection.)

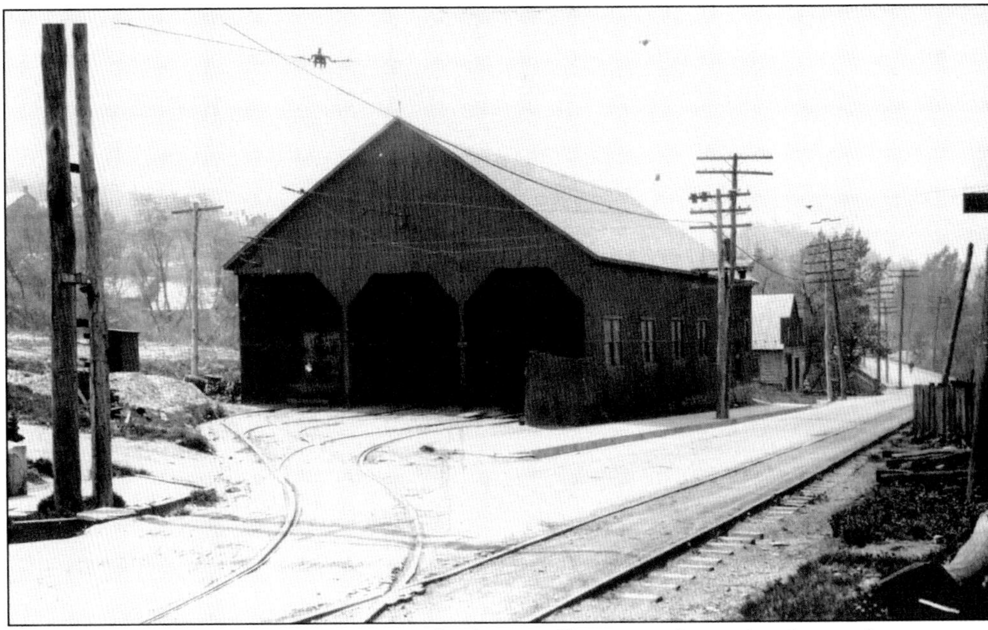

The Lehigh Valley Transit Company's trolley barn in Slatington, located at the southwest corner of Fifth and Church Streets, was built in 1910. (Courtesy of Jim Layland.)

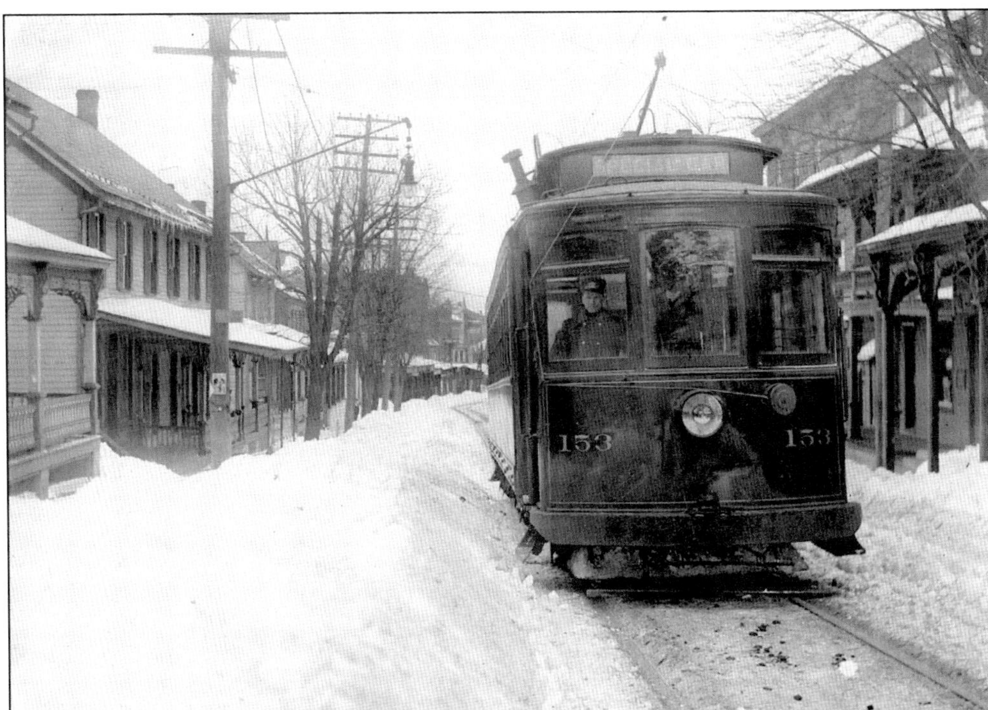

The Lehigh Valley Traction Company car No. 153 is on snow duty in this c. 1920 photograph on Main Street in Slatington, near the present location of the Shack. (Courtesy of Jim Layland.)

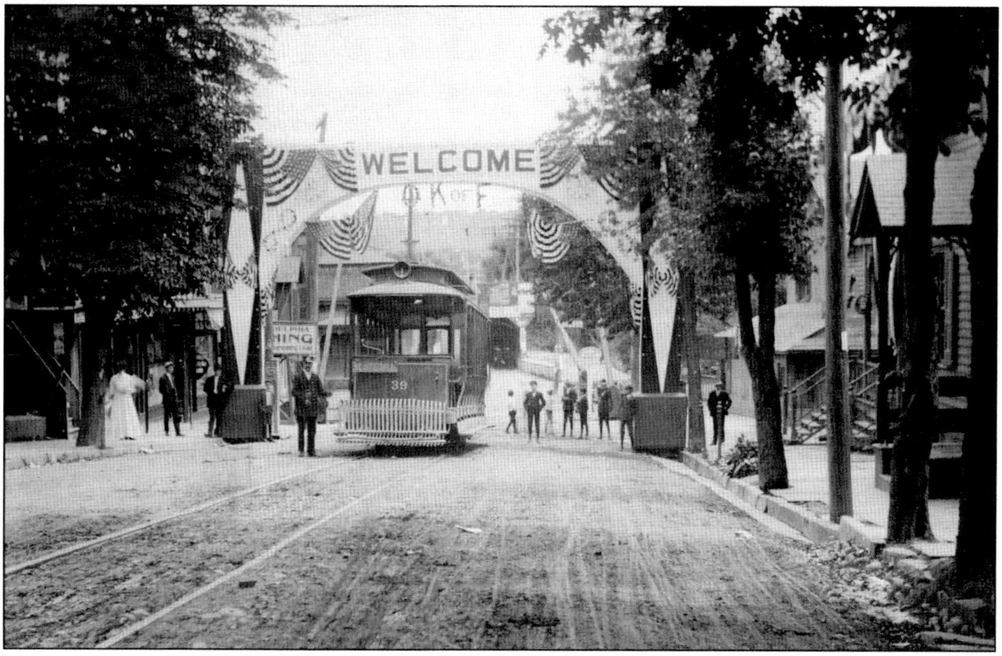

The Lehigh Valley Traction Company's trolley, seen here at lower Main Street in Slatington, is on its way to Slatedale. To the left of the trolley is half a sign for Ike Ginsberg's Philadelphia Clothing Store. (Courtesy of Larry Hillborn.)

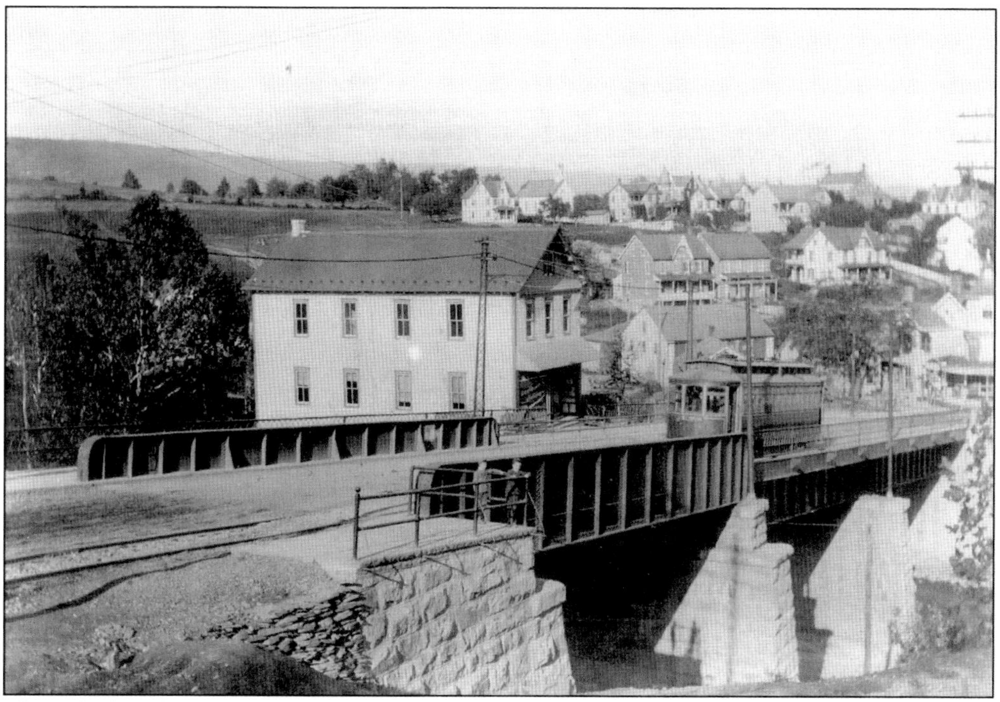

The Lehigh Valley Traction trolley climbs the hill on Main Street, crossing the bridge over Trout Creek. The News Publishing Company can be seen to the left. (Courtesy of Jim Layland.)

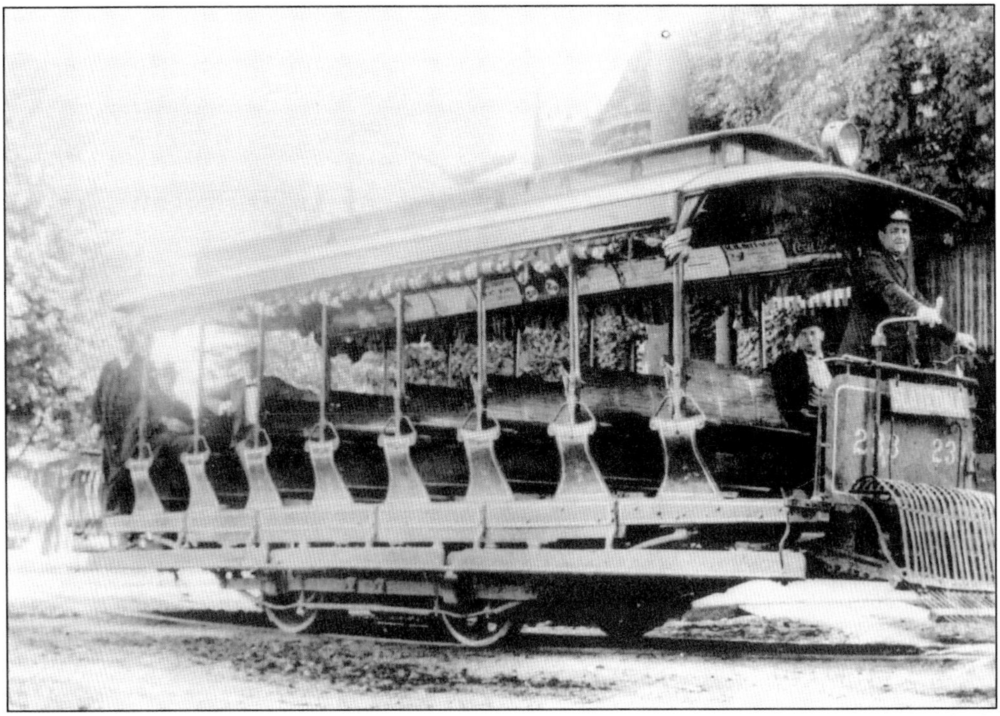

Gordon Dornblazer is the motorman, and Edward Laudenslager is the conductor of the Lehigh Valley Transit Company's summer car. (Courtesy of Northern Lehigh Future Focus Collection.)

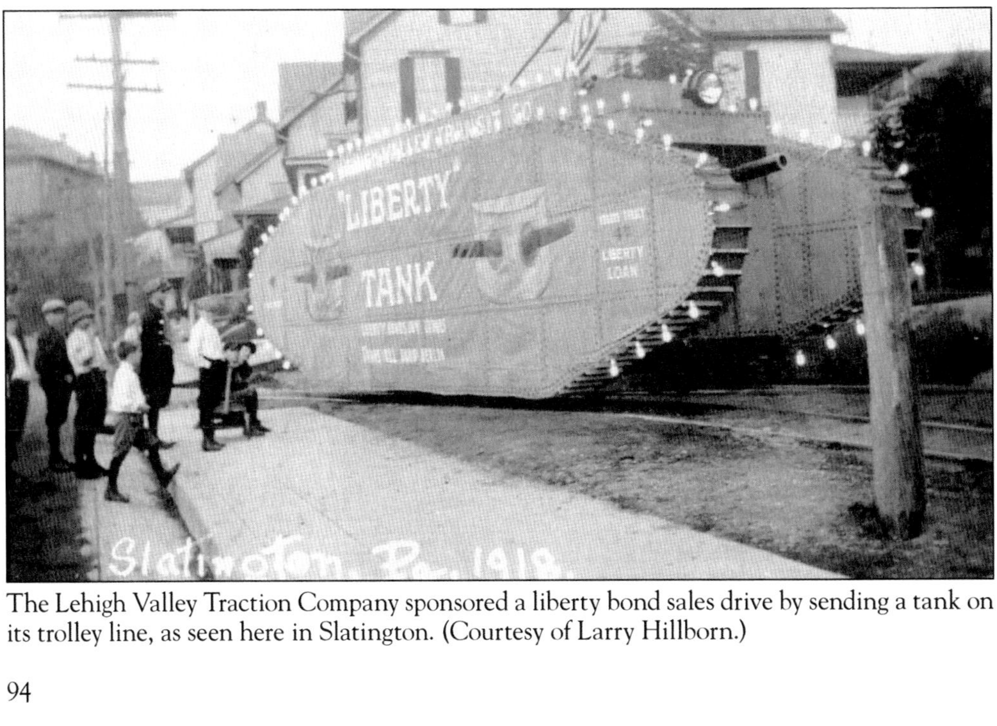

The Lehigh Valley Traction Company sponsored a liberty bond sales drive by sending a tank on its trolley line, as seen here in Slatington. (Courtesy of Larry Hillborn.)

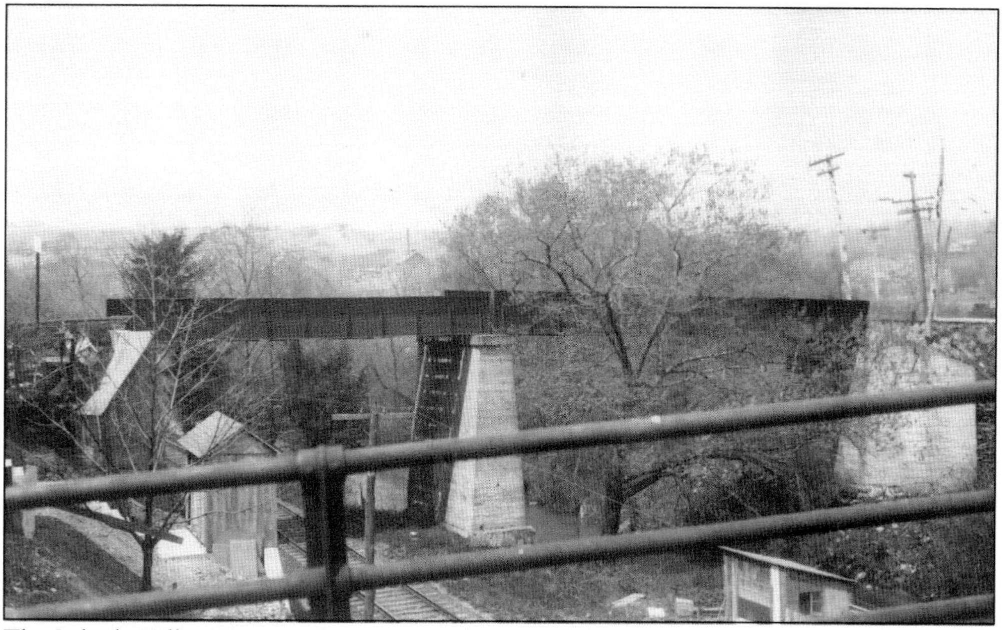

The Lehigh Valley Traction Company tracks crossed the railroad in Emerald on this bridge. The pillars for the bridge can still be seen behind St. Peter's Evangelical Church in Emerald. (Courtesy of Jim Layland.)

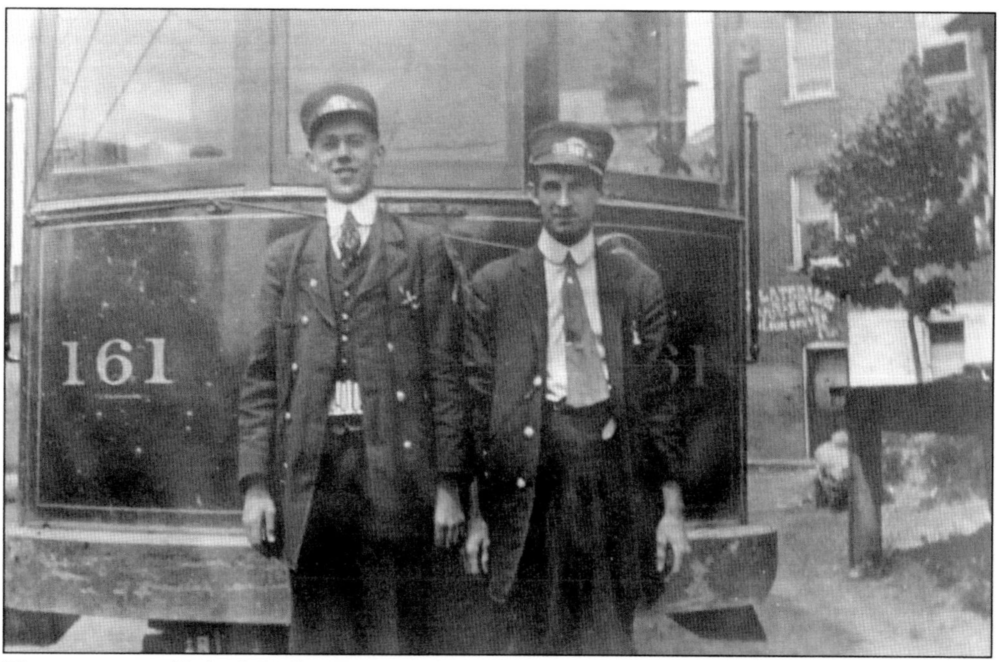

The operators of Lehigh Valley Traction Company car No. 161 are seen here in Slatedale at the end of the line. (Courtesy of Jim Layland.)

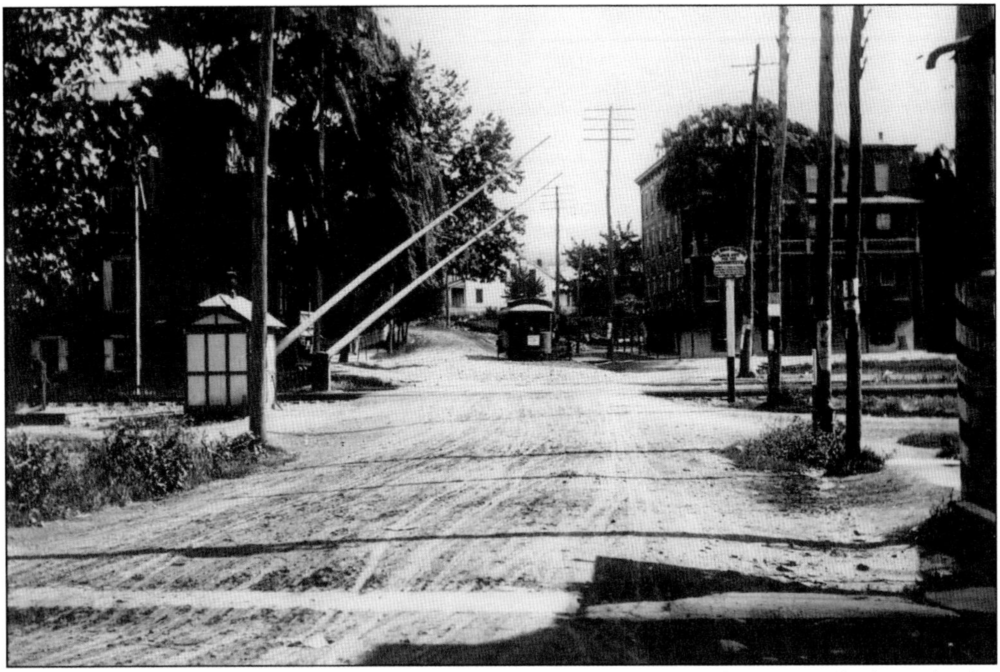

The Blue Ridge Traction Company trolley sits on Main Street in Walnutport, which marks the end of its line. The trolley line ran from Danielsville to Walnutport. (Courtesy of Palmerton Camera Club, Northern Lehigh Future Focus Collection.)

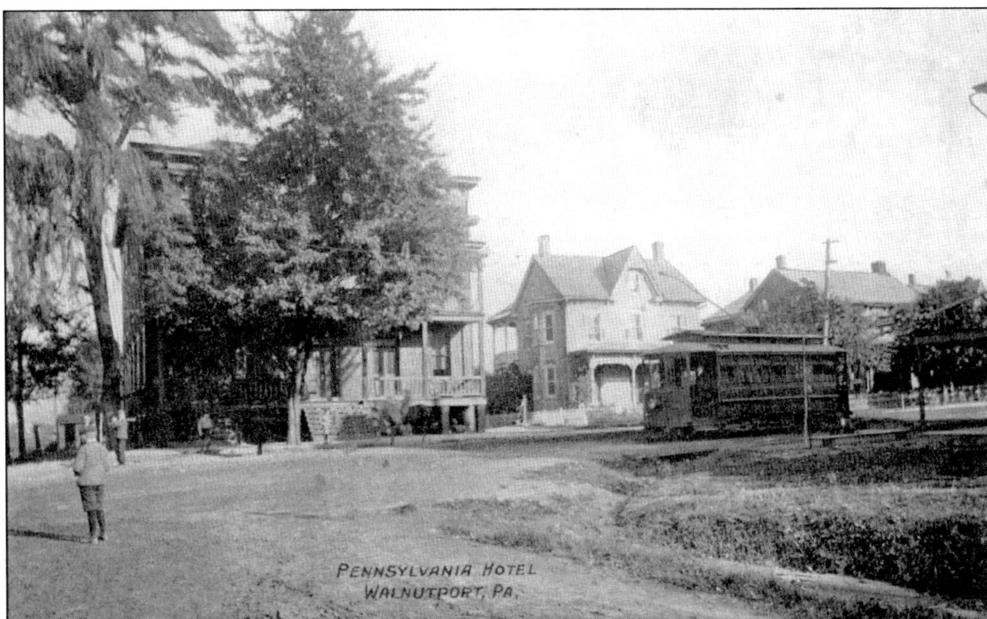

The Blue Ridge Traction trolley is visible to the right in this 1908 view of the Pennsylvania Hotel in Walnutport. (Courtesy of Kayleigh Billings.)

Five

THE SLATE INDUSTRY

The Pennsylvania Slate District runs from Lynn Township, Lehigh County, to the Delaware River. The 40-mile distance is divided into four different areas: Lehigh, Bath and Chapman, Bangor and Pen Argyl, and Delaware.

The first slate discovery in the Lehigh area was made at Rockdale in Whitehall Township in 1828. In 1831, a quarry opened north of Walnutport on John Benninger's farm. In 1844, three men searching for slate deposits along the Lehigh River noticed slate leaning against a barn owned by Peter Heimbach, who said it had come from John Benninger's farm. The three men—Owen Jones, William Roberts, and Nelson LaBar—obtained a lease to Benninger's property and, in 1845, opened a quarry. In 1845, Benninger also opened a quarry. Later these quarries were owned by the Heinbach Slate Company.

In 1845, the first quarry in Slatington opened after Owen Jones discovered slate on Jonas Kern's property. Called the Tunnel Quarry, it was located just north of the Slatington Borough/Washington Township line. William Roberts leased the property for 15 years with permission to quarry and manufacture slate shingles. The quarry operated until 1866.

In 1848, George and Nelson LaBar opened the first quarry in Slatedale. The Locke Quarry, situated just north of town, was later operated by the Locke Slate Company.

Jacob Papay and his sons John, Thomas, Stephen, and Michael, and his son-in-law Stephen Babyak, started the Papay and Babyak Slate Quarries in 1934. The first quarry the company opened in Lehigh Gap was unsuccessful because of the poor slate quality. The group next leased property in Berlinsville, operating there until the quarry became too deep to remain profitable.

The company moved from Berlinsville to Slatedale and leased land from the Wilson Rex estate, working those quarries until they became too deep. In 1944, the company purchased a quarry in Slatedale and soon after became the Penn Big Bed Slate Company.

In 1948, the Penn Big Bed Slate Company was incorporated. In 1956, the company purchased the National School Slate, which manufactured furniture and blackboards, and sold it in 1975. The firm, which runs a quarry adjacent to the earlier Slatedale quarries, is the only remaining operational quarry in the Lehigh area.

In all, 129 quarries existed between Slatedale and Danielsville. The vast slate deposits drew many European immigrants, particularly the Welsh. German farmers also worked in the quarries to supplement their farm income.

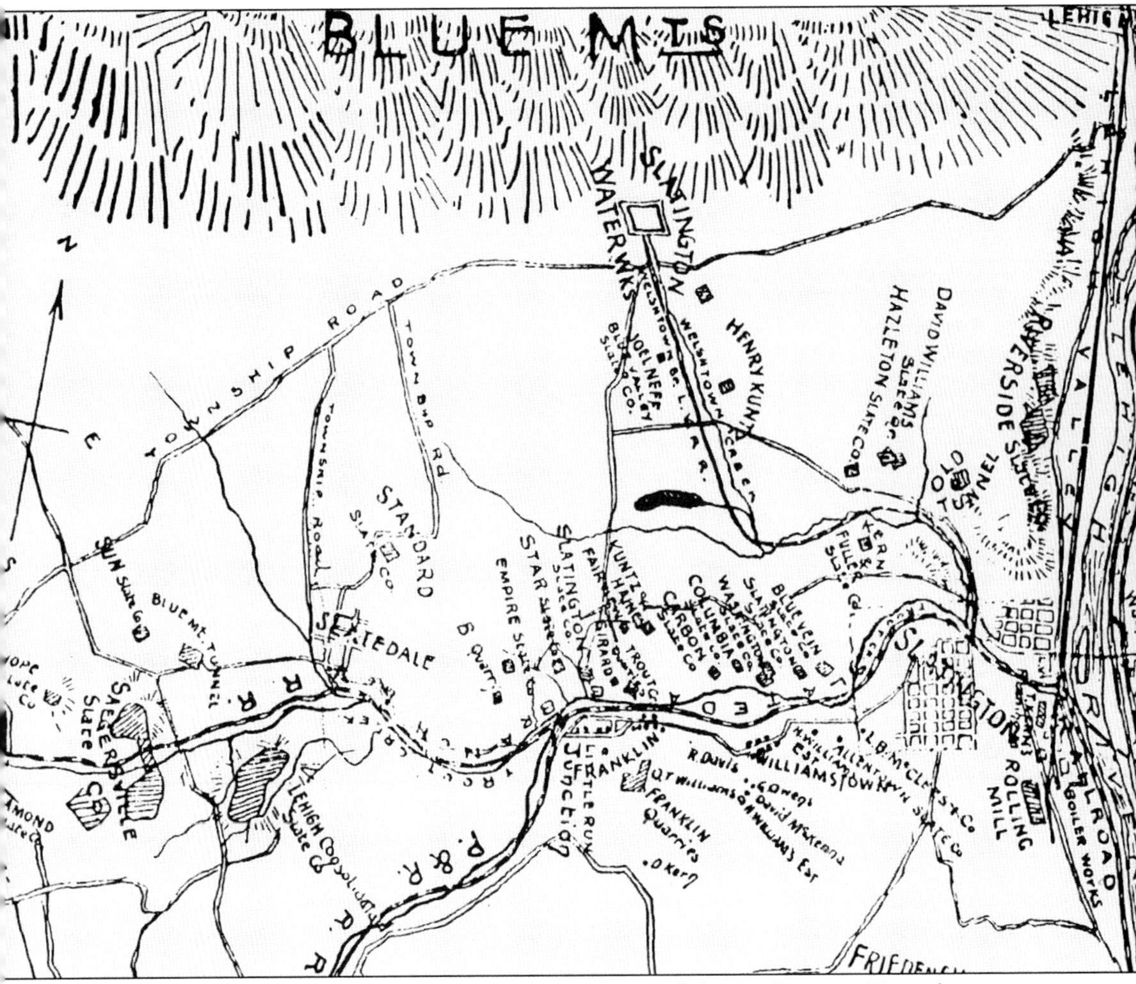

This map shows the slate quarries in the Slatington and the Washington Township region.

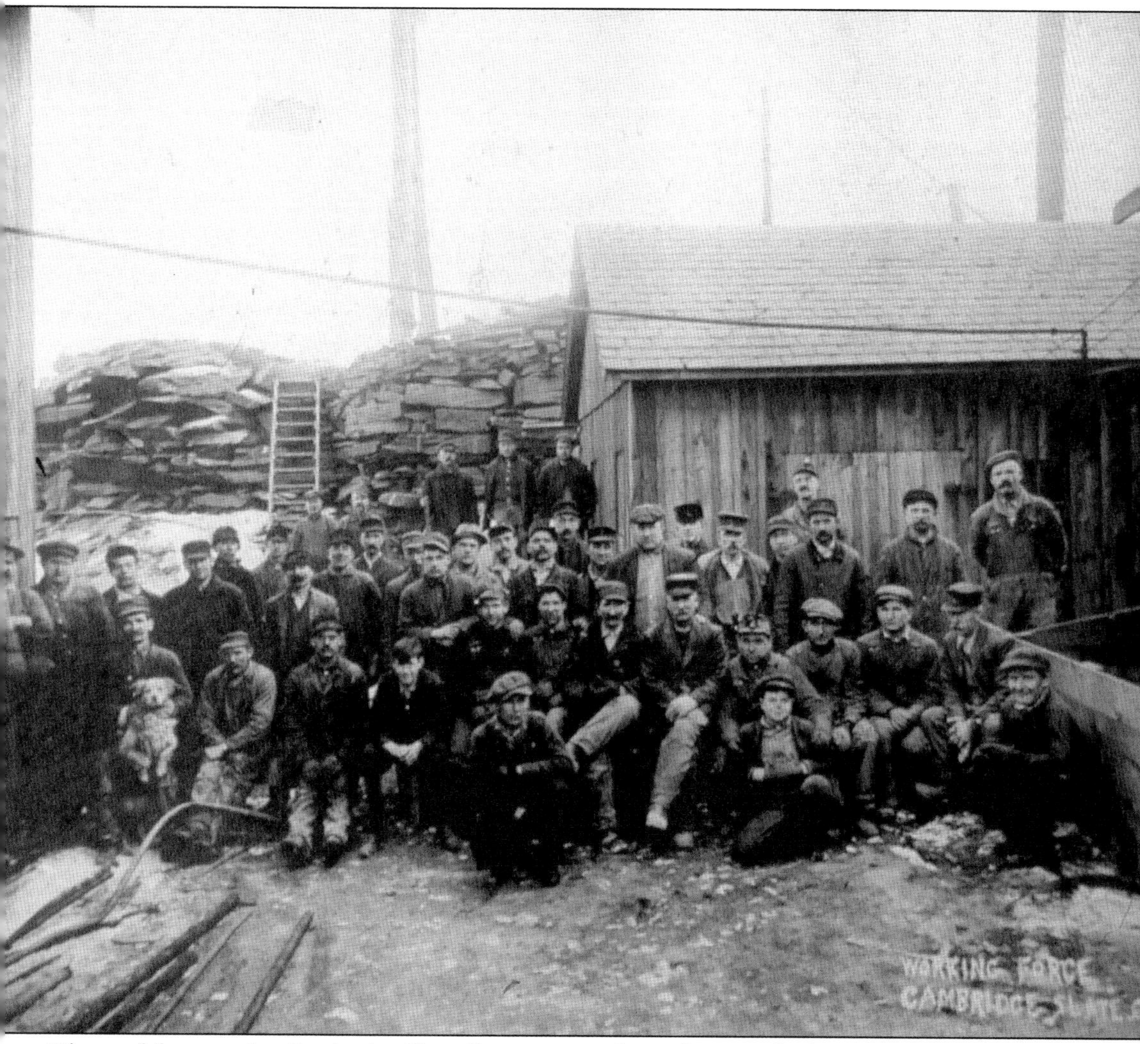

The workforce at the Cambridge Slate Quarry poses for a photograph. (Courtesy of Northern Lehigh Future Focus Collection.)

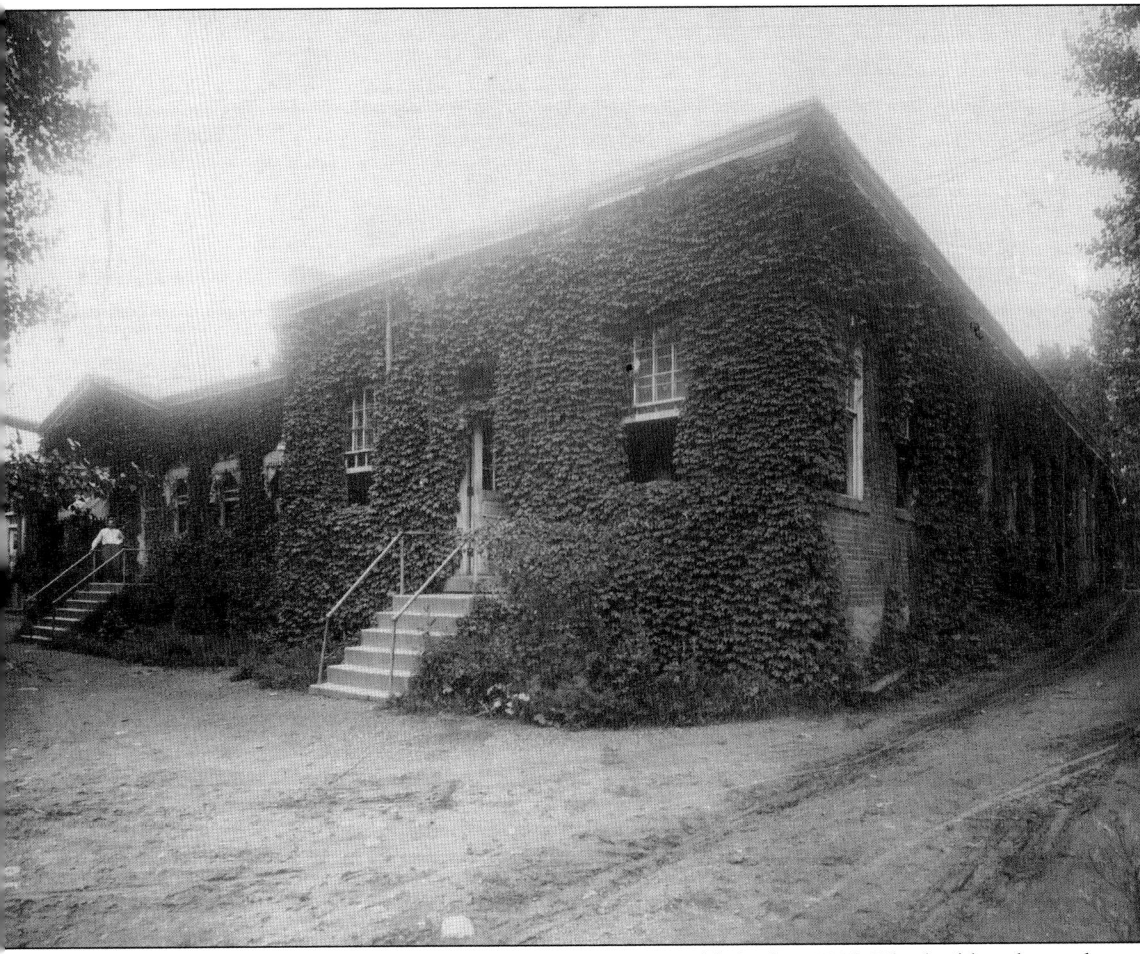

The National School Slate Factory in Slatington was established in 1885. The building burned down around 1977. (Courtesy of Larry Hillborn.)

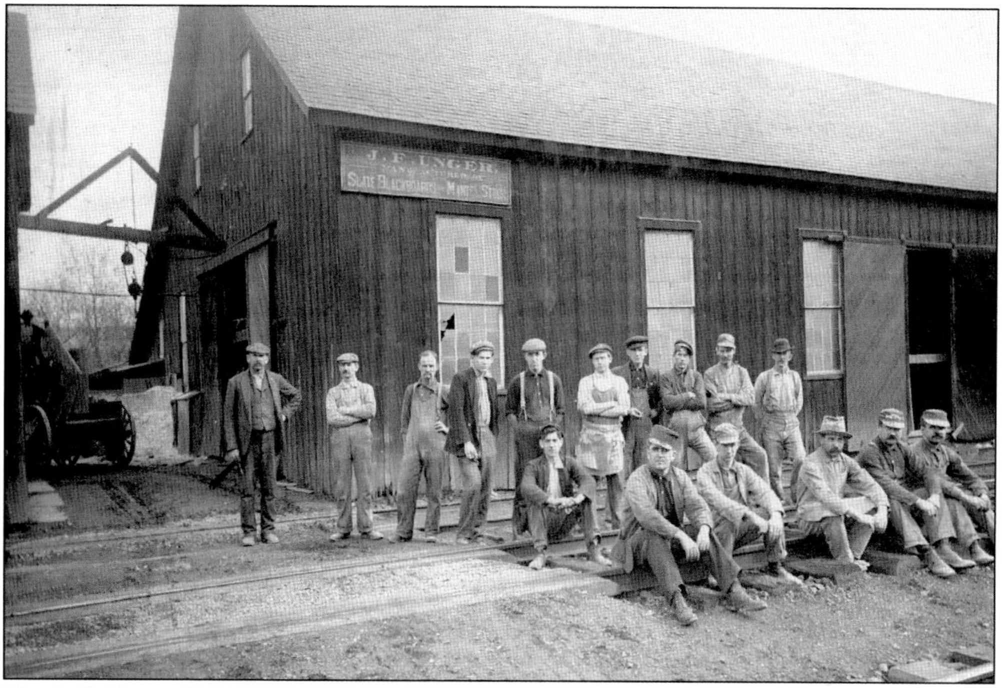

The J. F. Unger Slate Factory workforce takes a break outside the building. The back of the photograph states, "The first one is Howard's daddy, Edward Shoenberger." (Courtesy of Larry Hillborn.)

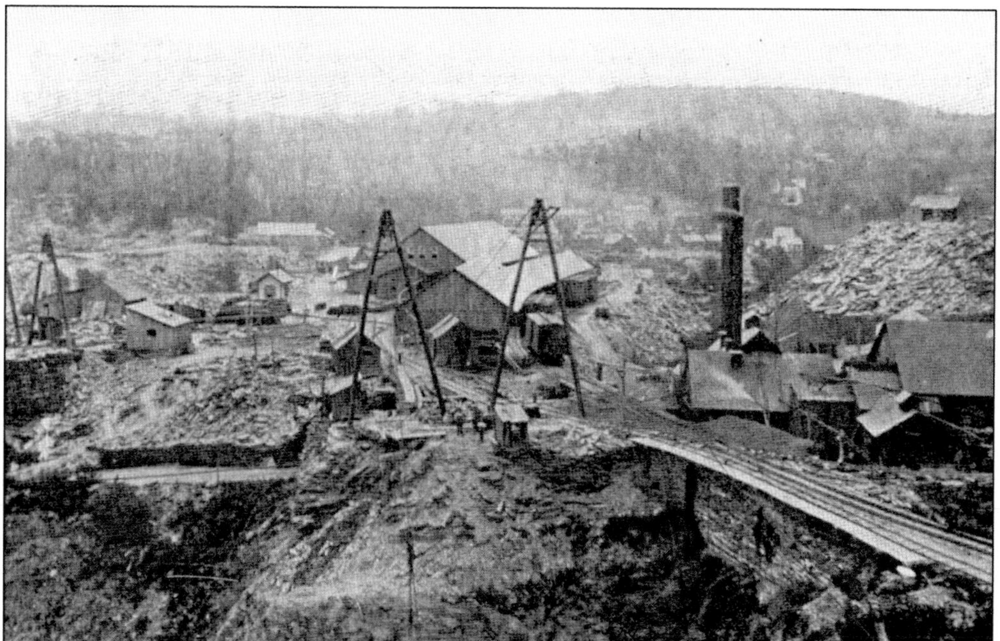

The Carbon Slate Quarry in Slatington is shown in this *c.* 1907 view. Ellis Owens, Robert G. Pierce, and Joseph Richards started the firm in 1888, and they operated the Franklin Tunnel, the Carbon Tunnel, and the Penn and Custard Quarries. The Custard Quarry, located out near Rextown, closed in 1911. (Courtesy of Larry Hillborn.)

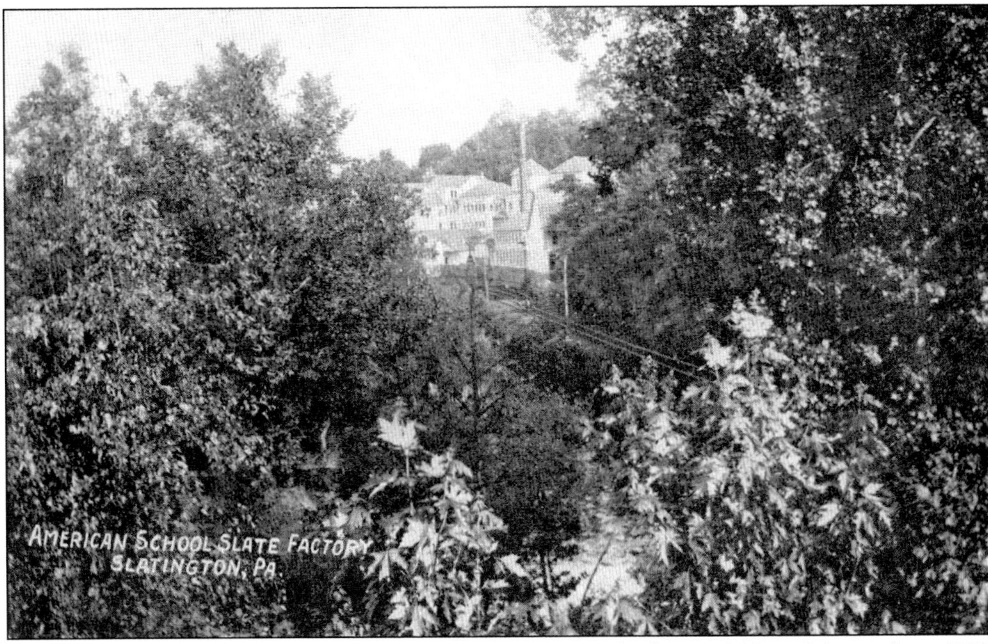

The American School Slate Factory in Slatington was built in 1908 and burned in 1923. (Courtesy of Larry Hillborn.)

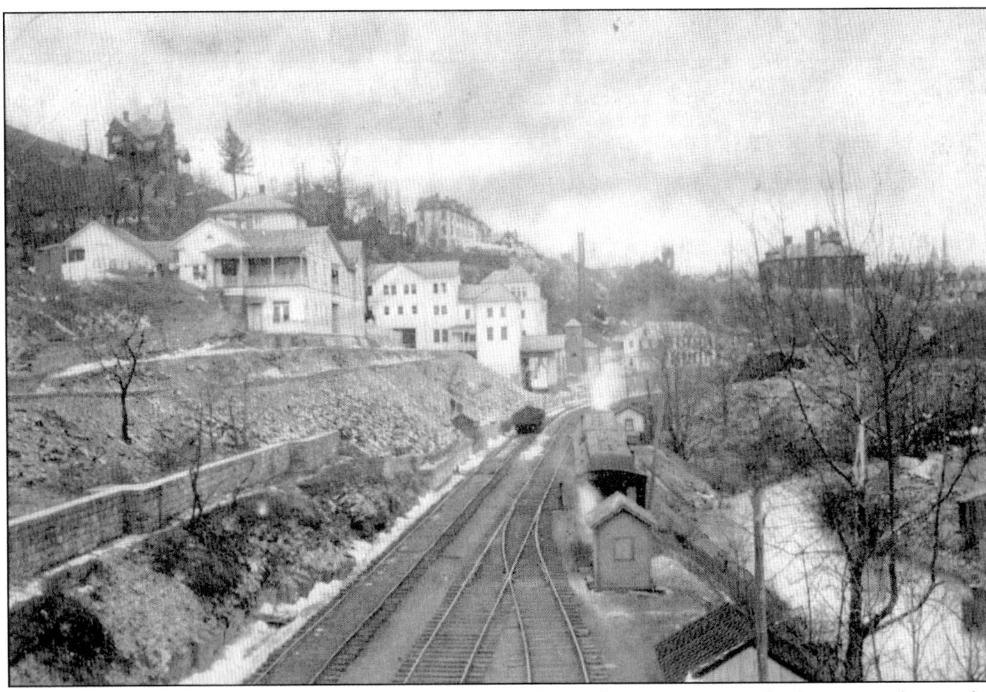

The American School Slate Factory is on the left in this 1906 view, looking north on the Lehigh Valley Railroad Slatedale branch. The shorter building along the tracks to the right is the Bachman Brothers Slate Company. The building was used as an umbrella factory, dye works, and the Slatington Textile Company before it burned in 1915. The Lincoln School building also appears on the right. (Courtesy of Kayleigh Billings.)

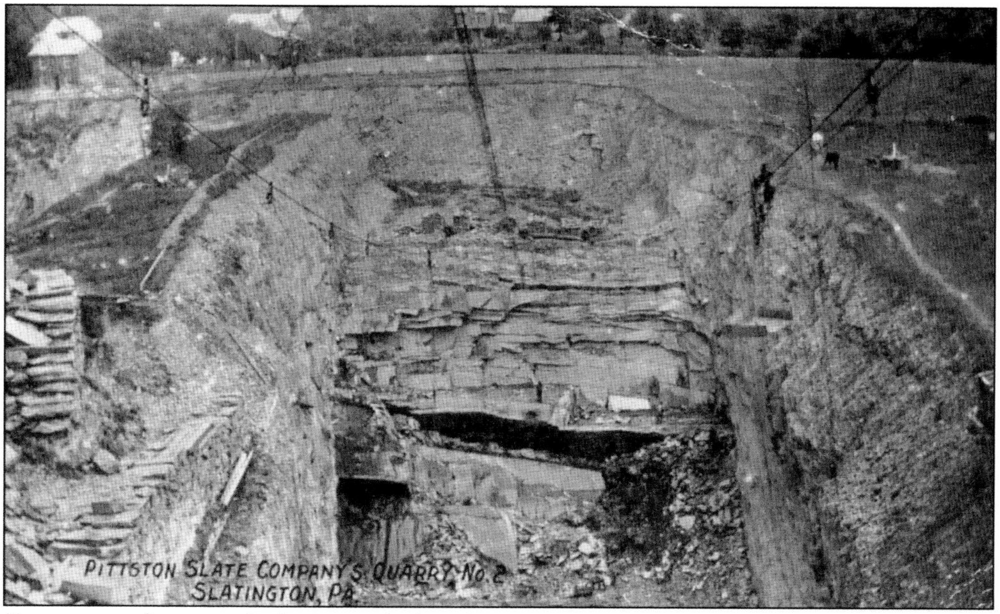

One can see down inside the Pittston Slate Quarry No. 2 in this c. 1907 photograph. (Courtesy of Larry Hillborn.)

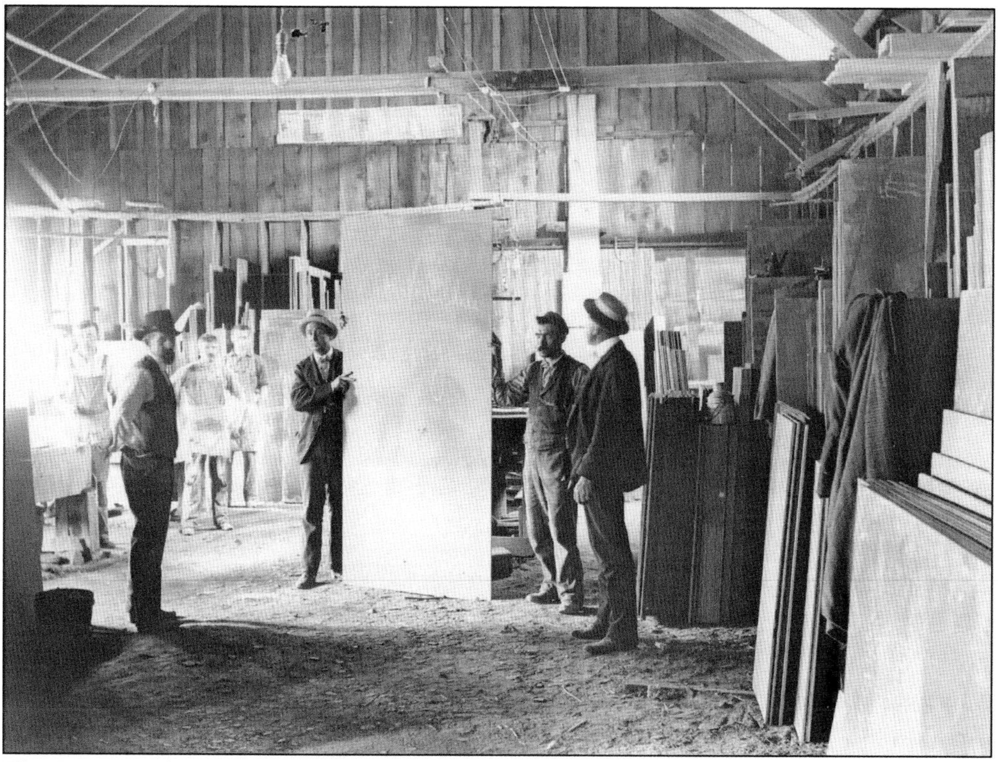
The Pittston Slate Quarry workers show off some of their blackboards. The Pittston quarry was located on Welshtown Road, near where the turnpike crosses. (Courtesy of Slatington Public Library.)

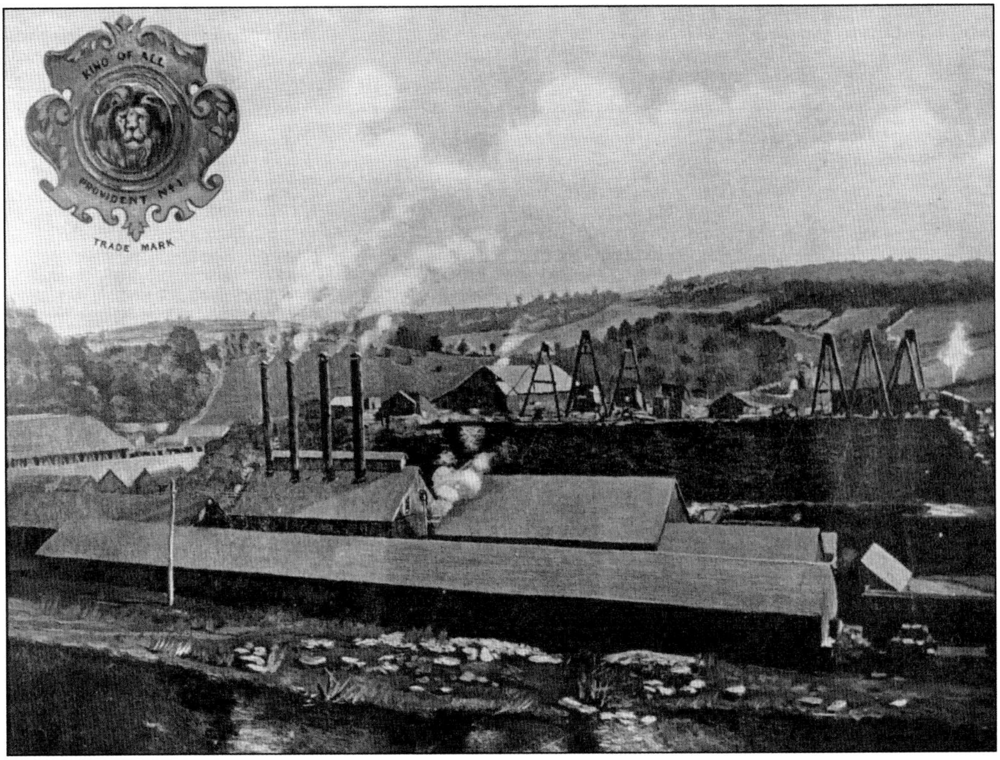

The Provident Slate Company's Washington Quarry is shown in this publicity photograph. (Courtesy of Slatington Public Library.)

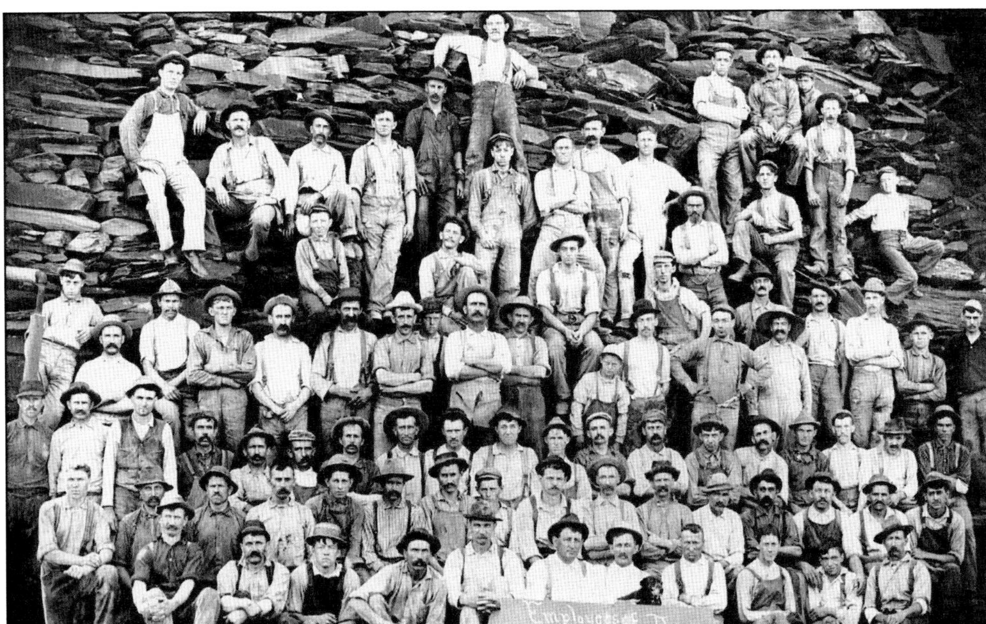

The Provident Slate Company's employees gather for a group photograph. (Courtesy of Slatington Public Library.)

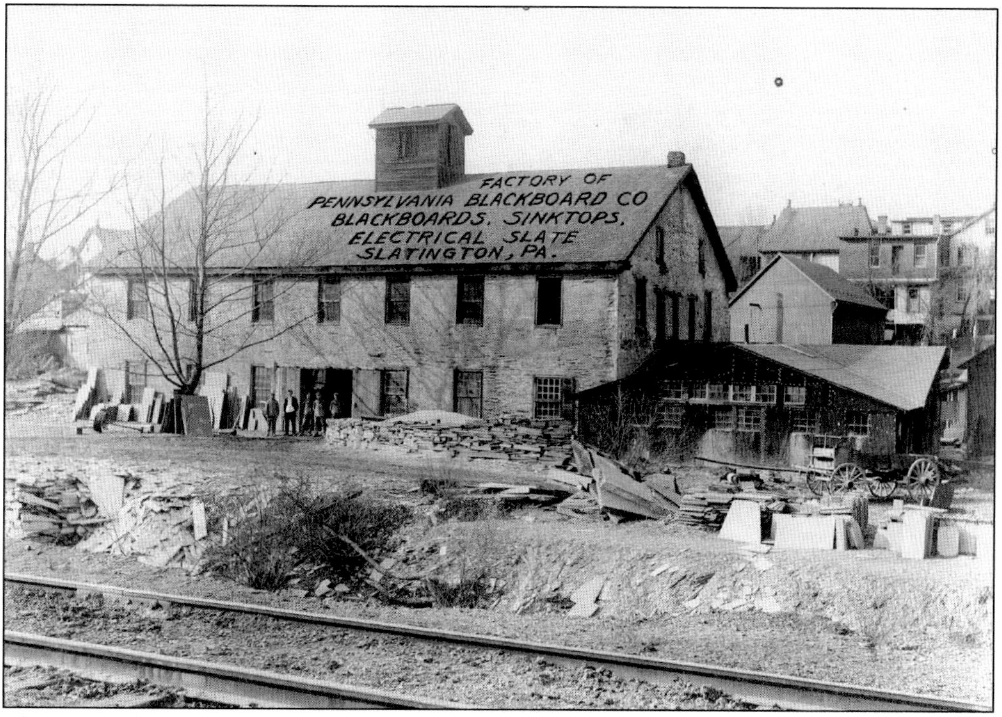

The Pennsylvania Blackboard Company's factory was located in Slatington. (Courtesy of Slatington Public Library.)

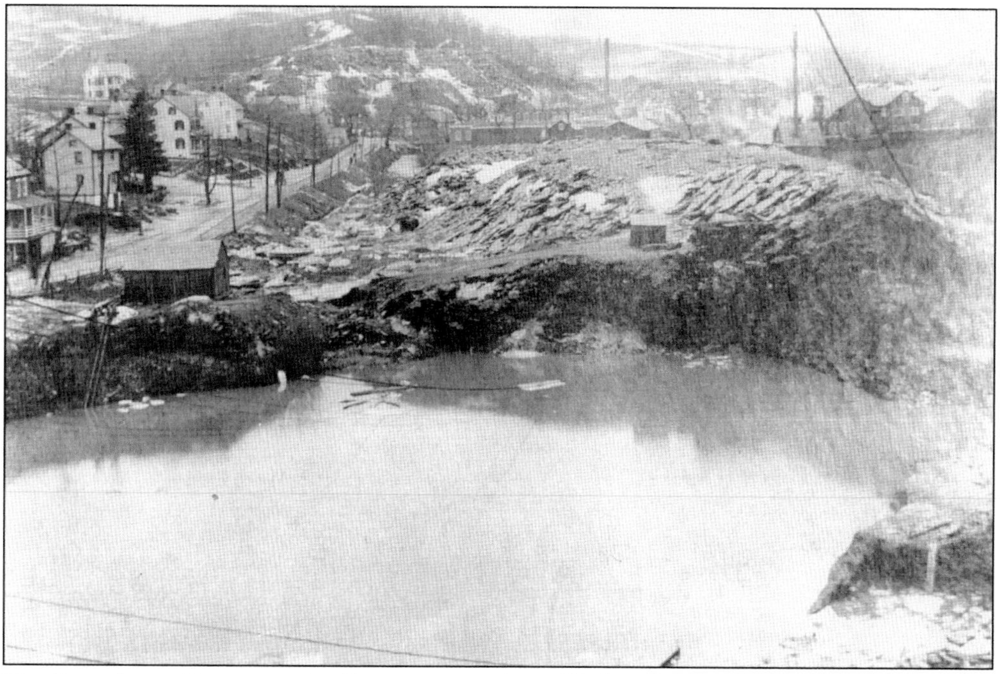

The Penn Lynn Quarry site in Slatington was later filled in for the construction of an Acme store. High Hughes started the Penn Lynn Quarry in 1864. Later Daniel D. Jones and C. M. Town owned it. (Courtesy of Slatington Public Library.)

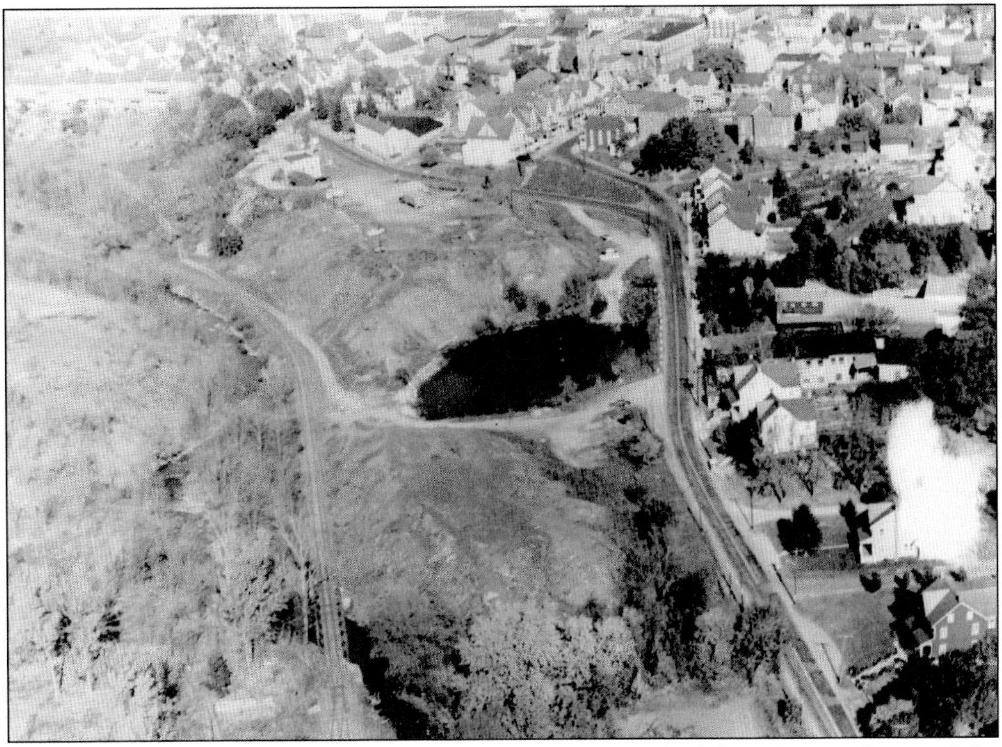

The Lehigh Valley Railroad Slatedale branch can be seen to the left in this aerial view of the Penn Lynn Quarry. The railroad bed is now the Slate Heritage Trail, thanks to the work of trail committee members Peter Papay, Darrin Heckman, Thomas Papay, Ted Kistler, Jeff Kunkle, Barry Latshaw, Eugene R. Mayberry, Jim Layland, and Edward Hartman. (Courtesy of Slatington Public Library.)

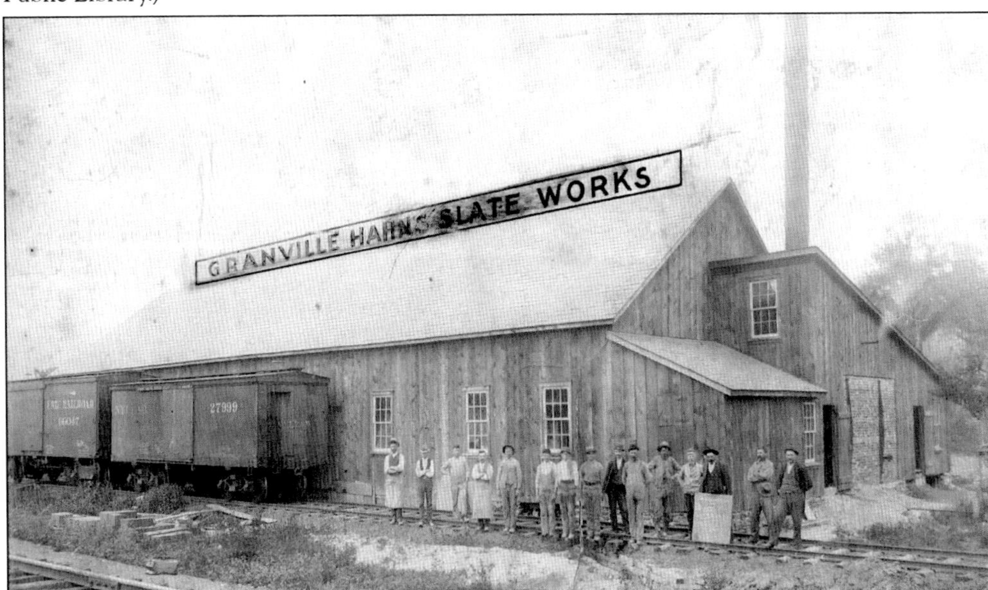

Granville Hahn's Slate Works in Walnutport was located where the American Nickeloid factory now stands on Cherry Street. (Courtesy of Larry Hillborn.)

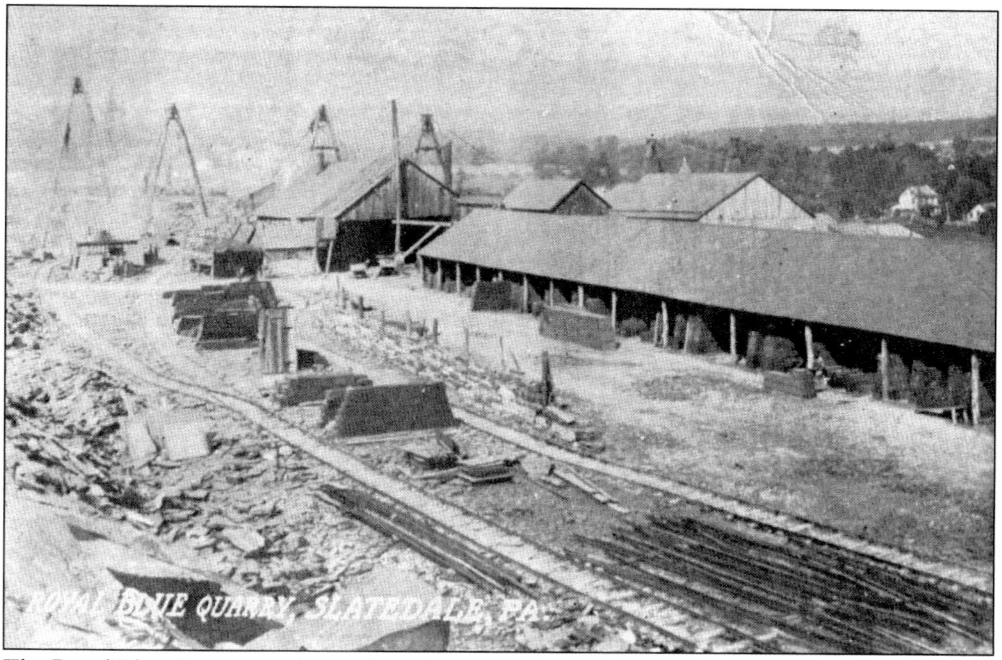

The Royal Blue Quarry was located in Slatedale. (Courtesy of Larry Hillborn.)

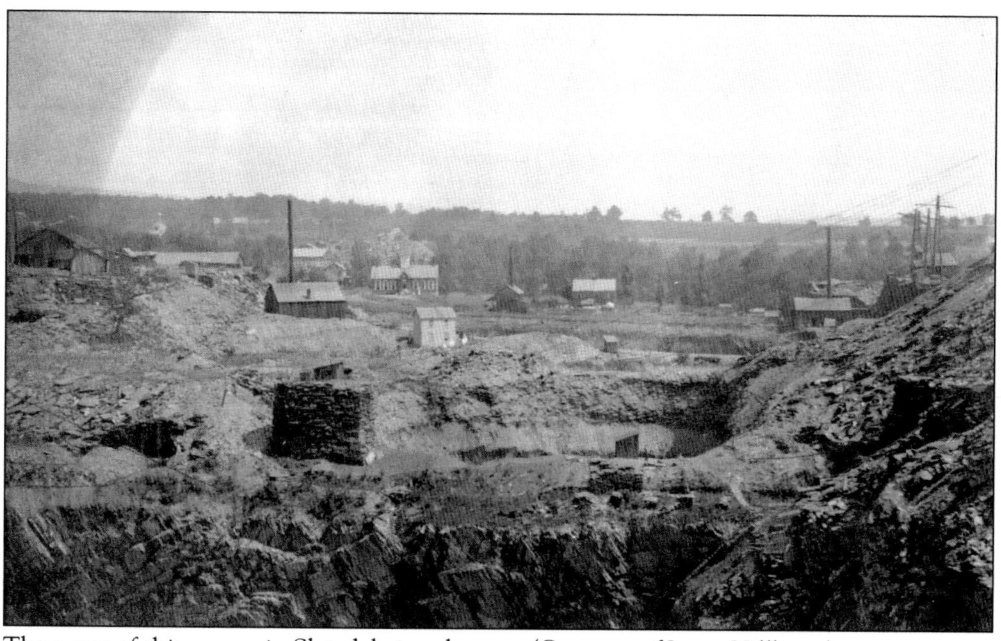

The name of this quarry in Slatedale is unknown. (Courtesy of Larry Hillborn.)

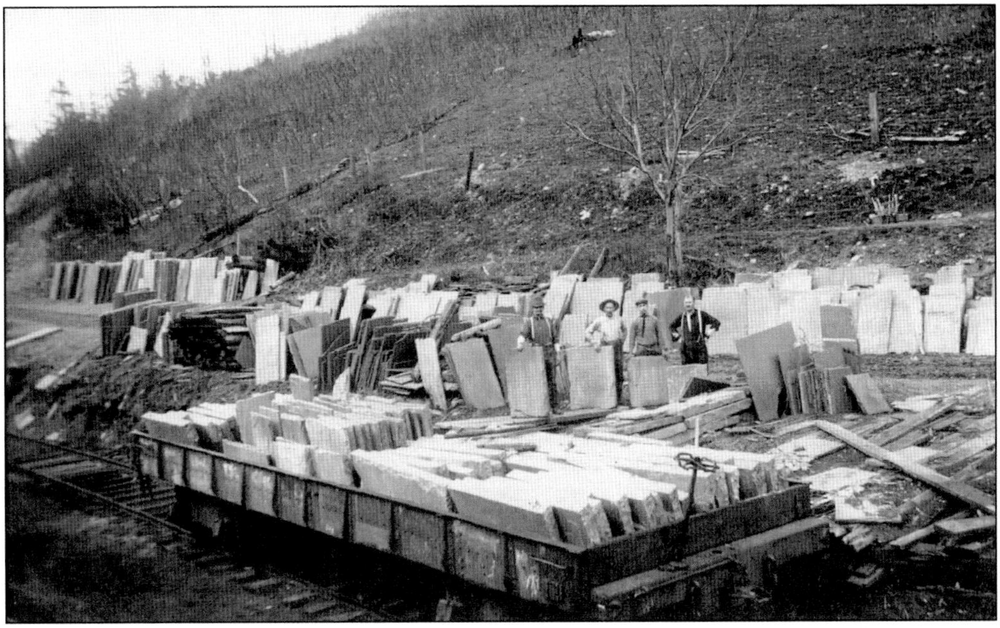

A railcar is loaded with slate for transport out of Slatedale. (Courtesy of Larry Hillborn.)

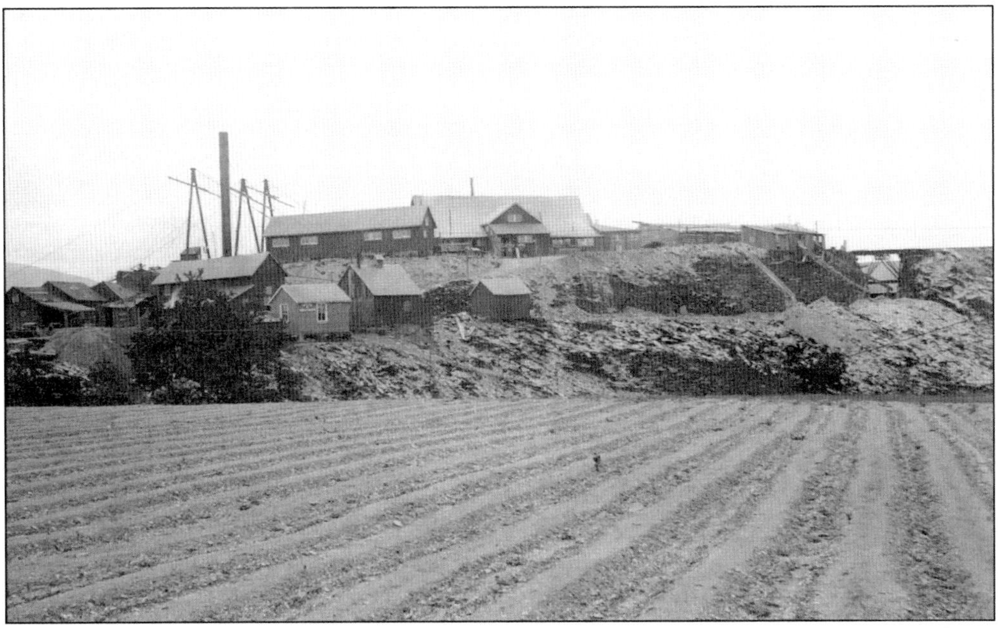

This photograph of the Thomas H. Shenton Slate Company in Slatedale was taken on March 20, 1911. (Courtesy of Larry Hillborn.)

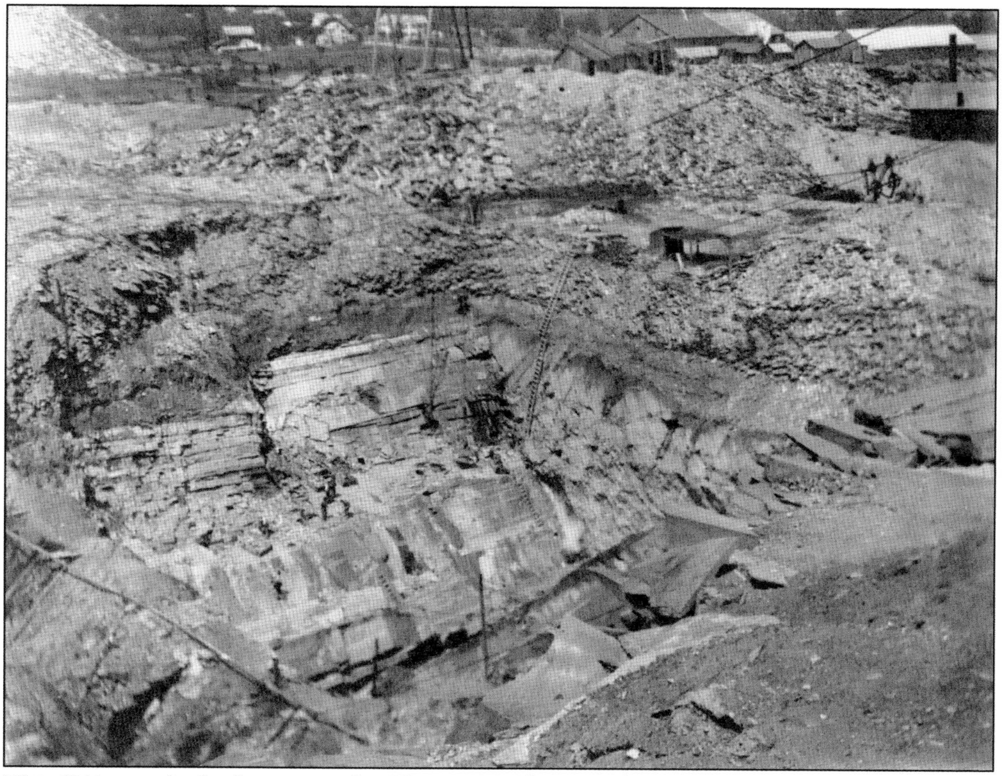

This 1911 view looks down into the Thomas H. Shenton Slate Company Quarry. (Courtesy of Larry Hillborn.)

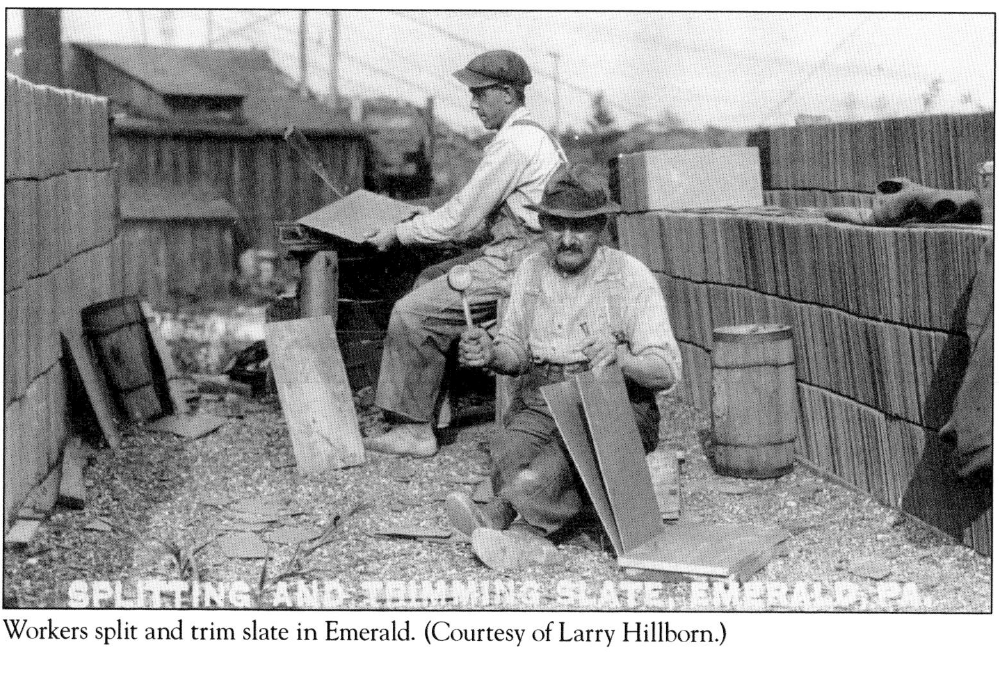

Workers split and trim slate in Emerald. (Courtesy of Larry Hillborn.)

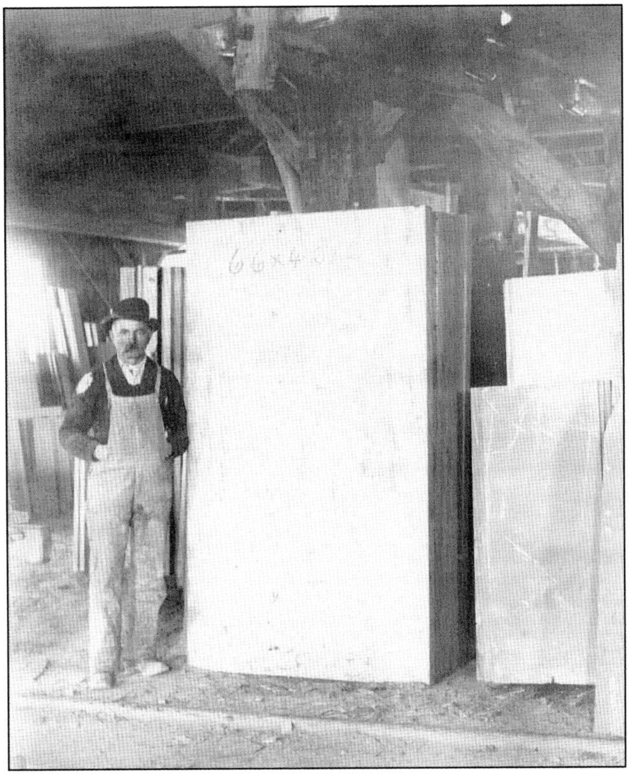

John Bloom stands next to some slate from Krum's Quarry. Bloom was the foreman. (Courtesy of Slatington Public Library.)

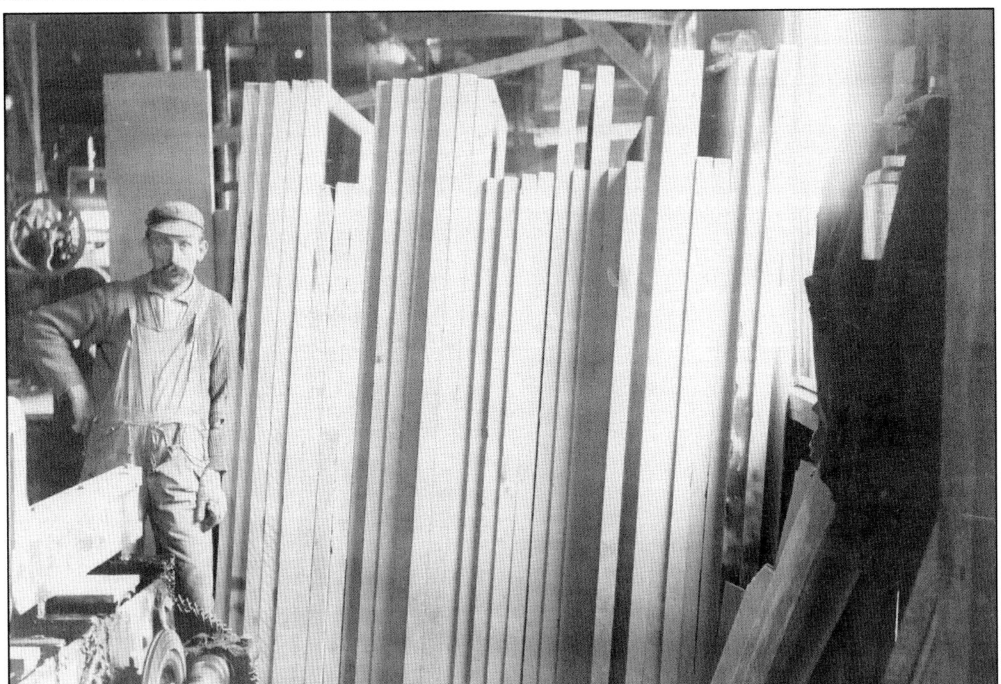

Albert Sechler is shown in this 1899 slate factory photograph. (Courtesy of Slatington Public Library.)

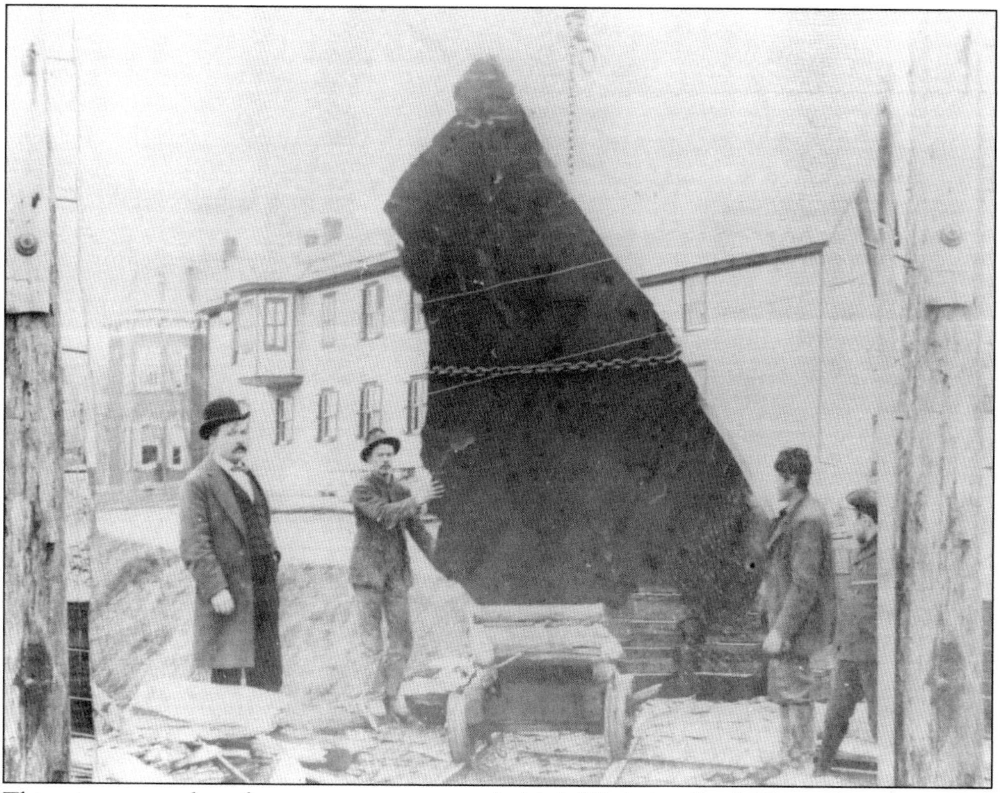

This view was taken from a stereoscope card titled "Hoisting Rock Slate, Slatington, Pa." (Courtesy of Slatington Public Library.)

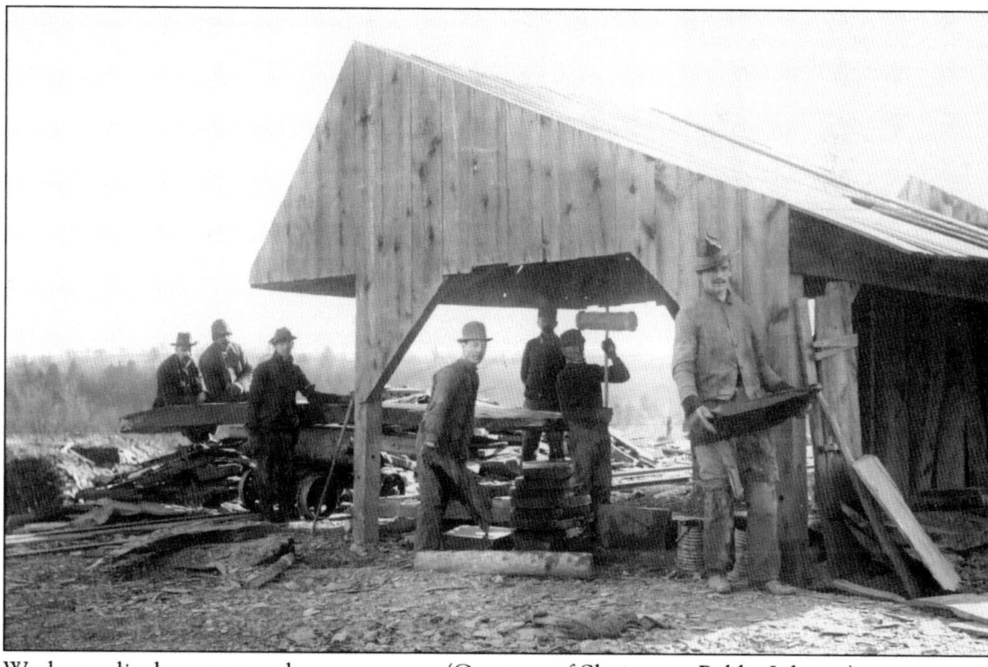

Workers split slate at an unknown quarry. (Courtesy of Slatington Public Library.)

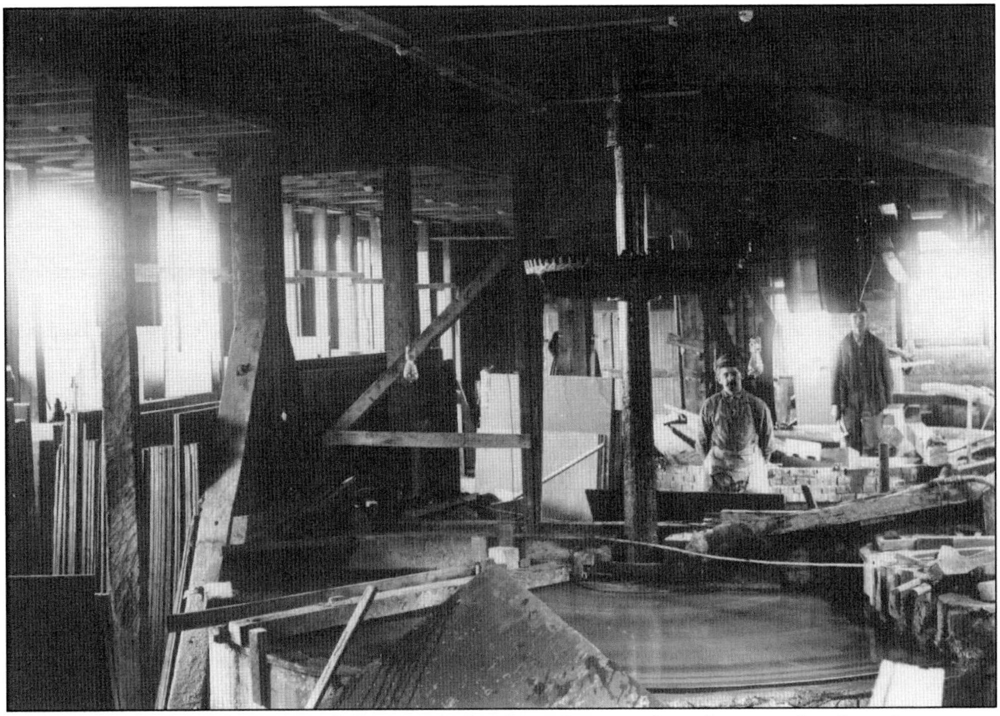

Slate of various sizes is seen piled around the shop floor in this photograph of workers at an unknown slate quarry. (Courtesy of Slatington Public Library.)

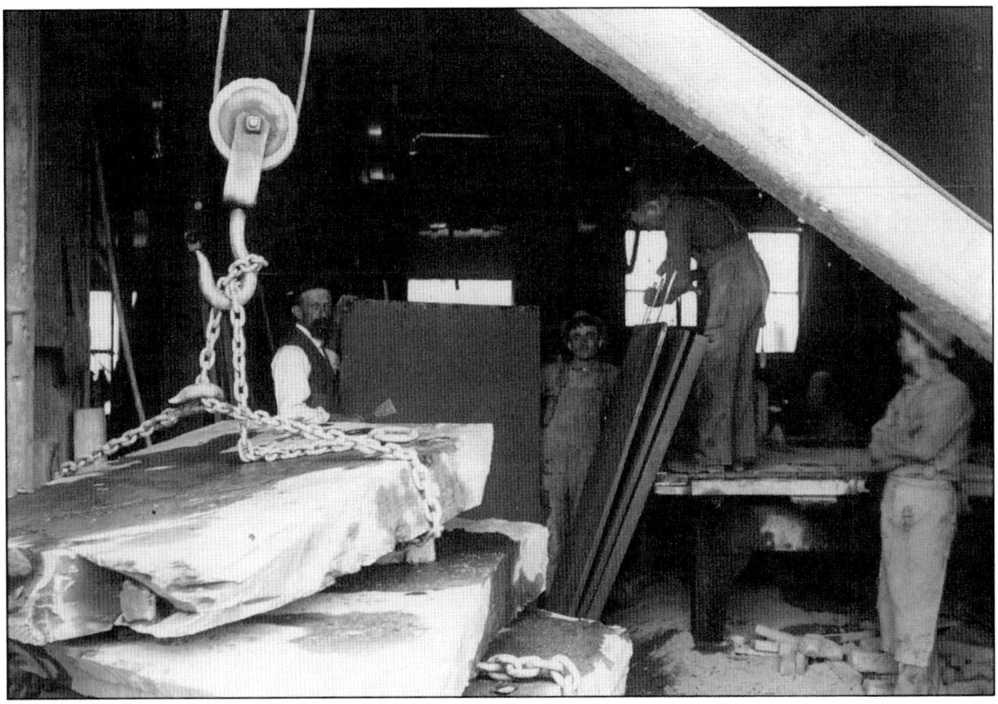

Machinery provides muscle for the lifting of slate to be cut and split. (Courtesy of Slatington Public Library.)

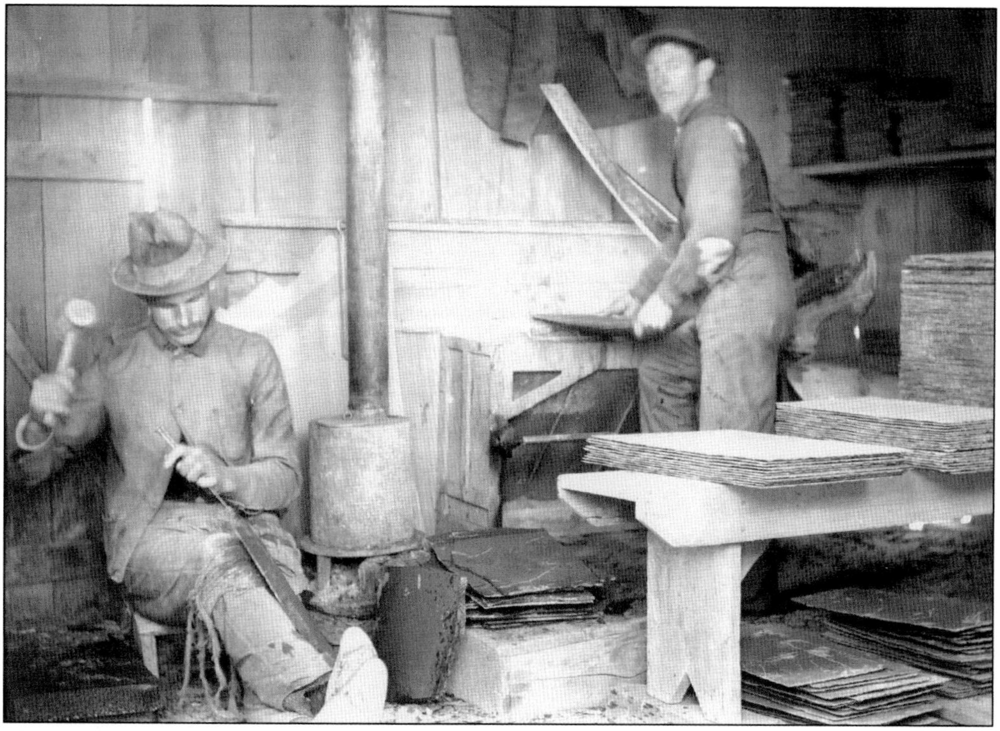

Slate workers split and trim slate to make roofing shingles. (Courtesy of Slatington Public Library.)

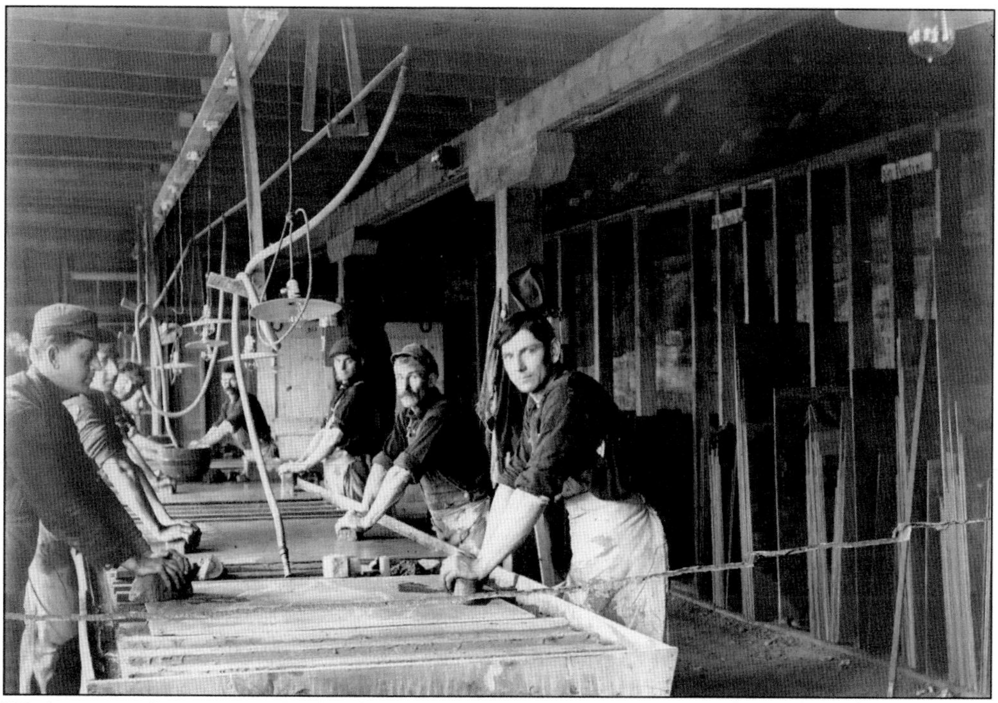

Workers man their stations for the slate finishing operation. (Courtesy of Slatington Public Library.)

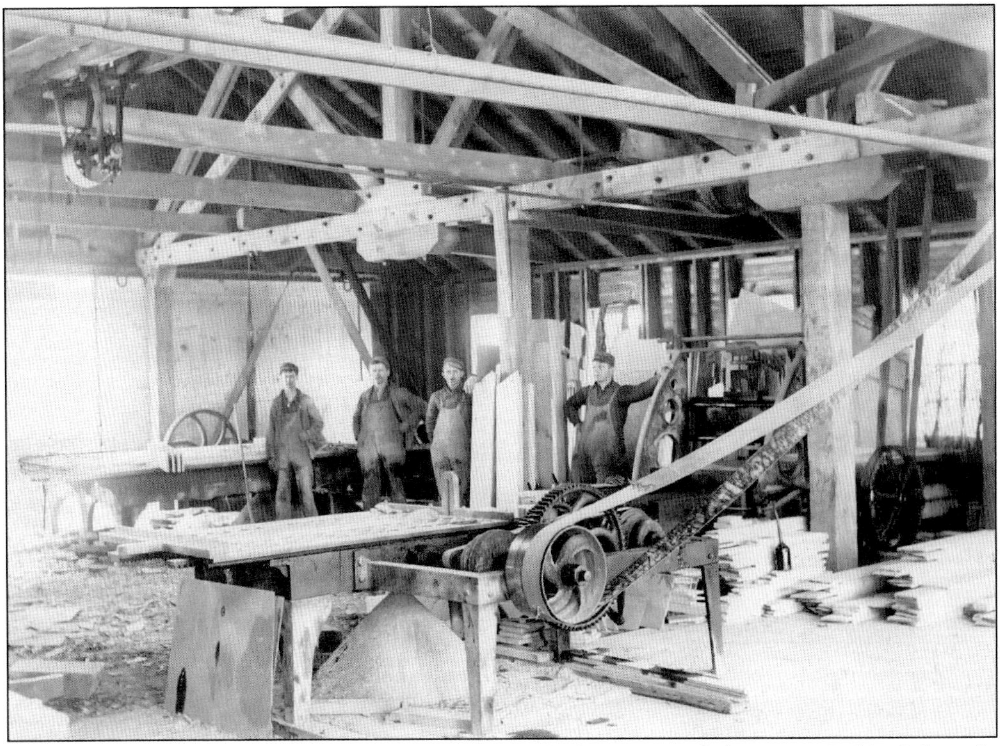

Slate factory workers take a break for this photograph. (Courtesy of Slatington Public Library.)

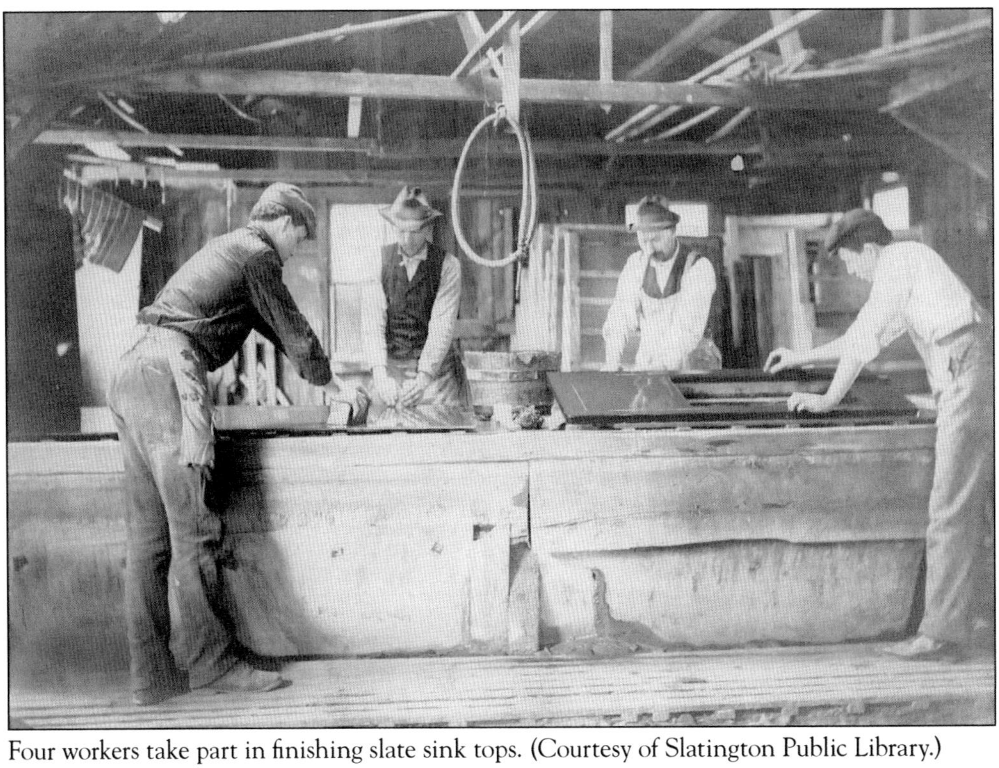

Four workers take part in finishing slate sink tops. (Courtesy of Slatington Public Library.)

Six

Schools, Sports, and Bands

Prior to 1868, school was held in various locations, including the Old Stone Mill in Lower Slatington, the Welsh church on West Church Street, the Presbyterian church, the home of Moses Kuntz, and on the second floor of the Lehigh Slate Company store in Slatington.

In 1868, a schoolhouse measuring 47 feet by 50 feet and two stories high was built at Second and Main Streets for $7,000. The White House School on Lincoln Avenue in Walnutport was completed in 1870. Two years later, property in Emerald was used for a school, and three years after that, another primary school opened in McDowell Hall in Slatington.

In 1879, and again in 1883, additions were built to the schoolhouse at Second and Main. In 1890, the 50-by-50-foot, two-story brick building was constructed on Fairview Avenue in Slatington to house four grammar school classrooms.

In 1897, a new high school was built on Kuntz Alley. In 1905, the Franklin School House was built in Emerald, followed by the construction of the Roosevelt Elementary School on Walnut Street in Slatington in 1906.

In 1911 and 1912, the Slatedale Elementary School was built on Grant Street and was enlarged in 1954. In 1916, a new high school went up on the site at Second and Main Streets.

During the summer of 1952, the Slatington and Walnutport School Districts merged to form the Blue Valley Union School District. In the summer of 1953, the Blue Valley Union and the Washington Township School Districts entered into a joint agreement, calling themselves the Northern Lehigh Joint Schools. In the summer of 1966, Blue Valley Union and Washington Township School Districts merged to form the Northern Lehigh School District.

In 1954, Peters Elementary in Friedens was built, and an addition was constructed in 1966. In 1959, a new high school was built on North Diamond Street in Slatington.

In 1966, the Franklin School House in Emerald was sold. In 1975, the White House building in Walnutport was sold, and the Lincoln Elementary building was demolished. In 1980, the Lincoln Elementary School property and the Smith Hall athletic complex were sold to the Lehigh County Housing Authority. In 1981, the Slatedale Elementary building was sold, and the new high school was built at 1 Bulldog Lane in Slatington. In 1982, the old high school at Main and Second Streets was sold, and the Smith Hall athletic complex was demolished. In 2001, the old high school was demolished.

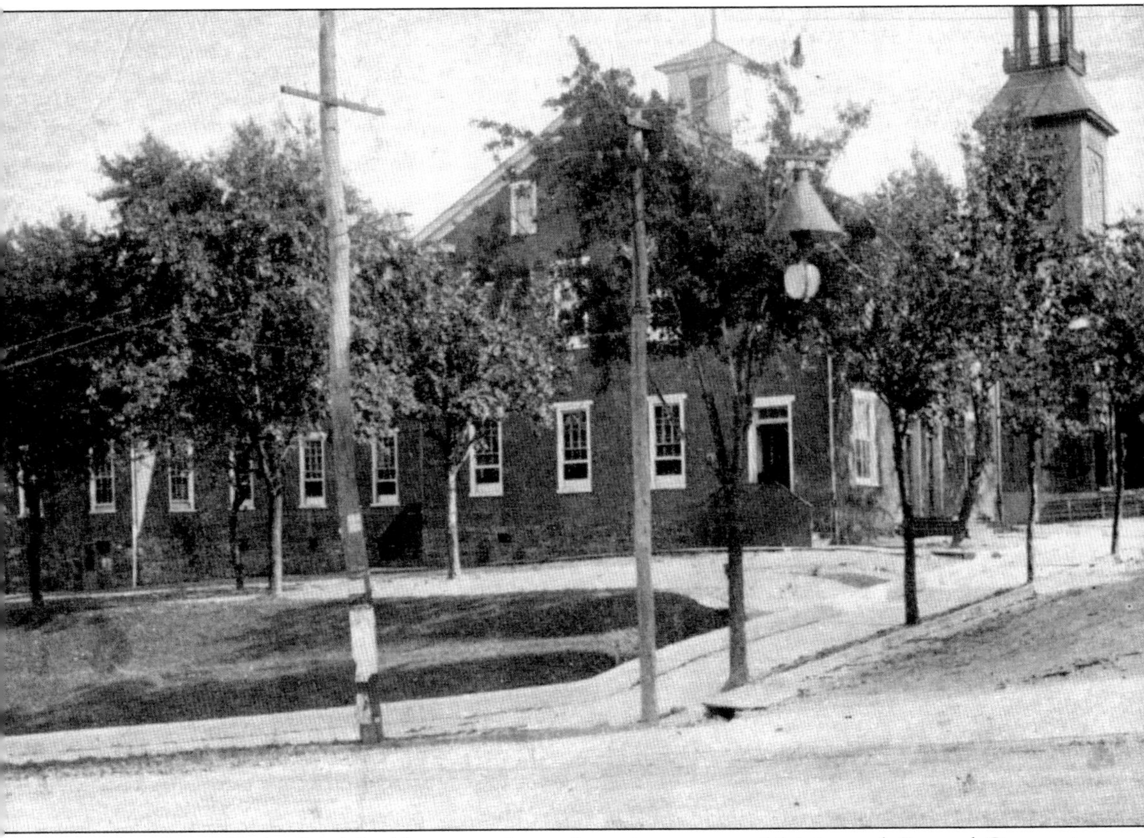

The First Ward school building was located at the corner of Main and Second Streets in Slatington. (Courtesy of Larry Hillborn.)

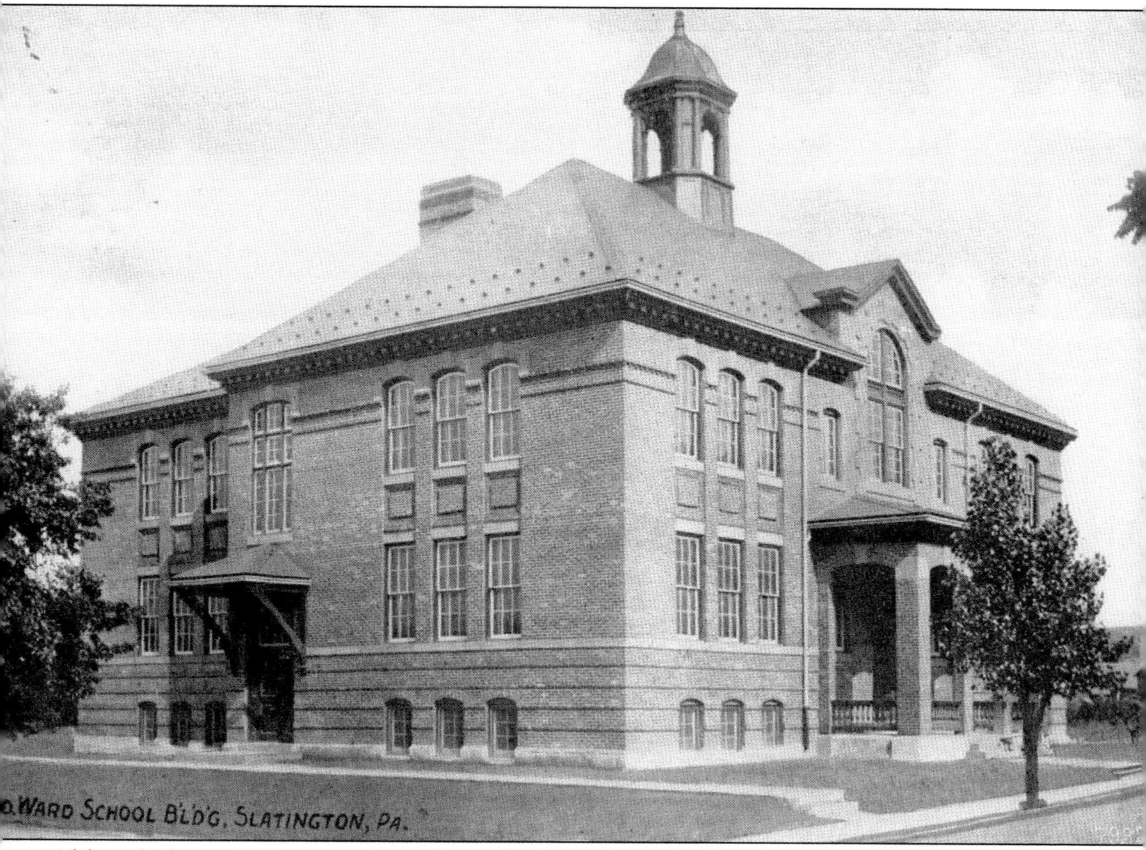

Although this c. 1907 postcard says this is the Second Ward school building in Slatington, it is actually the Third Ward school building, constructed in 1906. (Courtesy of Larry Hillborn.)

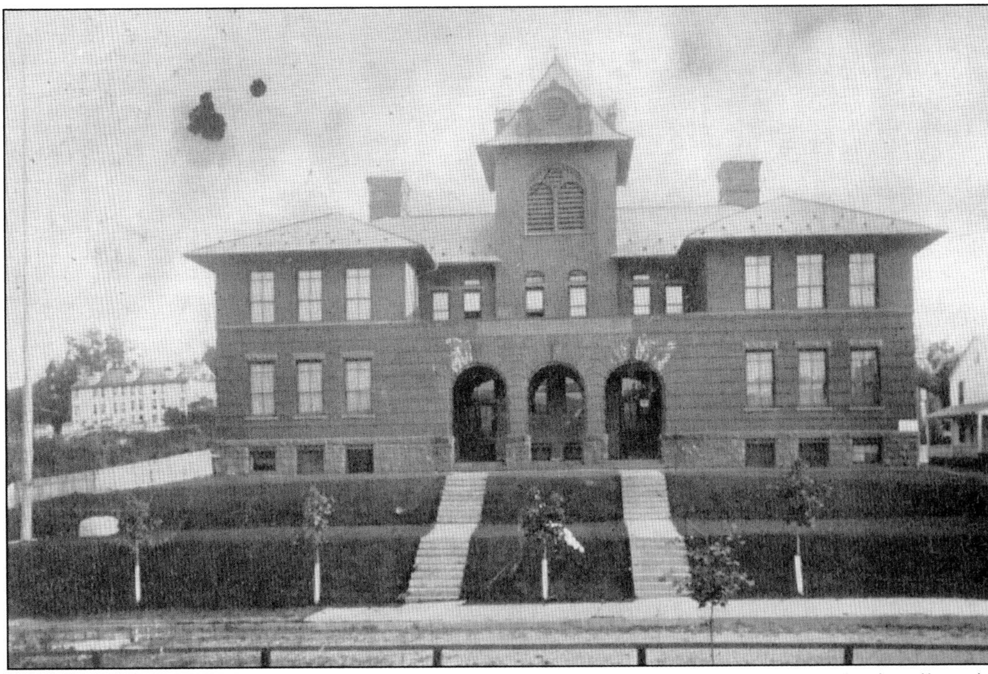

Slatington High School, built in 1897, is shown here around 1907. (Courtesy of Kayleigh Billings.)

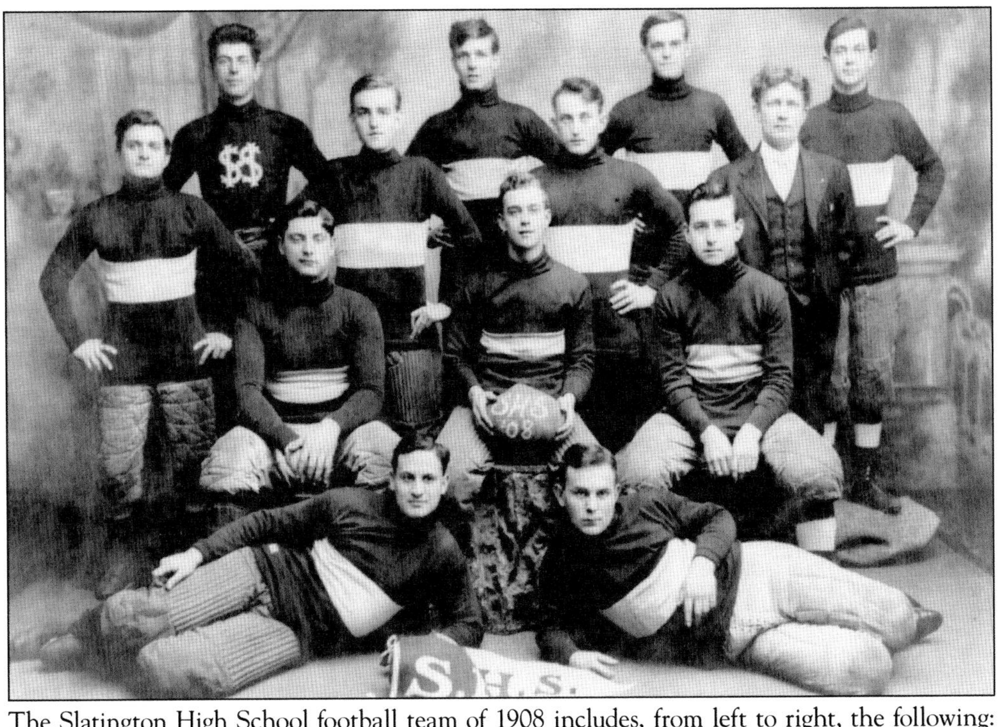

The Slatington High School football team of 1908 includes, from left to right, the following: (first row) P. Schertzinger and G. Minnich; (second row) A. Maxwell, D. Sewell, and W. Neff (captain); (third row) C. Beebe, G. Morgan, N. Kuntz, D. Davis, W. Handwerk, M. Hankee, I. Baker, and coach R. Morgan. (Courtesy of Northern Lehigh Future Focus Collection.)

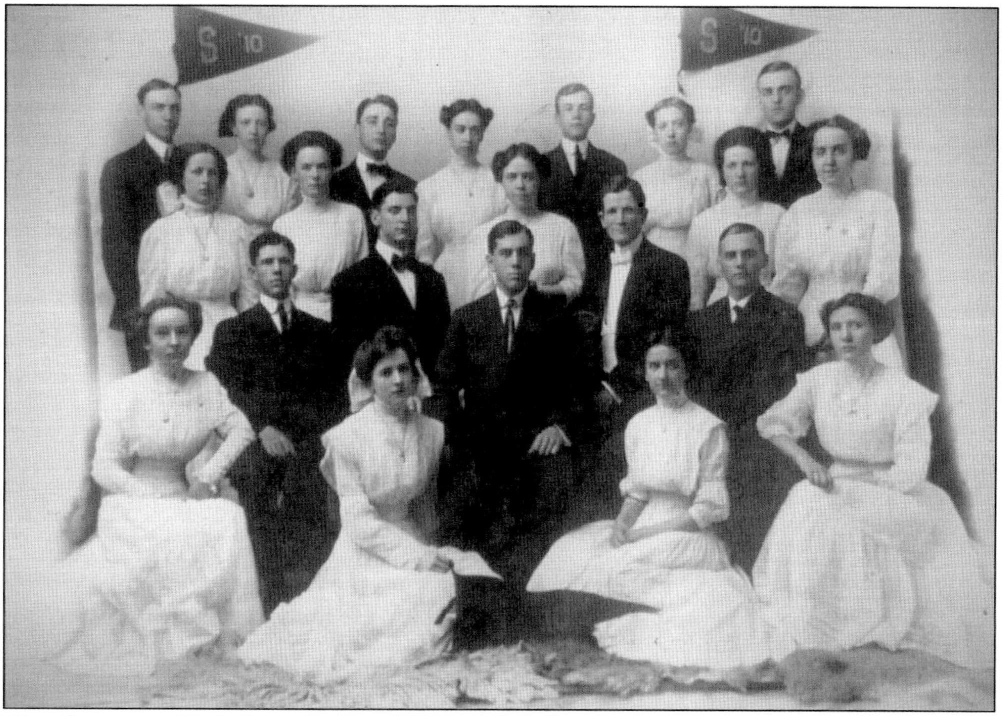

The Slatington High School class of 1910 included a total of 21 students, according to this photograph. (Courtesy of W. S. Merkle, Northern Lehigh Future Focus Collection.)

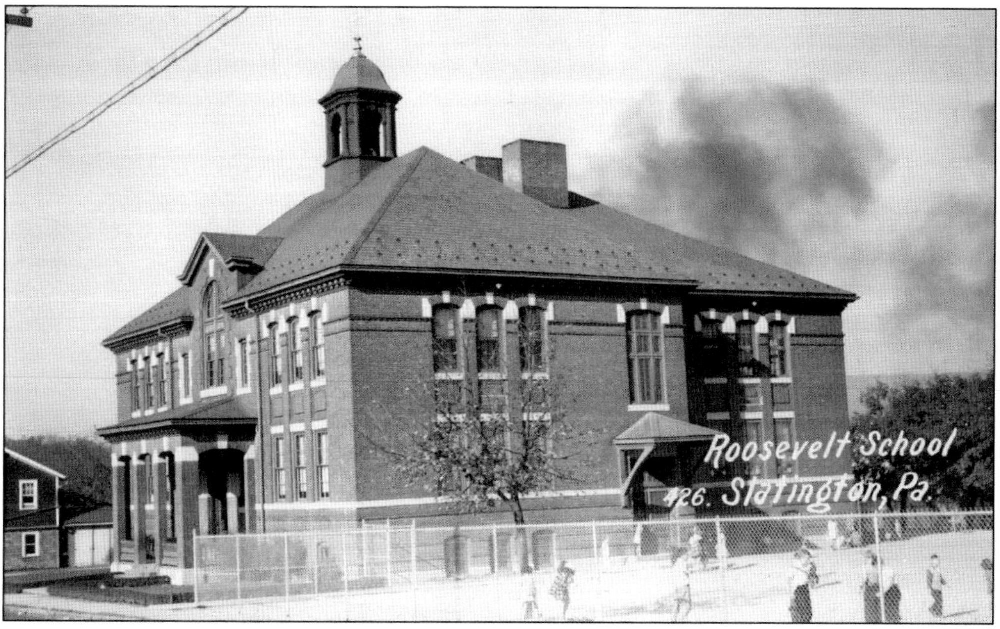

This is how the Roosevelt School appeared in 1950. (Courtesy of Larry Hillborn.)

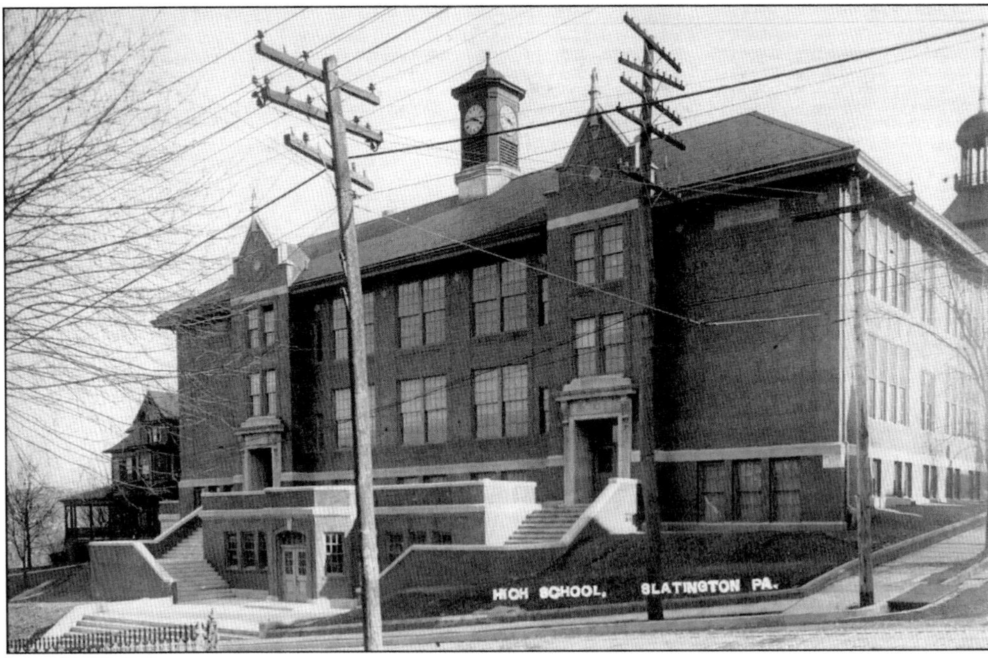

Slatington High School was constructed in 1916. (Courtesy of Larry Hillborn.)

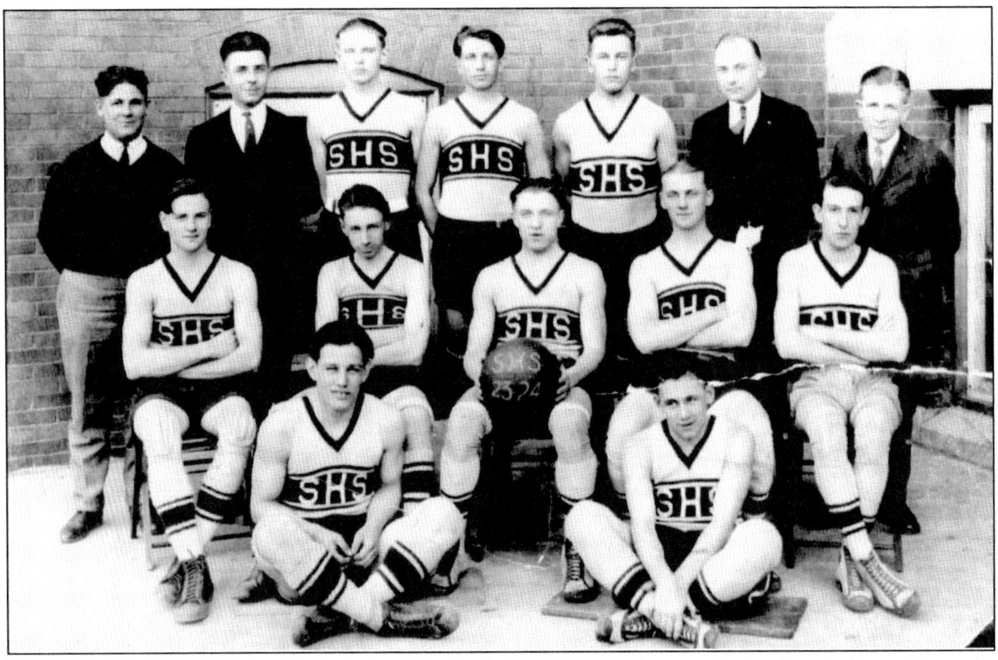

The 1923–1924 Slatington High School basketball team members include, from left to right, the following: (first row) William Beidelman and John McLaughlin; (second row) Lloyd Williams, Samuel Newcomer, Donald Roper, Walter Kelchner, and Charles Rasbridge; (third row) Izzy Schwartz, Richard Schoffstall, Howard Shenton, Dick Newcomer, Harrison Dilliard, coach Norman Smith, and Prof. J. W. Snyder. (Courtesy of Northern Lehigh Future Focus Collection.)

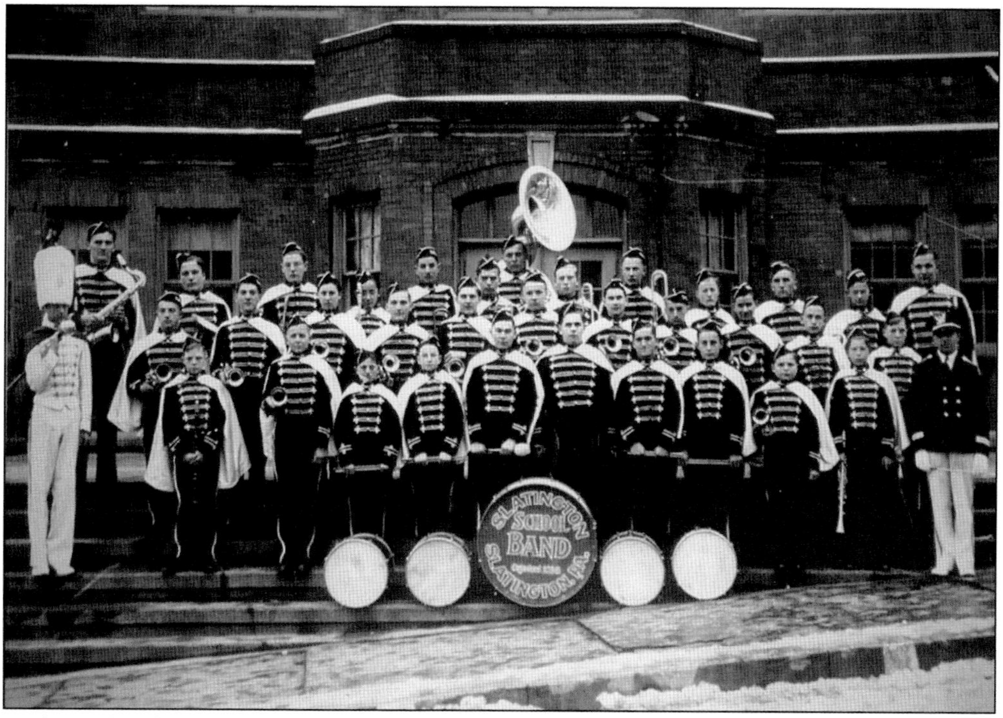

Paul Handwerk stands behind the bass drum in this 1936 photograph of the Slatington Band. (Courtesy of Paul Handwerk, Northern Lehigh Future Focus Collection.)

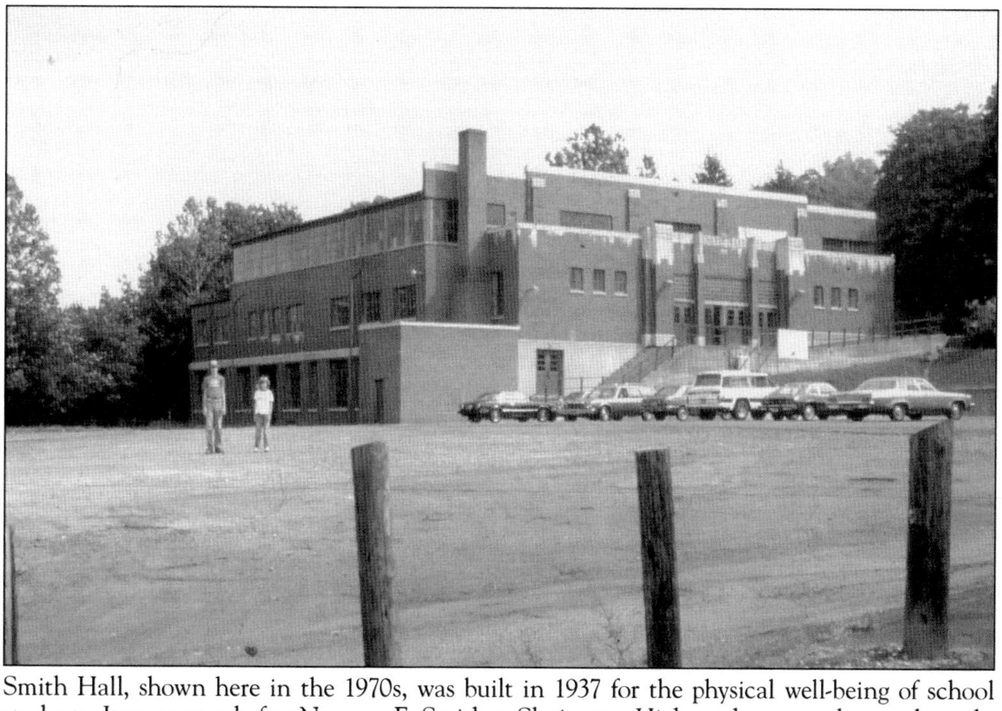

Smith Hall, shown here in the 1970s, was built in 1937 for the physical well-being of school students. It was named after Norman E. Smith, a Slatington High graduate, teacher, and coach. (Courtesy of Neil Kuntz, Northern Lehigh Future Focus Collection.)

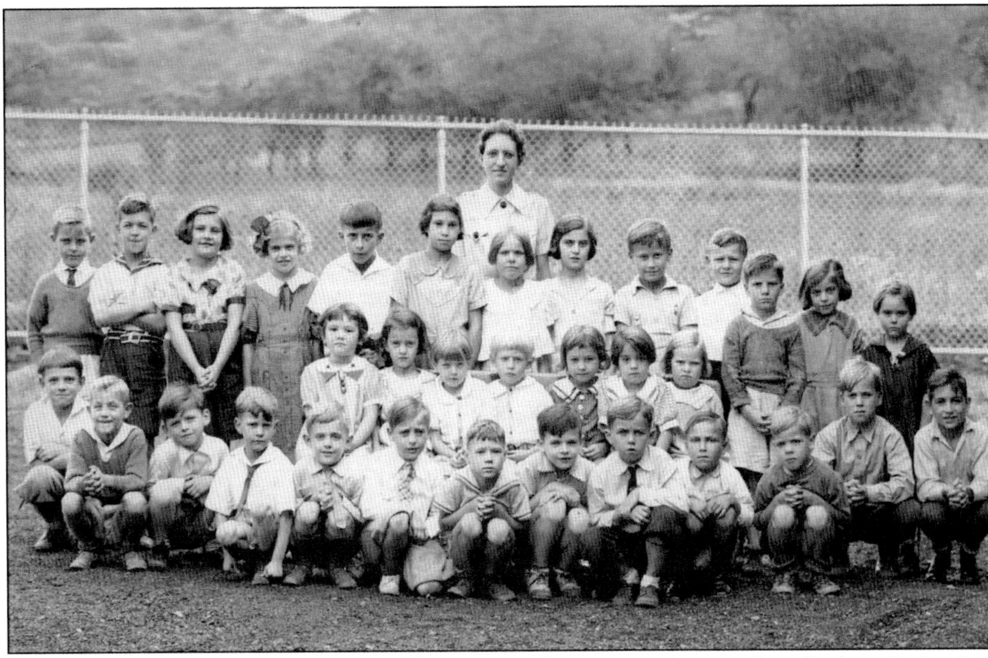

This 1937 class photograph shows students in grades one to four at the Newhart School in Walnutport. Martha Best is the teacher. (Courtesy of Everett Kaul.)

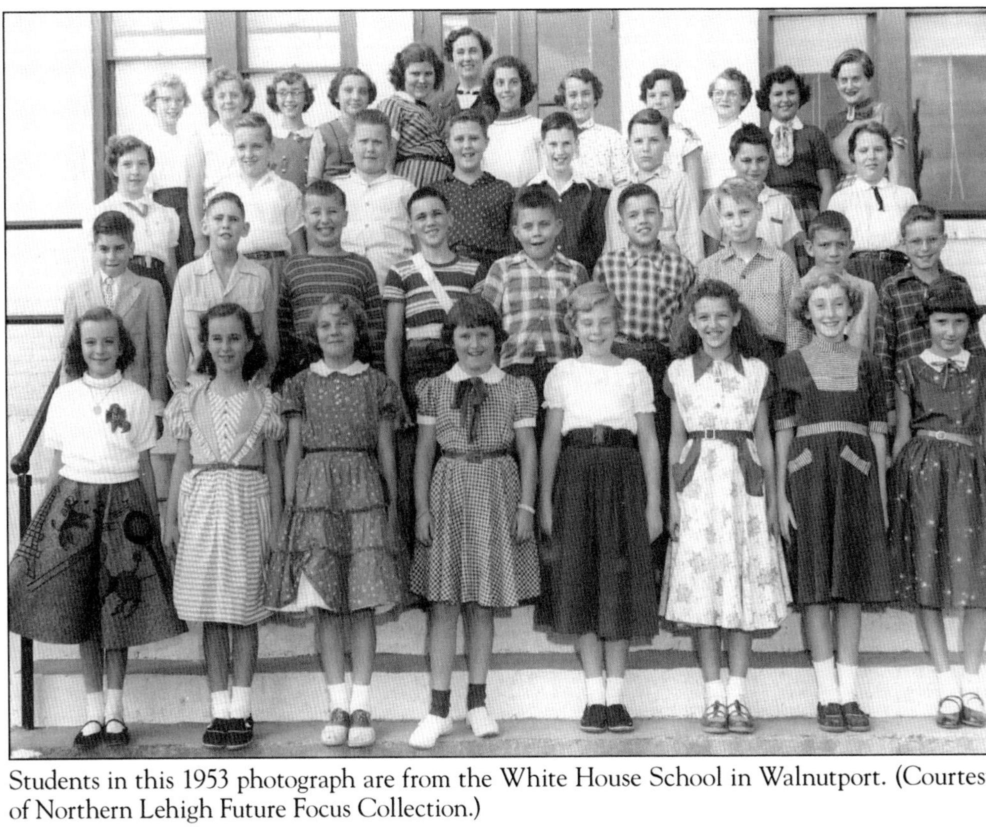

Students in this 1953 photograph are from the White House School in Walnutport. (Courtesy of Northern Lehigh Future Focus Collection.)

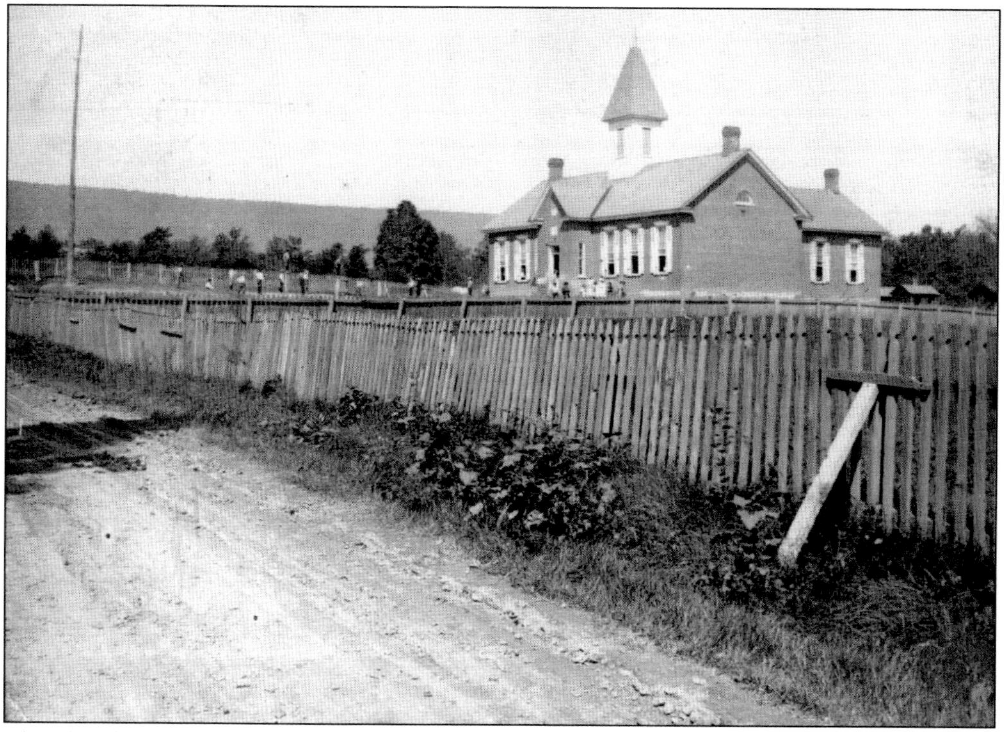

The Slatedale School is seen behind the fence. (Courtesy of Larry Hillborn.)

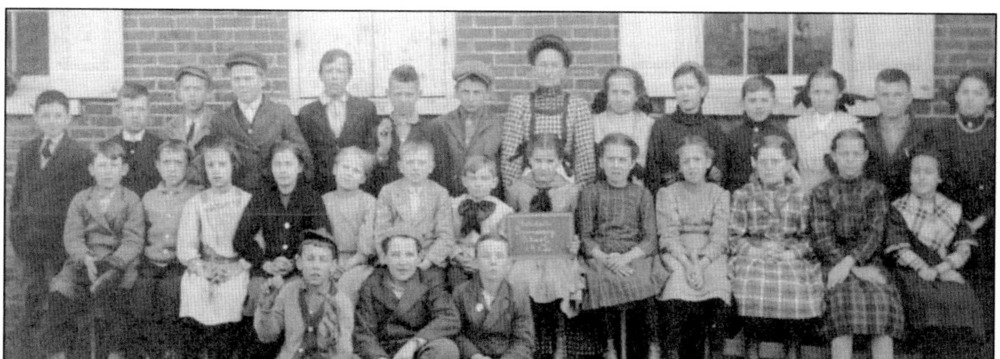

Students pose for this 1912 Slatedale Secondary School photograph. (Courtesy of Larry Hillborn.)

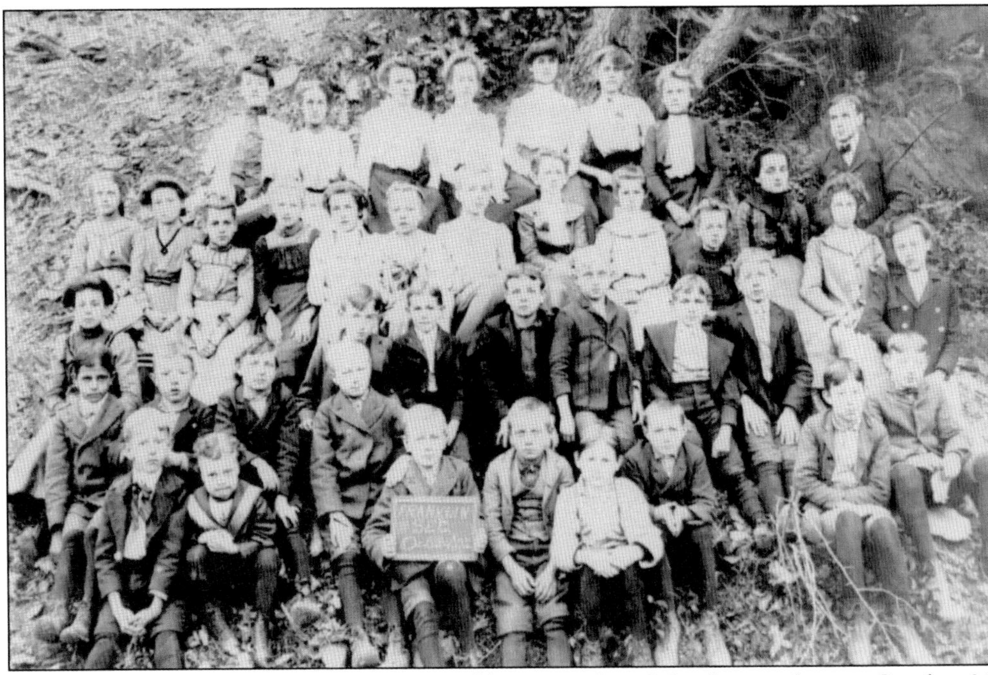

This photograph of the students at the Franklin Secondary School was taken on October 24, 1902. (Courtesy of Raymond Holland Regional History Collection, Northern Lehigh Future Focus Collection.)

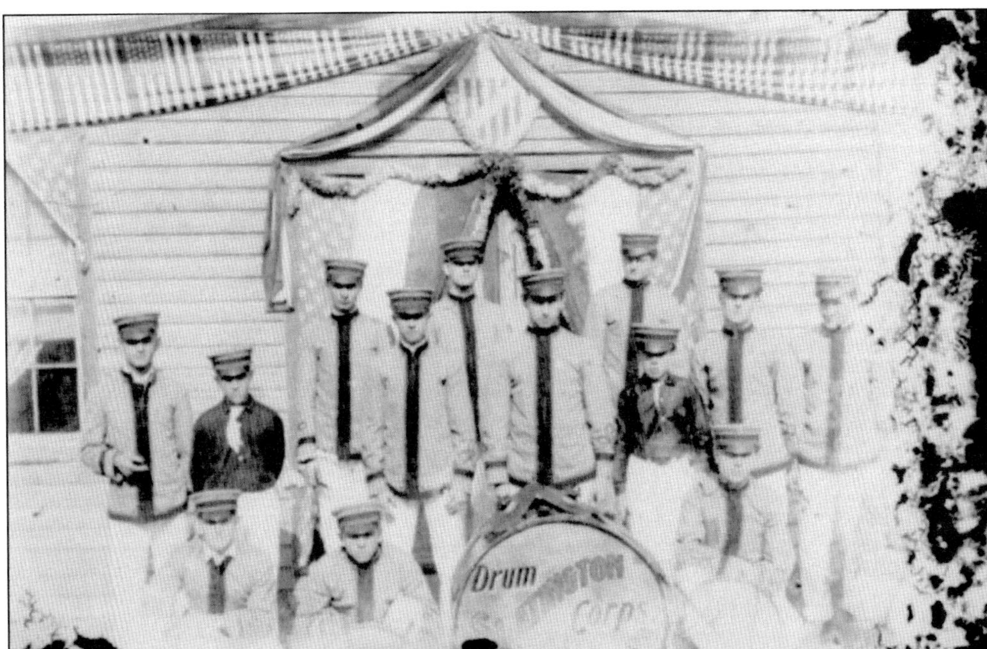

The building behind the Slatington Drum Corps is located on Dowell Street. The photograph was taken around 1910. (Courtesy of Raymond Holland Regional History Collection, Northern Lehigh Future Focus Collection.)

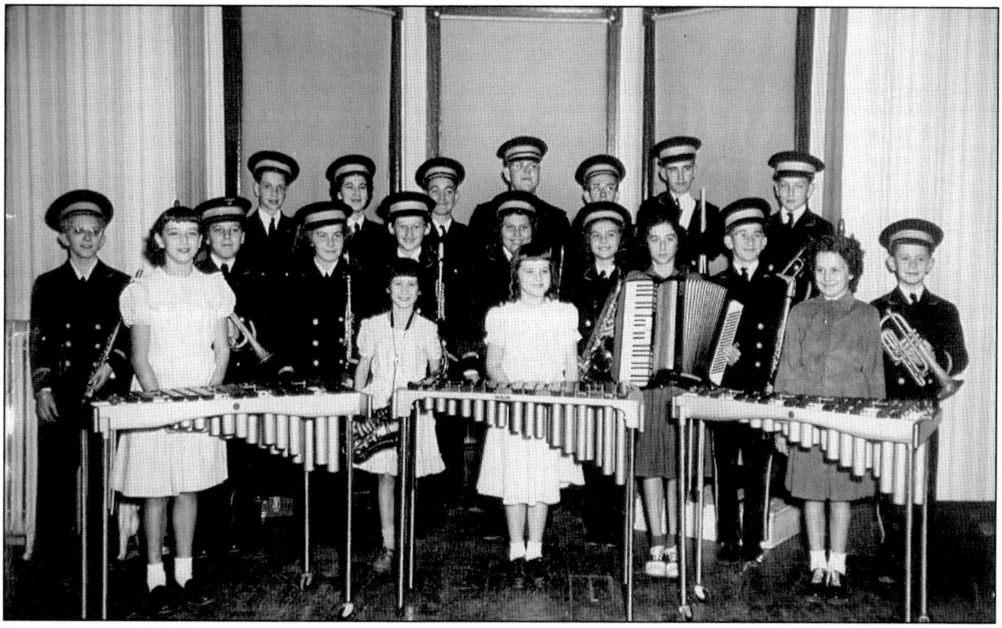

The 1947 Slatedale Junior Band poses for this photograph on the second floor of Ballier's Hotel in Slatedale. They include, from left to right, the following: (first row) Corrine Evans, Phyllis Schneck, Ruth Carol Evans, Elaine Rex, and Sandra Ferber; (second row) Peter Kern, Carl Schleicher, Deanna Kern, Shirley Sowden, Caroline Ebert, Althea Hunsicker, David Blose, and Lee Haas; (third row) Gerald Kressley, Frances Blose, Donavon Bauer, Robert Balliet, David Kern, Richard Schleicher, and Joe Frantz. (Courtesy of Lee Haas, Northern Lehigh Future Focus Collection.)

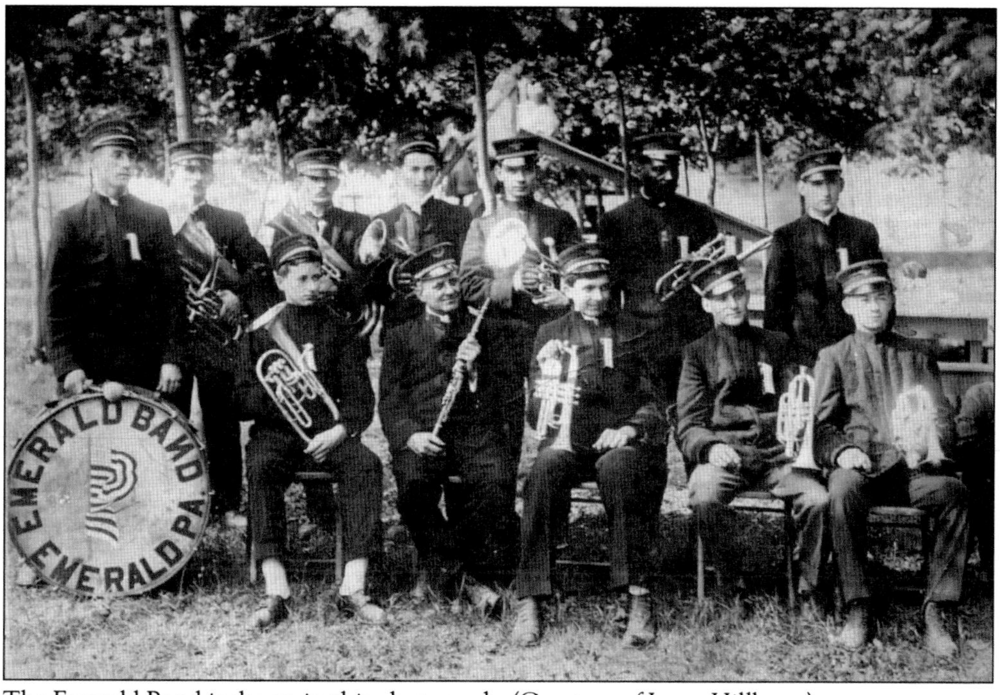

The Emerald Band is shown in this photograph. (Courtesy of Larry Hillborn.)

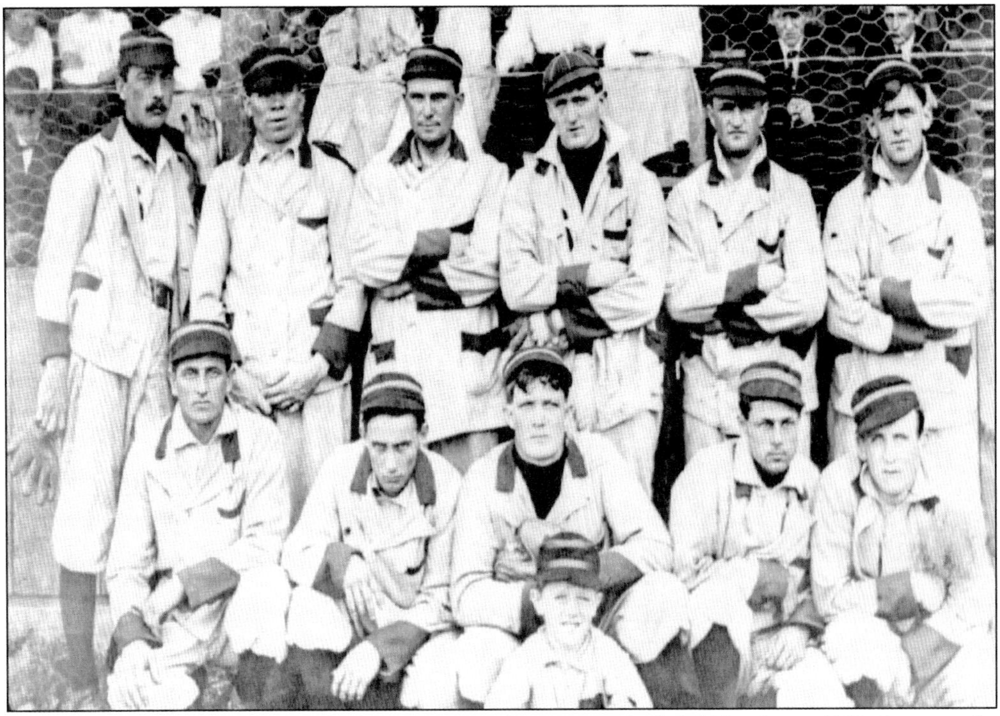

Members of the Slatington baseball team pose at the Victory Park field for this c. 1898 photograph. (Courtesy of Slatington Public Library, Northern Lehigh Future Focus Collection.)

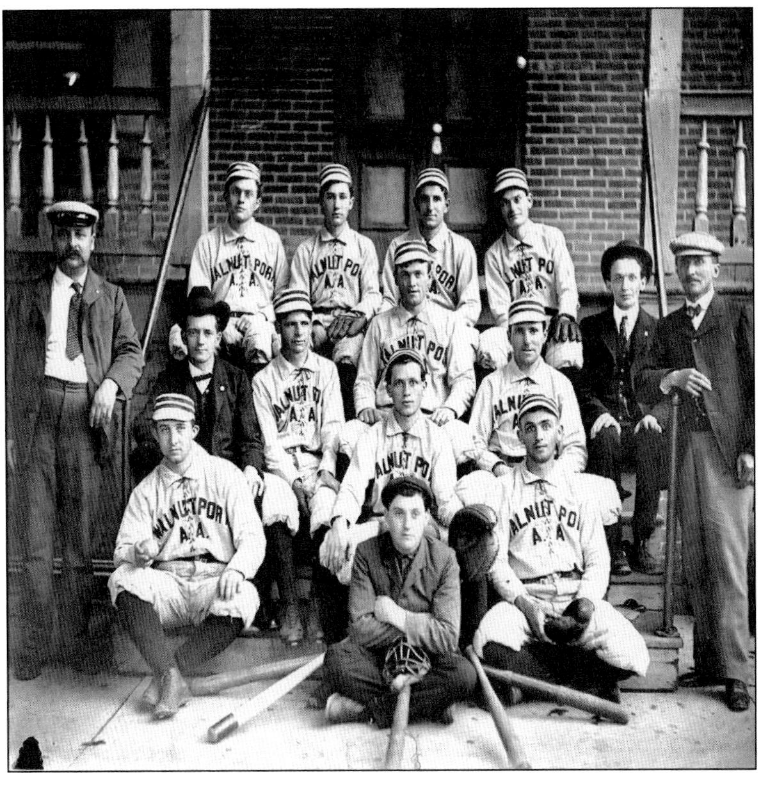

Walnutport also had its own baseball team. (Courtesy of Larry Hillborn.)

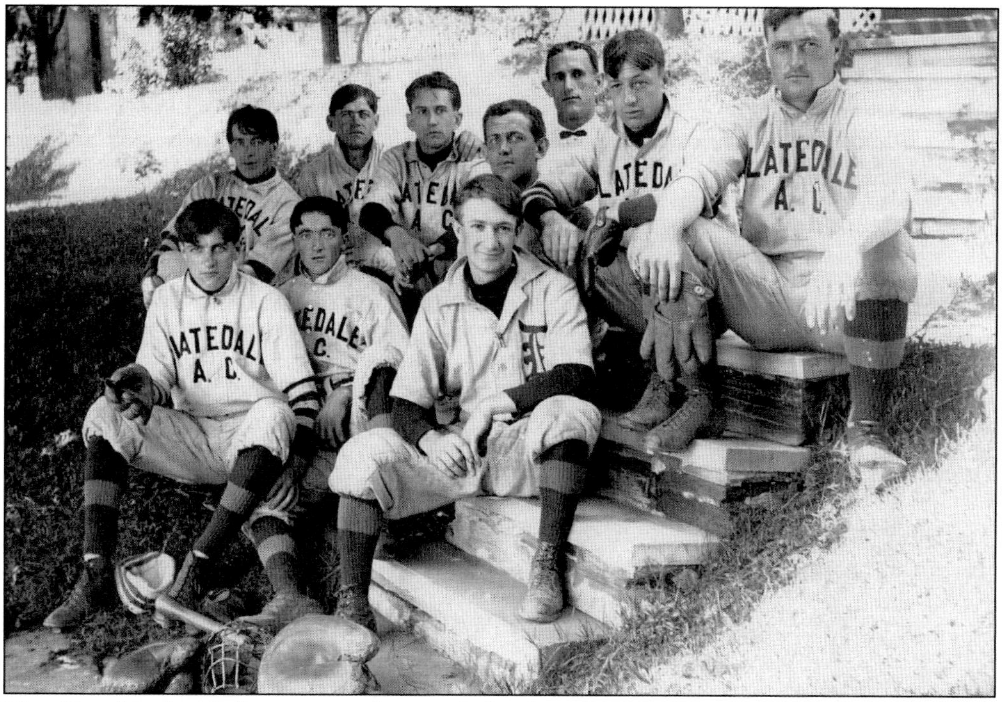

The Slatedale baseball team members include, from left to right, the following: (first row) Ellsworth Lewis, Billy Edwards, and Pie Jones; (second row) Chas. Morris, Bill Lewis, Walt Brice, Lewell Jones, Tom Jones, Tommy Williams, and Willie Blose (manager). (Courtesy of Northern Lehigh Future Focus Collection.)

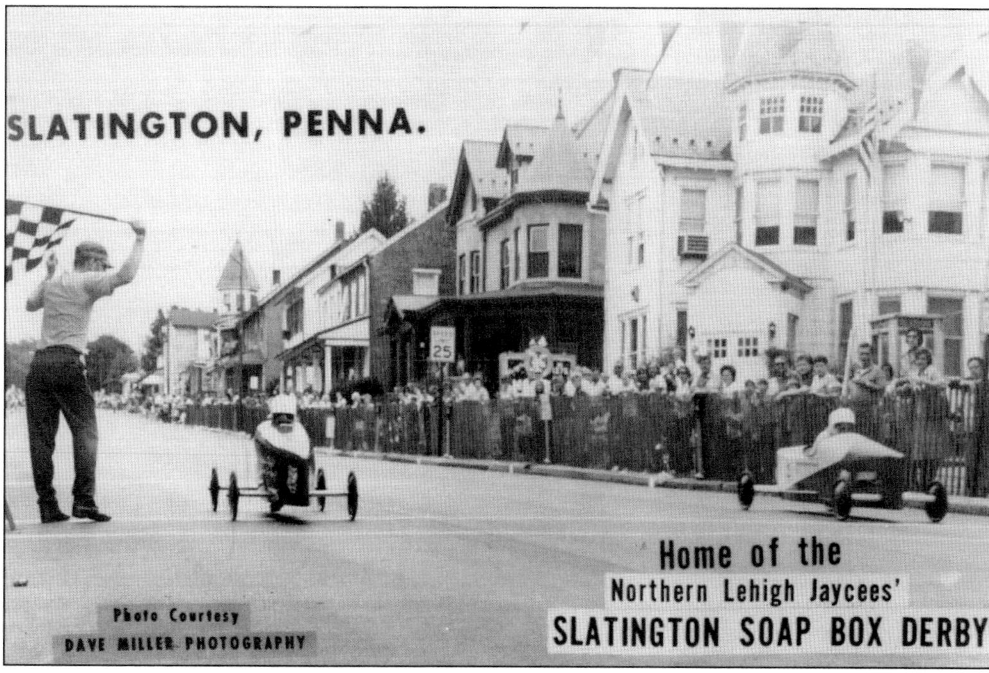

This postcard shows the Slatington Soap Box Derby that ran down Main Street. (Courtesy of Larry Hillborn.)

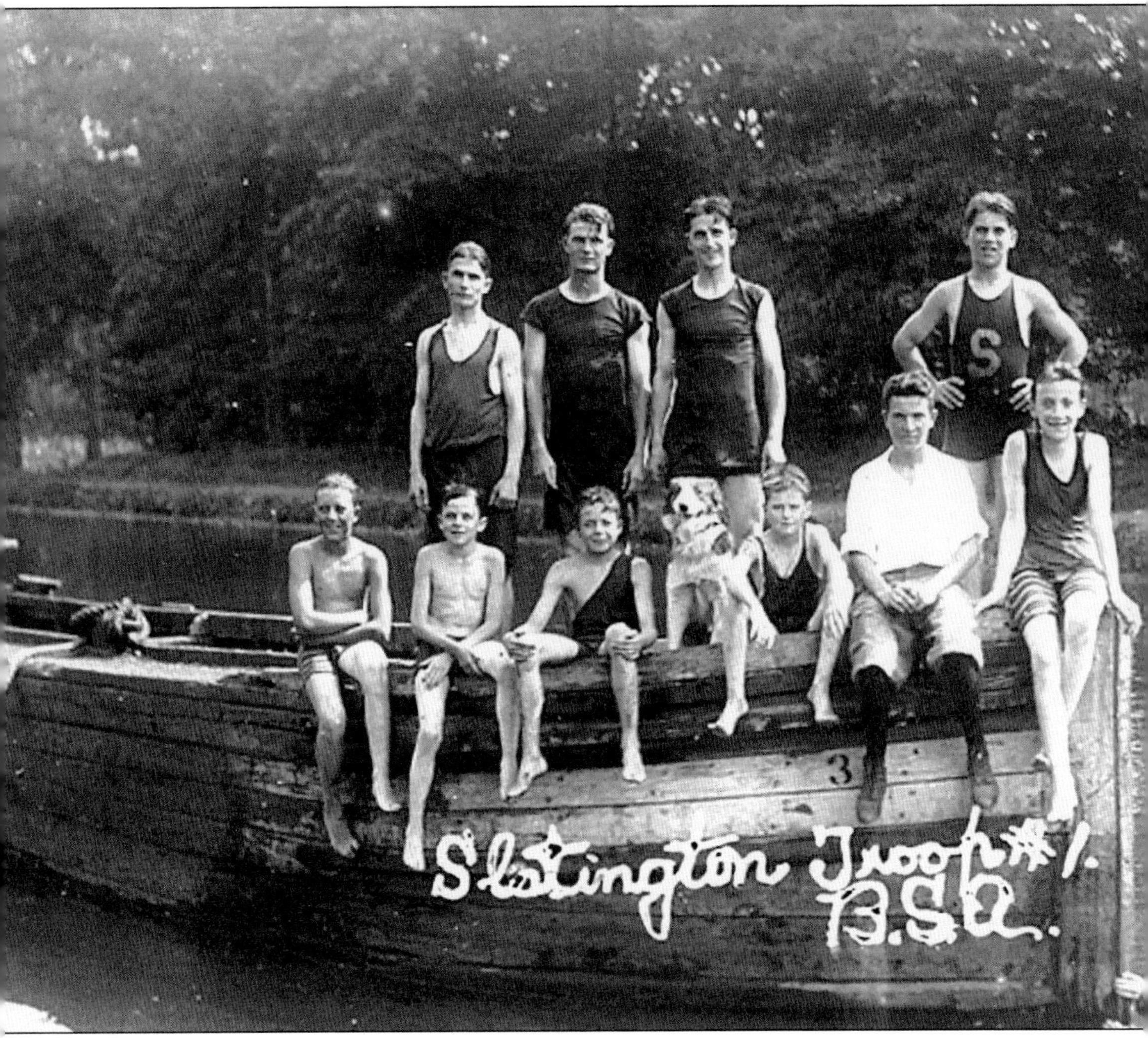

The Slatington Troop No. 1 Boy Scouts who swam in the canal during the summer of 1915 are, from left to right, the following: (first row) Edward Wright, Wallace Kern, Fred Williams, Russel R. Evans, and Wesley Jones; (second row) Mathew Meagher, Earl P. Meagher, Edward Meagher, and Mike Blefko. The boy in the white shirt is unidentified. (Courtesy of Everett and Marilyn Kaul.)